ENDORSEMENTS FO
BY GOD

Randy Schuneman has been a canvas for the weathering grace of God. As a pastor, writer, seer, husband and father—he has known the gentle breezes of prosperity and the harsh bitter winds of brokenness. And yet he remains faithful, steadfast and sewn together. I pray that you will allow the words of this book to seep into your soul and resurrect your hopes and dreams. Thank you Randy for teaching us all how to hand God the pieces of our heart and let him make us whole."

> – Randy Phillips, Founder of Phillips Craig and Dean

In *Sewn Together by God*, Dr. Schuneman presents a fresh perspective into the depth and richness of the Bible. Using the Seamless Robe of Jesus as a word picture, Randy shows how the Bible is tied together by numerous threads. These repeated themes enable the reader to see the Bible through "new eyes." Any reader will be blessed by the powerful message of this book.

> – Dr. Stan Toler, Bestselling author and speaker

Whether you are an amateur or an accomplished Bible student, this book will send you excitedly back to read and enjoy the greatest "love letter" ever written on a wider and deeper level of understanding. I dare you to read *Sewn Together* and not want to be counted among the Bereans who "receive the Word with all readiness of mind and search the Scriptures daily" (Acts 17:11).

> – Leonard Sweet, Bestselling author, professor (Drew University, George Fox University, Tabor College), and chief contributor to sermons.com

It is not often a book has a life-changing effect before it is even read. For that matter, before it is ever written. *Sewn Together* was that kind of book for me. It has been several years ago now I was in the early stages of my ministerial studies when I met my friend

Randy Schuneman for dinner in Oklahoma City. As he began to explain his passion for what would eventually fill the pages of this book, something changed in me. Having grown up in the church learning the Bible in pieces, I had never heard anyone explain the beauty and symmetry of the absolute seamlessness of God's Word. I'm glad the book is finally done. Just wish he hadn't waited so long.

> – Dave Clark, Legendary lyricist, author and wordcrafter

I heartily commend the book *Sewn Together by God*, by Randy Schuneman. The author writes from a background in ministry in which he has known both professional success and personal suffering. The author explains how God has sewn the Bible a "warp and woof" pattern that makes it seamless.

> – Rob Staples, Professor of Theology Emeritus at Nazarene Theological Seminary, author and preacher

What a refreshing, creative, insightful book! Randy Schuneman's understanding of Scripture as the living, breathing Word of God and his extraordinary insight into familiar passages are evident on every page. Regardless of whether you are an interested seeker, new Christian, or "seasoned saint ..." this book is for you"!

> – Ron Benefiel, Dean, School of Theology and Christian Ministry at Point Loma Nazarene University and former President of Nazarene Theological Seminary

Sewn Together by God

First published by Sonpowered Press in 2015
Sonpowered Books
Edmond, Oklahoma
www.sonpoweredbooks.com

ISBN 13: 978-0-692-41697-6

For more information, please visit
jennieshoe.com and randyschuneman.com

To Micah & Breth,

Sewn Together by God

Driven by His Wind,
Randy Schuneman

RANDY SCHUNEMAN

Sonpowered Books
Edmond, Oklahoma 2015

CONTENTS

DEDICATION

<small>THIS BOOK IS DEDICATED TO:</small>

My mother, *Millie Schuneman*, who made sure our family read a chapter from Egermeir's Bible Story Book each night for family devotions. She used that same book to read to her third grade students every morning for 30 years. Although it is worn, that book still sits beside me as I write these words. Along with Dad, Mom was beside me when I prayed to accept Jesus into my heart. I can still hear her voice as she has prayed daily for me all my life.

Jay Rader, whose hunger to understand the Bible taught me how to read it from a fresh perspective. Jay thanks for spending that "year of Monday mornings" with me. You taught me more than I ever taught you.

Terry Guilfoyle, who challenged me to think outside the box. We did not always agree on the answer, but the depth of our friendship allowed us to smile and say, "I think you are wrong about that! This is what that passage means."

Jessica (Jessie) Lee Bates Wilson, who always asked the most amazing questions during our studies the last semester of her senior year in High School. Jessie listened so well that four years later when I shared pre-marital counseling with her and her husband Tyler, I saw Jessie's face light up as we went over truths from studies we had done four years before. She remembered!

Dr. Leonard Sweet, my mentor and my lead "pneumanaut" (a Spirit-driven traveler). He became my cheerleader and encourager when I questioned writing this book. He challenged me to become a fellow "pneumanaut," to step out into the journey of writing down what God has laid on my heart.

My late father, *Don Schuneman*, who died during the writing of this book. Dad has always been my favorite theologian, even though his lessons were mostly taught during our pickup rides to the farm. I miss that traveling classroom, but I like that God told you, "You did a good job and it was time to go home." Dad taught me why biblical principles matter. Dad, the consistency of your

Christian walk enabled people to say, "If you want to understand what it means to be a Christian, read your Bible, go to church and ask Don Schuneman." I know God told you, "Well done, thou good and faithful servant." Thank you "Mr. Schuneman."

FOREWORD

NOT LONG AGO I WAS LEADING A TEEN GROUP WHEN ONE OF THE young men shared a recent discussion from his American History class. He was excited to talk about their study of the "Jesus Movement" of the 60's. I responded with laughter as I revealed, "I was there." I remember the struggle we had with the relevancy of the church. The organized church, meaningless ceremonies, and religion in general was all being questioned. Although there were no negative statements about Jesus, He was being placed in an unusual package, with some even wondering if He was missing and we did not know it. The driving force of our heart was to return to Jesus. I am not sure how to evaluate the theological liberalism of that hour. Did the lack of a strong biblical belief create the vacuum or absence of Jesus? Did the church become an organization or club without the strong presence of Christ? What we discovered then is what we are discovering now! All the organizational wrappings do not matter when Jesus is present. I do not refer to the idea of Jesus or His doctrine, but I refer to the "person" of Jesus. We cannot tolerate a religion without Him!

That was true in the days of the early Church. The role of the apostles was singular: "And with great power the apostles gave witness to the resurrection of the Lord Jesus" (Acts 4:33). This was the agenda for the first recorded business meeting of the early church. They needed to fill the apostle vacancy created by the betrayal and death of Judas. The purpose behind this issue was "one of these must become a witness with us of His resurrection" (Acts 1:22). However, they were not merely witnessing about an event or even testifying to actually seeing Him. As they told of Jesus' resurrection, He was present. His Spirit touched the lives of the listeners. They were not moved by the effectiveness of the speech or the personality of the speaker; they were confronted with the presence of Jesus. Over the years I have noticed that the first issue in moving away from biblical belief is to undermine the Scriptures. To shape our theology to what we believe, we must adjust the

Scriptures. The Scriptures define Christianity! If a person wants to set aside the Scriptures, we have no argument, because that is their right. However, we do not call that Christianity. Jesus and the Scriptures are a singular issue. The Living Word and the Written Word are interactive. According to Jesus, the Trinity God exposed His heart, His nature. This exposure became the Scriptures. The Second Member of this Trinity leaped from His throne into our world; He submitted to the Scriptures. The Scriptures formed and shaped everything He did. Therefore Jesus fulfilled the Scriptures, the revelation of God's heart (Matthew 5:17-20). If you want to know what God is like, look at Jesus. If you want to understand Jesus, comprehend the Scriptures. Jesus, a Man, is calling us to do the same as He did.

In allowing the Scriptures to shape our lives, we become the body of Christ in our day. The Scriptures are not ancient literature; they are the functioning, beating heart of God. They are the fingers of Christ molding us into His image. *Sewn Together by God* is a powerful statement of this truth. Randy Schuneman captured and exposed this reality to my heart once again. My longing is for you to saturate in this truth and find the presence of Jesus!

– Stephen Manley

A LOVE LETTER FROM GOD

How would you respond if you received a love letter from God? Whether it is enclosed in an envelope or downloaded on your electronic device, imagine you hold in your hand a personalized letter from the heart of God. The Creator of the universe is inviting you to join Him in a personal relationship! With the touch of an icon or the opening of a page, God wants to reveal to you how to know Him and walk with Him daily. This letter is filled with adventure, romance, mystery, wisdom, scandal, history and even a talking donkey. Most importantly, this letter reveals how deep and far God's love has reached out to you! How would you respond? Would you:

- Display it unopened on your coffee table?
- Lay it by your favorite recliner to read at your convenience?
- Leave it zipped up in a nice leather cover?
- Only open it on Sundays?
- Not open it, because you are sure it is too hard to understand?

The Bible is God's love letter to you! It is not sixty-six fragmented books, but *one seamless love letter that is so tightly woven that only God could have sewn it together.* The unity of the Bible enables us to start anywhere in Scripture and move backward and forward without losing sight of God's message to us. Whether God is speaking to Abraham, Moses or the Apostle Paul, the message of salvation remains the same. This plan of reconciliation between you and God will cost God everything! Through Christ, God will shed His Blood not only to show the depth of His love for us, but also the depth of our sinfulness.

The message of this Letter is so simple that a child can understand it. It is also so deep and complex that we can spend a lifetime of study and never understand it completely. No matter what age you are, there will always be those moments when it feels as if a verse jumps off the page. The Bible was meant to be a source of *delight*, not *drudgery*. Through the ministry of the Holy Spirit, God wants to "guide you into all Truth" (John 16:13a). God's intention is to draw you into the only Story that can *change your life!*

The Bible has never been more available than it is today. With the development of the Internet, more resources are available on our smartphones than the libraries of all pastors combined. With the YouVersion app, it is possible to have almost every version of the Bible at your fingertips. We can read, listen to and see the Bible in every format imaginable. Mini-iPods are being used to take the Gospel to people who have never heard the Bible. The *Jesus Film* is being used to bring millions to Christ. We can do word searches without knowing Hebrew or Greek. We can even hear a British voice correctly pronouncing those pesky Old Testament names!

In light of the abundance resources we have, can I ask you a personal question? Are you continually learning more insights from the Bible? Do you have an insatiable desire to know more about God's Word? Or do you find reading the Bible to be duty rather than a joy? Would you find it difficult to even locate your Bible right now? Wherever you are in your spiritual journey, my hope is that in the time we spend together, the Bible will come alive in your heart and mind. May you hear the divine "Whoosh!" of God moving on every page.

The Purpose

If the Bible was a tapestry, Jesus would be the central focus of the design. In their book *Jesus: A Theography*, Leonard Sweet and Frank Viola point out, "In a word, Jesus is the thread that holds all Scripture together."[1] Jesus is woven into the fiber of every page of the Bible. From the Creation Story in Genesis 1 to John's vision of heaven in Revelation 22, the divine thread of Jesus is intricately sewn into the Bible.

However, a tapestry cannot be completed unless a variety of threads are used to enhance its beauty. The Bible is filled with

---

1   Leonard Sweet and Frank Viola, *Jesus A Theography*, (Thomas Nelson, Nashville, Tennessee), page xiv.

thousands of threads that enhance the person and message of Christ. We will be using the term "thread" to describe repeated truths that can be found throughout the Bible. The desire of my heart is that this book will help each reader get excited about The Book, God's written word. I also hope you will begin to see what God is doing "behind the scenes." Threads tie passages together. For example, the thread of a *garden* ties the Creation Story (the Garden of Eden) to the Empty Tomb (the Garden Tomb) to the Heavenly Garden in the book of Revelation. Following a thread makes each passage come more alive by enabling to see details we may not have noticed before.

This book is a *primer*. This is not an exhaustive volume on all the threads in the Bible. My purpose is to introduce the reader to some of the major threads and show how they add depth and dimension to our knowledge of Christ. There may be times when you think, "Why didn't he write a chapter on…?" My goal is to keep this book short enough that it will be both quick and easy to read. The main challenge in writing about the Bible is trying to keep what I am learning as compact and concise as possible. After nearly 15 years of study, I realize I have only scratched the surface. This book is meant to be a "starter kit."

My target audience can be divided into two-groups: people who have read the Bible and people who have not read the Bible. I am writing to Sunday School teachers who are preparing to teach Sunday School this Sunday. I am writing to Pastors who are at times chomping at the bit to share what God has laid on their heart, and at other times are breaking out into a cold sweat Saturday night as they struggle to find a text. I am writing to those who sit through worship service checking off the items on the Order of Worship until the service is over.

I am also writing to those who have a mental block about understanding the Bible. I am writing to that person who never has opened a Bible. I am even writing to that teenaged boy on the back pew that passes notes to girls rather than listening. I want to include children as well.

Wherever you fit into those categories, here are my hopes for you. When you have finished this book, I hope you will be hungry to know God and learn more about His Word. God did not communicate to us in hidden codes. He is not trying to confuse us. Through the Holy Spirit, God wants "lights to come on" as the Holy Spirit illuminates the eternal Truth that can change our lives.

I also hope you will see the unity of the Bible. It is one book. It is not a collection of unrelated writings. In fact, every passage is tightly connected to the rest of Scripture. The story of Abraham and Isaac on Mount Moriah is directly connected to the Cross. Jonah's deliverance from the belly of the Whale on the third day is directly connected to the Resurrection. The Tabernacle and the Temple are filled with the story of Jesus. The context of each verse is broader than just the verses before and after the passage. Every passage of Scripture should be read with God's "bigger picture" in mind.

I want to help you become a "self-feeder." Just as we cannot survive physically on one or two meals a week, we cannot survive spiritually on one sermon and a Bible Study per week, no matter how great they are. Many of the insights that I will share in this book were given to me by people who never stood behind a pulpit. God wants you to take advantage of opportunities to hear sermons and enjoy a Bible study, but He also wants to talk to you through His written Word on weekdays too.

Although it may sound strange, I am praying there will be times as you are reading this book when you will stop and say, "Wait a minute! I am not so sure about that!" When that happens, grab your Bible or your smartphone and check it out. Talk through the passage with someone else. Ask the Holy Spirit to illuminate or enlighten your mind as you seek the meaning of a passage and how it can change your life. Through His written and Living Word (Jesus), God wants to change the person that you are.

Finally and most importantly, my hope is that you will encounter Jesus Christ in a deeper way than ever before. The writer of Hebrews says this about God's written Word,

> For the word of God is living and active. Sharper than any double-edged sword, it penetrates even to dividing soul and spirit, joints and marrow; it judges the thoughts and attitudes of the heart. Hebrews 4:12

What the Bible will do is bring you face-to-face with Jesus Christ, I promise!

The Process

This journey began long before I realized I was on it. While I was pastoring in Flint, Michigan, I was invited to teach a college adult studies class entitled "Biblical Perspectives" for Spring Arbor College (now Spring Arbor University). The goal of the class was for each student to read the Bible from Genesis to Revelation, review some of the familiar Bible stories like Abraham or Moses and discuss a few of the major themes of the Bible, such as the Covenant. Our time limit was six classes in six weeks! I had 24 hours of class time to take on the whole Bible!

Then something began to happen to my students. Each one was required to write a six-page reflection paper on what they had learned from the module. With the exception of the first class, someone always wrote about how God had changed their lives. Some started attending church after years away. Others even testified to the fact that they had begun a personal relationship with Christ! There were stories of forgiveness and healing from broken relationships. It was easy to realize that my scatter-brained approach to teaching was not responsible for those changes. I never made an evangelistic appeal either publicly or privately. Somehow, in spite of me, the message of the Bible had reached the student's lives!

Then, something began to happen to me, too. I taught this course for three different schools about twenty times in fifteen years. As I walked each class from Genesis to Revelation, I began to see more patterns and connections. Each time I taught, there was something fresh that came out of my preparation and the questions from the class. Students would come to me and share insights that made me think, "How could I not have seen that?" Their feedback shook me out of my "Bible expert" mindset. My learner's heart opened up again.

Over those same years, God brought people into my life who challenged me to dig deeper in my search to know Him better. I was able to watch the Bible come alive in the lives of people who had never read even one verse before. God brought people who weren't afraid to lovingly say, "Pastor, I don't agree with how you explained that passage." One of those people, Terry Guilfoyle became a friend who would not let me "blow smoke" by giving him a pat answer to his questions. We developed a friendship were we could kindly say to each other, "You are wrong on that!"

This process crystallized for me one day when Jay Rader came to ask if I could help him understand the Bible in a one-on-one format. Jay had been raised in the Church and had owned a Bible all of his life. As familiar as he was with the Church, he had a deep desire to understand the Bible in a better way. We committed to meet one hour every Monday for a year. My plan was that we would begin with Genesis by letting Jay write down questions from his reading. Genesis and Exodus went fairly well. When we approached Leviticus, I started the session by suggesting we skip over to Joshua since Leviticus was rather boring.

I will never forget Jay's response. He said, "I have already read Leviticus. I know you said it was boring, but I found it very interesting. By the way, "What is a Gershonite?" I had no idea, so we googled it. A quick search led us to Levi's three sons: Kohath, Gershon and Merari.

Just so you will know, during the forty years of wandering in the wilderness, the Israelites had to move the Tabernacle several times. So that each move was orderly, the Kohathites were responsible for carrying the holy things of the Tabernacle. The Merarites were responsible for disassembling and carrying the poles and frames of the Tabernacle. The Gershonites were responsible for carrying the curtains of the Tabernacle. Exciting, right?

The simple discover of the Gershonites led us to look at the colors of the curtains (scarlet, blue and purple represent Jesus as our Prophet, Priest and King). I realized that the four living creatures in Revelation 4 (lion, ox, man and a flying eagle) were present in the four banners for the twelve tribes of Israel (Lion of Judah) and Ezekiel 1. The colors, the symbols woven into the curtains and the furniture inside the Tent of Meeting shouted the name of Jesus. By the time we got finished that day, I was excited about how God provided seacow skins (Exodus 25:5) for the covering of the Tent of Meeting from the plunder of the Egyptians before the Exodus began! (You had to be there!)

I tell you that to say that I do not come to you as an expert, but as a co-learner. I am on this journey with you! I want to learn from you as you have new insights about what you are learning. I would love to engage pastors and congregations in this conversation. If you would like to communicate, contact me through my website, randyschuneman.com. Let's talk!

My Perspective

So that you will know up front, I am conservative in my perspective of the Bible. I believe the Bible is God's sacred Word. I believe that God is the Creator of the universe. And that Jesus' death and resurrection is the only hope we have for our salvation. I believe in the Virgin Birth. I believe there is a Heaven and a Hell. God even directed the canonization process of both the Old and New Testament. I do not apologize for my position. I have seen the power of God's Word transform too many lives to believe otherwise.

God wants to talk to you daily through His Holy Spirit and His Written Word. The Bible demands a response. Neutrality is not an option!

THE SEAMLESS CONCEPT

THE SEAMLESS CONCEPT

The first time I remember hearing the word "seamless" was during a visit to a CPA friend of mine. When I walked into his office, I immediately noticed Nathan had two monitors on his desk sitting side-by-side. I had to ask, "Nathan, why do you need two monitors?" It seemed like a waste to me.

Nathan's response got my attention when he said, "These monitors are seamless. Most of the times, I need to have multiple charts and documents where I can see them simultaneously. I used to have to minimize one document to read the other. Now I can just move it over to the other screen until I need it."

I walked over to Nathan's side of the monitors and watched as pulled up a picture of his family. With his cursor, he moved the picture back and forth from one screen to the other. I had just bought my first LED monitor. Needless to say, I was impressed. I envisioned all the ways I could use seamless monitors in sermon preparation. Then I was reminded I could not afford such an expense.

On the way home, I got to thinking about how I had begun seeing a seamless concept in the Bible. Old Testament stories like Abraham could be moved from Genesis 12 to Romans 4, since Paul used the story of the calling of Abraham to deal with the issues in the church at Rome. Or how about Elijah's prayer in I Kings 18:37-46 being used by James in James 5:17 to remind the Church of the power of prayer? Jesus even used the story of Noah in Genesis 11 as a part of His Olivet Discourse in Matthew 24:37.

That day, I did not see as clearly as I do now how the Old Testament spills over into the New Testament and the New Testament builds off the Old Testament. I just knew that the idea of seamlessness had piqued my attention. Then I started hearing the word "seamless" used in a variety of ways. From seamless gutters to seamless mergers, I realized the need in the world for smooth transitions tying the past to the present and future. Little did I know how much those two monitors would impact my understanding of the Bible.

In this section, I want to introduce you to the seamless concept of Scripture. I did not grow up thinking this way. I pastored for almost 25 years before I realized that I had made harder work than I needed to out of every sermon I had ever preached. While I was trying to parse every Greek word in the text, I found myself dreading the whole process. After six weeks and 15 sermons in my first pastorate, I was pretty sure that I had exhausted everything there is to know about the Bible. I could not think of anything else to preach! Forty years more of this? Preaching is so much easier now.

When I was ten, our pastor challenged everyone to read the entire Bible. I took the challenge. How hard could it be to read from Genesis to Revelation? I enjoyed Genesis and Exodus, but I hit a brick wall when I came to Levitcus and Numbers. Deuteronomy did not exactly thrill my soul either. I did not remember much of what I read, but I finished the job. Now, it is hard to read or hear a passage without seeing something I had previously missed.

There is nothing magical about what I am going to share. This is not a decoding device. It is just a fact that has helped me immensely enjoy both my preaching and private devotions. It is a reminder that the Bible is a book that man could not have fathomed. Join me on my journey!

REMOVING YOUR APPENDIXES

I GREW UP IN A VERY LOW-TECH PERIOD OF CHILDREN'S SUNDAY School. Unless you were blessed enough to have a film-strip projector, there was no need for electrical outlets. My teachers had a limited arsenal of weapons to keep my attention. There was a black chalkboard, a flannel graph board with figures that represented Moses or Jesus, depending on the story. Later on, we progressed to a magnetic board with a two-sided background (one inside, one outside) for the paper figures that the poor teacher had to cut out each week. We had a supply of construction paper in various colors. You could smell the broken crayons and dried-up Elmer's glue. The table and chairs were well-worn.

However, there was one other item that completed the teaching tools. Somewhere near the Holman Hunt painting of Jesus knocking at the door was a poster known as The Bible Bookcase. Its sole purpose was to provide an aid to memorize the books of the Bible. The 39 books of the Old Testament were grouped into three categories: History (Genesis through Esther), Poetry (Job through Songs of Solomon) and Prophecy (Isaiah through Malachi). The first five books of the Old Testament (the Pentateuch) were clearly marked as The Law of Moses. The Major Prophets were separated from the Minor Prophets. Because the Bible is organized by literary types, not chronological order, several shades of color were used to distinguish the groupings. Most importantly to me, there were noticeable gaps between each grouping.

The New Testament took up the bottom two shelves and included five groupings: the Gospels (Matthew through John), History (Acts), Paul's Letters (Romans through Philemon), Other Letters (Hebrews through Jude) and finally Revelation. Although there were gaps between each grouping, poor Revelation looked like it had been put in solitary confinement. It stood by itself on the right of the last shelf with a large gap between itself and its neighbor, Jude.

I found tremendous comfort in the size of that final gap between Jude and Revelation. You see, the book of Revelation scared me to death! The thought of the Mark of the Beast, the Anti-Christ and the Second Coming of Christ kept me awake every night the summer before I started Junior High. I would kneel on my bed and look out my window to see if Jesus was coming back. Unfortunately, I did not realize my window faced the west and Jesus would be coming from the east. I would be the last person to know when the Second Coming took place.

My thought was that the book of Revelation was an *appendix* to the rest of the Bible. There was no sense in worrying about a book that only applied to "the last days." If we were supposed to worry about Revelation, why was it placed all by itself? Unfortunately, I read a lot more into the chart than was intended. I examined the different colors, the standing up/lying down of some books and especially the gaps that brought me to some very wrong conclusions.

First, I thought *the Bible is disconnected.* What else could the gaps represent? Obviously, the Law of Moses has nothing to do with the Gospels. In fact, the Law apparently had nothing to do with the Prophets either. Even the Major Prophets were distanced from the Minor Prophets. Why did it matter if we knew that someone "begat" someone else? I knew the basic stories of Abraham and Isaac on Mt. Moriah, David and Goliath, the Flood and Daniel in the Lion's Den. Between Sunday School class and our families nightly devotions, I was almost a Bible expert, right?

When it came to the New Testament, I could recite facts about the life of Jesus. I knew about Bethlehem, the Cross and Easter. Of course, the Gospels were important because they told the story of Jesus. But what did Jesus' ministry have to do with the Apostle Paul? Why did we need four Gospel accounts, instead of just one? These questions did not bother me as long as Revelation did not come into play, knowing about Jesus was good enough for me. I thought that each book of the Bible was an entity of its own.

I thought *the Bible was fragmented.* Within each grouping, individual verses could be torn out of the Bible without concern for context. Even in college, I was taught it was enough to just read the verses immediately before and after the verse. As a pastor, I took a verse or passage of Scripture and examined it for every Greek word I could find. Eventually, I even found three words that began with the same letter so I could build my three-point sermon. I could quote John 3:16 years before I discovered John 3:17. I memorized Psalm 23, but did not discover Psalm 22 until I examined the words of Jesus on the Cross. Even as a pastor, I thought I was responsible to pick up the pieces of the Bible and wring out the truth inside each one.

The One-Year Bible also affirmed the fact that anyone can take an Old Testament verse and a New Testament verse, plus a short devotional, with an end result of reading the whole Bible without it being too painful. It never crossed my mind that the two passages might be connected. Getting the reading done was the goal.

To make matters worse, I received a Bible Reading chart from my Great Aunt Josephine. Now I had the freedom to skip around from Exodus 5 to Acts 15 to Malachi 3 to I Kings 13 in order to get my chapters completed. If I read three chapters each day from Monday through Saturday and five on Sunday, it was the same thing as starting from the beginning of a book. Dropping in and out of Bible stories is okay, I thought, as long as you cross off the chapter.

I thought *the Old Testament has nothing to do with the New Testament.* We proudly proclaimed, "I am a New Testament Christian." I had numerous copies of just the New Testament or the New Testament plus Psalms and Proverbs. The Old Testament became *optional reading.* Growing up in the Church, I felt like I had a head-start on other people. I knew the main Old Testament stories. I could now focus on the New Testament.

I thought the *Bible was written in chronological order.* I took it for granted that *when* something happened was not an issue. I was not sure why we needed I and II Chronicles when we already struggled with the confusion of knowing which one was a "good king" or "bad king" from First and Second Kings. Why bring it up again? I did wonder why Ezra and Nehemiah were rebuilding the Temple when Solomon had just built it.

Finally, I thought *the Bible has exciting stories, but overall it is not exciting.* I have a friend named Mark who frequently visited my office on his day off. One thing was always clear during each visit: Mark was excited about some new insight he learned from the Bible. Whether it was the Covenant Concept or Creation, Mark talked so fast that I thought he would hyperventilate. My head was spinning like an F5 tornado by the time Mark left.

Then I began to understand why Mark was so excited. As I began to see the threads that Mark was discussing, familiar passages took on new life. I became the one talking so fast! As you begin to see how interwoven the Bible is, my prayer is that you will get excited too.

As we begin this journey together would you do me a favor? In your mind, push all the books on the Bible Bookcase as close together as you can. Remove any appendix that you have created. Stand them all up and close the gaps. See them as one unit with the most powerful message that we have ever known ... God has acted in Christ to redeem a lost and dying world!

Let's begin the journey!

THE SEAMLESS TIES THAT BIND

IN FEBRUARY 2008, I HAD THE PRIVILEGE OF VISITING ISRAEL. I was able to see first-hand the places that I had read about since I was a child. The places that I had only seen in pictures now came alive before my eyes. When I stood by the Sea of Galilee, I dipped my feet into the same water that Jesus had walked on. I stood on the hillside where Jesus preached the Sermon on the Mount. I could almost see Joshua watching the flood waters of the Jordan River parting as I listened to those same waters flowing at the place where Jesus was baptized.

Seeing the eastern wall of Jerusalem from the Garden of Gethsemane enabled me to see in my mind's eye Jesus entering the city on a donkey's foal during His Triumphal Entry. In Jerusalem, I walked through the Upper Room, stood at Golgotha and walked into the Empty Tomb. Our group took a walk down the crowded streets of the Via Dolorosa.

I took thousands of pictures of places like Bethlehem, Capernaum, Armageddon and the Eastern Wall. When I got home, my friends started getting that "deer in the headlights" look when I approached, because they knew I would overwhelm them with pictures. However, one of the most meaningful moments happened in a place where taking photographs was not allowed.

During our tour of Jerusalem, we were taken to a museum that houses part of the Dead Sea Scrolls. I am sure you know that the Dead Sea Scrolls were one of the greatest biblical discoveries of our time. Discovered between 1947 and 1956 in the caves west of the Dead Sea, these scrolls of the scribes of a place called Qumran were found in clay jars in various caves. The jars preserved the scrolls of the Old Testament so well that they are the most complete copies of the Old Testament we have.

Because they are so fragile and priceless, this partial collection of Dead Sea Scrolls was placed behind very thick protective glass and displayed with as little light as possible. As our group was admiring the display, a museum moderator approached us and asked us, "Would you like to know how these scrolls were put together?" Of course, we did.

The moderator explained, "The scrolls were copied page by page. Each page was overseen by four other scribes who carefully examined each one. Small mistakes would be corrected by wiping the ink away. If there were too many mistakes, the whole page would be wiped clean." Then he added, "When the page was flawless, the page was taken and *sewn into the previous page.*"

A light came on for me! The seamlessness that I had been grappling with since that day I saw Nathan's dual monitors became picture perfect. The Bible is seamlessly sewn together by God! It was not fragmented or disconnected. In fact, there is no book on earth that has ever been so beautifully interwoven. Each verse is sewn into the others. There are *threads* that bind the Bible together from Genesis to Revelation. Once you begin to recognize these threads, the familiar passages we know begin to jump off the page! Unfamiliar passages became easier to understand. *The Bible is seamless!*

Looking at the Bible as one seamless book transformed my study of the Bible. Looking at a passage in isolation was no longer an option. I began to examine Scripture with a different set of lens. Like pulling a thread on a sweater, I realized that when you examine one verse of Scripture, the whole Bible moves. Let me share a few of those changes in my thinking.

The Bible is one unified book.

Whatever passage you are studying is a part of the whole. Every verse has a purpose in the bigger picture of God's message to us. The genealogies with all the difficult names, the Sacrificial System with its meticulous details and even the book of Revelation all play a role in God's redemptive plan for His ultimate creation of man.

Just like the Dead Sea Scrolls, the Bible is sewn together tightly with hundreds of threads that permeate each word. You cannot look at any verse in isolation or within the immediate text only. The Passover meal is setting the stage for the Last Supper. The Garden of Eden is sewn into the Garden of Gethsemane and the Empty Tomb. Grace is knotted into the message of Ezekiel.

The Exodus cannot be separated from the Cross. Every piece of furniture in the Tabernacle and later the Temple are telling the Story of Jesus.

The Bible has one unified message.

Everything in the Bible centers on the Christ Event (Jesus' Birth, Death and Resurrection). Seven hundred years before Jesus' birth in Bethlehem, the prophet Isaiah proclaims the hope we have in Christ (Isaiah 6:9). The Psalmist David describes the events of the Cross so clearly in Psalm 22. David begins that psalm with the words spoken from the Cross—"My God, my God, why have you forsaken me." Every passage is either leading up to the Cross or reflecting back on it. I love this Facebook post from Leonard Sweet: "Every biblical story has The Whole Story nestled within it."[2] *That Story is Jesus!*

I have always loved James Taylor's song "Fire and Rain." I have listened to it hundreds of times. However, I had a chance to listen to it using my iPod earbuds recently. Although I have listened to the song hundreds of times, for the first time, I heard the cello part that undergirds the whole song. I cannot listen to that song now without hearing that cello part. The cello made the lyrics stand out even more. I heard the words more clearly than I ever have before. That is the purpose of all the threads that we will examine. Each thread amplifies the person and ministry of Jesus.

You can start anywhere in the Bible and move backward and forward.

Although I would certainly recommend reading every book of the Bible from beginning to end, it is possible to start with the story of King Ahaz in II Kings 15 and work backward or forward from there. I always suggest starting with the Gospel of John, but you can start with the book of Jonah. The message of the Bible does not have Stop signs. It flows from the beginning of the Bible to the end and back. If you do not have a Bible reading game plan, I

---

2   Leonard Sweet, Facebook post for June 8, 2014

highly recommend you develop one. I would challenge you to read each book from the first chapter to the last. Keep a notepad by you as you think of questions you would like to ask a Christian friend. Focus more on *what* you are reading more than *how much* you read.

The Old Testament is interwoven into the New Testament.

The book of Malachi is not a bookend. There is a bridge between Malachi and Matthew. A proper understanding of the Old Testament is absolutely necessary to understand the New Testament. If you do not understand the Old Testament, you will misinterpret the New Testament. The Passover, the Exodus, the Tabernacle/Temple and the feast days are all interwoven into the ministry of Jesus. The defeats of the King of Og and the King of Sihon serve as a marker for both Old and New Testament passages.

Every verse in the Bible is sewn to all the other verses.

We will examine this more closely later in this book, but one of my favorite examples of this fact is the use of the phrase, "On the third day." So many events happened on the third day: Abraham sees Mount Moriah on the third day. Jonah is delivered from the belly of the whale on the third day. The wedding in Cana is on the third day. Most importantly, Jesus' Resurrection takes place on the third day. All of those verses work together.

The threads that tie the Bible together are visible.

We will not be looking for hidden secrets. You do not have to be a Bible scholar to identify what is going on "behind the scenes." It is a matter of keeping our eyes and ears open for things we may not have noticed before.

The Bible is a book of relationships, not a book of religion.

The Ten Commandments were never meant to be a checklist for righteousness. When the Bible is seen as a book of religion, we find ourselves trying to save ourselves through our good works. The end result is frustration from seeing that no matter how hard we try, there is always someone trying harder.

I will be using several metaphors throughout the book. For example, you will notice I use the metaphor of music quite often. Before we begin our study, let me introduce you to the main metaphor of this book—The Seamless Robe of Jesus.

THE SEAMLESS ROBE

WHEN THE SOLDIERS CRUCIFIED JESUS, THEY TOOK HIS CLOTHES, dividing them into four shares, one for each of them, with the undergarment remaining. This garment was seamless, woven in one piece from top to bottom.

> "Let's not tear it," they said to one another. "Let's decide by lot who will get it." This happened that the scripture might be fulfilled which said, "They divided my garments among them and cast lots for my clothing." John 19:23-24

Had we been present at the Crucifixion, it is doubtful that we would have even noticed it lying crumpled on the ground. Our eyes and ears would have been overwhelmed by the sounds of the blood-thirsty crowd surrounding us. Their intense hatred permeated the air, so hell-bent were they on watching the Innocent One on the middle Cross suffer and die. Ironically, the pious chief priest and religious leaders were at the forefront of this feeding frenzy. Any sense of justice and mercy had been overcome by an irrational desire for revenge. The ones who claimed to be closest to God were willing to sell their souls to Rome in order to see the end of threat to their power that Jesus caused. As the crowd mocked and spit on Jesus, even the criminals hanging next to Jesus joined in the taunting.

If we had been close enough, we may have been able to hear Jesus' voice as He spoke to His Father and His disciples from the Cross.[3] If we had been listening, we could have heard Jesus preach His final sermon from the Cross. For an unrepentant crowd, Jesus prayed, "Father forgive them, for they do not know what they are doing" (Luke 23:34). To a repentant criminal dying beside Him, Jesus responds, "I tell you the truth, today you will be with me in Paradise" (Luke 23:43). To Mary, Jesus says, "Dear woman, here is your son" and to John, "Here is your mother" (John 19:26-27).

---

3   The Seven Last Words of Christ will be listed in the Appendix.

As the sky darkened and the earth began to shake, Jesus cried out, "My God, my God, why have you forsaken me" (Matthew 27:46)? So He might wet His lips to strengthen His voice, Jesus tells the soldiers, "I am thirsty" (John 19:29). In a voice of triumph, Jesus shouts, "It is finished" (John 19:30). And like a child falling asleep in His Father's arms, Jesus whispers, "Father, into your hands I commit my spirit" (Luke 23:46). History is changed forever!

While this Heavenly Conversation takes place and the salvation of all mankind hangs in the balance, the transaction at the foot of the Cross may have gone unnoticed by most eye-witnesses. The four Roman soldiers in charge of crucifying Jesus were simply gathering their reward for a hard day's work. They were divvying up Jesus' clothing. As the soldiers cast lots for the final piece of clothing, one soldier's life would be changed forever.

The first choices were made quite quickly. Jesus' *sandals* that John the Baptist said he was unworthy to untie (John 1:27) would have been an easy choice. Little did the he soldier know he held the sandals that had held the very feet of God. In the Sermon on the Mount, Jesus had used *His outer robe* to serve as an object lesson of selflessness (Matthew 5:40), but the soldiers selfishly grabbed for what they wanted. Just hours before, Jesus had used *His turban* to cover His Head as He initiates the Lord's Supper in the Upper Room (Mark 14:15). *The belt* encompassed God in human flesh, but the soldiers could only see a trophy of their military service.

The final choice would provide a mathematical problem for the soldiers. There were four soldiers and five pieces of clothing. All four soldiers realized that the seamless robe Jesus wore was a garment of great value, but *only* if it was left in one piece. If this special garment was divided into four pieces, it became nothing more than pieces of cloth. The only solution was to cast lots to see who would take the Robe home. These soldiers had no idea that they were fulfilling the words of the Psalmist David when he wrote, "They divide my garments among them and cast lots for my clothing" (Psalm 22:19).

A seamless robe was both costly and distinctive. Not just anyone could sew a seamless robe. Johnny Pope writes,

To those tailors and seamstresses, we have something that stands out. Someone had taken the extra effort to make a seamless inner tunic for our Lord … this kind of a garment is valuable. The quality of the material chosen was durable and costly to withstand often wearing.[4]

Usually sewn by a man's mother, the seamless robe was more than a specially handcrafted garment. It was visible evidence of a mother's love. It was the last gift a mother would give to her son before he left home. How heartbreaking it must have been for Mary to watch that special gift be gambled away before her very eyes! It is immediately following the dividing of Jesus' clothing that Jesus speaks to Mary these words of comfort, "*Dear woman, here is your son.*" And to John, Jesus says, "*Here is your mother*" (John 19:26).

As Jesus' and Mary's eyes meet, Jesus bids farewell to the one person who had experienced His earthly ministry from beginning to end. The once-scared teenage virgin now stands by the Cross as a broken-hearted mother about to lose her promised Son. Jesus' words remind Mary that the love they have shared will continue. Although Jesus would no longer be her son, He will always be the Son of God. Jesus will no longer be her right-hand man, but He will sit at the Right Hand of the Father.

Why is the seamless robe of Jesus such a good word picture for understanding the Bible? Of all the Gospel writers, John alone is close enough to the Cross to see the Roman soldier's actions. Although he sees all five items of clothing, he only comments on one. A seamless robe would have great spiritual significance to a Jewish man. The design of this Robe is patterned after the seamless robe of the High Priest (Exodus 28:31-32). Through Jesus' Seamless Robe, the Bible is enveloping the Greatest Story ever told!

This small detail given only by John serves as a wonderful word picture to help see so many parallels between the Seamless Robe and the Bible. Like the Seamless Robe, the Bible is telling the Story of Jesus. Let me give you seven ways in which the Seamless Robe parallels the Bible.

---

4   Johnny Pope, christchurchbaptistfellowship.com

1. Like the Seamless Robe, the Bible is a Seamless Work.

Using a *warp (up and down)* and *woof (side to side)* pattern, the weaver of a seamless robe would work the thread up and down and then side to side. The tightness of this pattern would make the garment into a single unit which was unable to be torn. The fashion of weaving would make it impossible to tell where one thread stopped and another one started. Even the neck opening had a reinforced collar which added extra strength. The beauty of the Seamless Robe is not found in examining one strand, but in seeing the Robe as one unified garment.

The Bible is an interconnected seamless book. Glen Hall is correct when he writes, "All things in God's holy word relate, interrelate, correlate, and prove each other."[5] God's Word is Eternal Truth that will stand the test of time. Although we live in an age of eclectic religion, our attempts to mix religions together will always fail. Jesus' words are still true when He says, "I am the Way and the Truth and the Life. No one comes to the Father except through me" (John 14:6). The Bible proclaims the truth that our salvation is through Jesus only, not through Jesus and something or someone else.

We can read and study individual verses, but seeing how these threads work together will enable us to see that the Bible is *"living and active and sharper than a two-edged sword"* (Hebrews 4:12a). There are no insignificant details in the Bible. Wherever you begin to read, you are stepping into the River of God as His hand moves throughout history. You can move backward and forward throughout the Bible, because it is one Story.

Glen Hall affirms this when he writes,

> Because the Word of God itself is a seamless garment, a seamless work, a seamless revelation, I can go to virtually any verse in any book of the Bible and begin to teach the plan of God for mankind, the plan which states that the entire history of mankind gives witness to the creation of man by God in His own image. We see this plan in the very first verse of the Bible, Genesis 1:1

---

5   Glen Hall, New Jerusalem: Eternal Home of God's Perfect Jewels, his overcomers, "A Seamless Garment." zedek.us/a-seamless-garment

wherein God declares, "In the beginning God created the heaven and the earth." The rest of the Bible explains this creation.[6]

If you allow the Holy Spirit to guide you, I believe He will enable you to have even familiar stories come alive in a new way. Hopefully, you will see the Bible move before your very eyes! You might even find that talking donkey in Numbers 22:28 showing up in the book of Revelation.

2. Like the Seamless Robe, the Bible is like a second skin of Jesus.

In reading articles on how a seamless robe was sewn, the phrase *"second skin"* was frequently used. The Seamless Robe formed the closest bond to Jesus of anything on earth. It served as Jesus' last piece of "armor" as He faced the onslaught of the combined efforts of the Jewish religious leaders and the Roman forces. If we could have examined the Seamless Robe, it would have been able to tell the story of Calvary. Jesus' essence is permeated throughout this garment.

The pink tinge on the Robe would have reminded us of the blood-like sweat that poured out of Jesus' skin as He experienced the weight all our sins on His shoulders at Gethsemane. The red, splattered blood stains told the story of the scourging that Jesus had experienced. As the soldiers scourged Jesus, they were skillfully trying to bring Him as close to death as possible without killing Him. It is by these stripes that we are healed! (I Peter 2:24) The blood stains around the collar of the Robe told the story of the Crown of Thorns as the King of Kings was mocked.

Along with the smell of Jesus' sweat, there would also be a tinge of the smell of the nard his friend Mary so extravagantly poured on Jesus' feet (John 12:1-8) two days before. The Seamless Robe served as a multi-sensory reminder of the story of Jesus.

The Bible wraps around the very being of Jesus from before the beginning of time into eternity. If you look carefully, you will be able to hear, see, smell and touch the One who has come to save you. The Bible was inspired to draw us into the Story. Jesus

---

6   Ibid.

is on every page, but so are we. We are present the day Adam and
Eve fell. We are the whining Israelites on the way to the Promised
Land. We are in the crowd shouting for Jesus to be crucified. By
the mercy of God, we can be those who are able to enter the Holy
of Holies.

3. Like the Seamless Robe, the Bible is a gift of love.

As has been mentioned, the Seamless Robe is most likely a gift
given to Jesus by His mother. Marshall Davis states, "… it was
likely a gift because Jesus was no weaver, and He had no money to
purchase such a garment. It is a sign of love for the One who was
and is love and died for love."[7] It was a clear message of love! It
cries out, "I love you!" The key was in receiving the gift. We must
be willing to confess our sins and humbly bow before Christ.

Although there are clear warnings about the consequences of
rejecting the message of the Bible, the purpose of God's Word is
to show each of us how to experience the love of God through a
personal relationship with Christ. Every reader of the Bible will
experience conviction through the Holy Spirit as the Word pen-
etrates their hearts. However, even the conviction that we feel is in
order for us to see our need to change by allowing Christ to work
in our life.

4. Like the Seamless Robe, the Bible presents Jesus as our High Priest.

In Exodus 28: 31-32, God gives the instructions for the High
Priest's robe. The robe the High Priest wore into the Holy of
Holies on the Day of Atonement was to be seamless with a rein-
forced collar, just like the robe of Jesus. Moses was instructed,

> Make the robe of the ephod entirely of blue cloth, with an open-
> ing for the head in its center. There shall be a woven edge like a
> collar around this opening, so that it will not tear Exodus 28:31-
> 32

---

7   Marshall Davis, *Spiritual Reflections:Meditations on culture, art and spiritual-
ity,* *"The Seamless Robe of Jesus."* revmdavis.blogspot.com/2010/03/seamless-robe-
of-christ.html

As Jesus prepares to be crucified, even His robe shouts that he is the final High Priest performing the final Sacrifice. Just as the purple robe and the Crown of Thorns placed on Jesus by the soldiers remind us that Jesus is the King of Kings, the Seamless Robe reminds us that Jesus is our High Priest.

The word "priest" means "bridge builder." The Bible proclaims that Jesus is the only Bridge to God. Throughout the book of Hebrews, the author celebrates Jesus as our High Priest. The author rejoices in the fact that Jesus has provided the means by which we can come into the presence of God on a regular basis when he writes,

> For we do not have a high priest who is unable to sympathize with our weaknesses, but we have one who has been tempted in every way, just as we are—yet was without sin. Let us then approach the throne of grace with confidence, so that we may receive mercy and find grace to help us in our time of need. Hebrews 4:15-16

As we will see, when Adam and Eve fell from God's grace, they did not have a way back to God. They were helpless to save themselves. The beauty of the message of the Bible is that before the foundation of the world God had the plan to reconcile us to Him if we were willing to accept His gracious offer.

5. Like the Seamless Robe, the Bible cannot be torn.

The fibers were so tightly woven together that it was impossible to tear. If the soldiers had decided to divide up the Seamless Robe, they would have faced more than just an economic problem. A seamless garment was built not to be torn. God's purpose in this design was to remind His people there would always be a High Priest. The position would be fulfilled in Jesus Christ.

"A seamless robe is out of place in a crucifixion scene. Normally at a death, robes were torn as a sign of grief. This robe is purposely designed not to be torn."[8]

The High Priesthood of Jesus is permanent. The Bible declares Jesus to be "a priest *forever*." (Hebrews 7:17) There never has been,

---

8   Ibid.

or will be any other Savior of the world than Jesus! At the Cross, the price of man's redemption is paid in full, once and for all. Never again will someone have to die for us. Jesus has paid the price for our deliverance from sin. Jesus offers our salvation as a gift we can receive freely through repentance of our sins.

Hall continues,

> Jesus wore a seamless garment at the time of his crucifixion for a reason and that reason was to show the world that God's Word has no patches, no tears, no seams; it is all of one. Hear, o world, the Lord your God, the Lord is ONE![9]

6. Like the Seamless Robe, the Bible leads us to the Cross

As the soldiers prepared Jesus for Crucifixion, they remove the Seamless Robe and an amazing transition takes place. Our High Priest becomes the Final Sacrifice. The Book of Leviticus with all of its meticulous detail is now fulfilled in this beautiful moment of God's plan of salvation.

In Levitical law, the High Priest entered the Holy of Holies once a year on the Day of Atonement. On that special day, the High Priest went behind the Temple Veil and stepped directly into the Presence of God. It was a moment so powerful that incense was used to enable the High Priest to withstand the brilliant light (Shekinah) Glory of God. The High Priest made not only a sacrifice for the Israelite people, but also for himself.

At the Cross, the embodiment of the Holy of Holies, Jesus Christ, sacrifices Himself; not for Himself, but for all of us who had no hope. Paul writes,

> God made him (Jesus) who had no sin to be sin for us, so that in him we might become the righteousness of God. II Corinthias 5:21

---

9   Glen Hall, *New Jerusalem: Eternal Home of God's Perfect Jewels, his overcomers, "A Seamless Garment."* www.new-jerusalem.us/a-seamless-garment

7. Like the Seamless Robe, the Bible belongs in the hands of those who need Jesus most.

In his classic novel *The Robe*, Lloyd C. Douglas tells the story of a Roman legate named Marcellus Gallio who is chosen to be in charge of the soldiers who will crucify Jesus. Marcellus becomes the one who wins Jesus' Seamless Robe. From that point in the story, Douglass follows Marcellus as he carries the Robe with him. The possession of the Robe brings Marcellus face to face with the story of Jesus. As hard as he tried, Marcellus cannot keep from telling others about the One who wore the Robe. In the end, Marcellus' life is changed by the power of the story of Jesus.

In reality, this precious Robe would go home with one of the very soldiers who escorted Jesus to His death. The presence of the Robe would give the soldier opportunities to tell the story of Jesus over and over again. As unfair as it may seem, Jesus' seamless robe belonged in the hands of those who rejected Him. What a beautiful symbol of Jesus' message and ministry! The very person who crucified Jesus received a symbol of the Savior of the World. The Cross reaches down to the vilest of sinners and the most self-righteous and brings the message of salvation!

It is impossible to separate the Living Word (Jesus) and the Written Word (the Bible). Apart from Jesus, the Bible becomes a book of rules and regulations. Apart from the Bible, Jesus and His teaching are open to man-made interpretation. The Holy Spirit weaves both the Written Word of the Bible with the Living Word of Jesus. What a joy to eye-witness the power of the Bible as Christ changes a person's life.

My prayer is that all of us will open our hearts to the leadership of the Holy Spirit. My goal is not to have you worry about whether a thread is a warp or woof thread, but to allow God to weave these Truths into your heart. Let's begin with the longer Warp Threads, those repeated truths that are sewn beginning in Genesis and ending in Revelation.

WARP THREADS

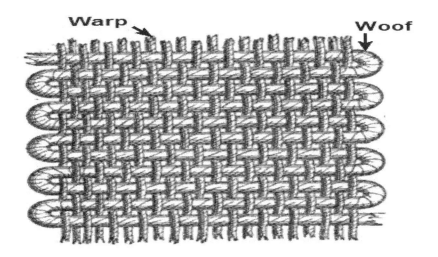

WHAT ARE WARP THREADS?

Captain Kirk sits nervously in his captain's chair on the brig of the USS Enterprise. Even though the force field has been activated, the ship is being rocked by a surprise attack from the Klingons. In a desperate voice, Scotty has just reported, "Captain, if we don't get out of here, she'll be breakin' up." Calmly, Mr. Spock adds, "Captain, it is logical that we would use the one weapon we have remaining." Seeing no alternative, Captain Kirk gives the command, "Warp speed ahead, Scotty!" The starship disappears in a flash of light and sound, past stars that are only streaks in the sky.

This Star Trek vignette has nothing to do with the next few chapters, except the word "warp." I just wanted the male readers to start with something familiar as we prepare for a short lesson on a sewing technique known as Warp and Woof. For this lesson, warp will have more to do with length than speed.

The design of a seamless robe was unique in that the sewing process began at the neckline. Starting with the collar opening, the threads were sewn up and down (warp) and then side to side (woof). The collar would be reinforced with further binding, resulting in a tightly-knit garment that could not be torn. There would have been a noticeable difference between a seamless robe and a common robe, both in design and price.

Although distinguishing between the two types of threads is not an issue, we will be defining warp threads as repeated truths sewn into the Bible from *Genesis 1 to Revelation 22*. Even if you cannot sow a stitch, you will recognize these biblical truths. Hopefully, you will see them in a new and deeper light.

We will be focusing on seven of these threads. I know you will find major threads that are not covered in this section. Our purpose is not to present an exhaustive list, but to introduce the reader to some examples that will open our eyes and minds to the bigger picture God is communicating.

We tend to have "tunnel vision" when we approach a biblical passage. It is like viewing the Mona Lisa, but focusing on one brush stroke of Da Vinci's masterpiece. Just remember that each thread is warping and woofing throughout your reading.

WHO'S IN CHARGE HERE?

In the beginning God created the heavens and the earth. Genesis 1:1

I WILL NEVER FORGET THE FIRST TIME I SAW THE PHOTOGRAPH later named "Earthrise." It was taken on December 24, 1968. The crew of Apollo 8 (Frank Borman, James Lovell and William Anders) was seeing something that had never been seen by human eyes. Being the first humans to travel beyond Earth's orbit, these men were the first to see the whole Earth and were the very first eye-witnesses to Earthrise, the Earth coming into view as you orbit the moon. Lunar Module Pilot William Anders snapped the picture that has become a classic. If you are not familiar with the photograph, take a minute to google "Earthrise."

The photograph took my breath away! At 15 years old, I had never seen anything so astonishing. Planet Earth looked so small when viewed from 93,000 miles away! I could not have imagined the photographs that are available to us today. By means of the Hubble Telescope, we are able to view galaxies we have never seen before. One of the galaxies is 300 million light years away and has a Cross-shape in the middle of it! If you want to see God's handi-work, I recommend that you to go to NASA.com.

Can you imagine the magnificent results produced each time God said, "Let there be …?" Our eyes would have been blinded by the brilliance and beauty of the vast colors that flashed before our eyes. Our ears would have been deafened by the sounds that filled every corner of the universe. Our minds could not have processed the millions of galaxies God hung in space that day. Time and space are spoken into existence.

The truth is we were not there! So God begins His love letter by introducing Himself to us. The Creation Story describes more than what God *did*. It is a description of who God *is*. The biblical thread that *God is our Creator* will serve as the framework for the Bible. James Houston puts it this way, "Creation is the *landscape* of the Bible. It sees God as the 'Maker of heaven and earth;' the Creator of all things."[10]

The first thing God wants us to know is that He is the Creator of the universe and we are His creation. This first thread is so important that God tells the story twice (*Genesis 1:1-2:4* and *Genesis 2:4-25*). God opens His conversation with us by establishing, "In the beginning, God created the heavens and the Earth" (Genesis 1:1). Echoing the Genesis Creation account, the Apostle John opens his Gospel account with these words.

In the beginning was the Word, and the Word was with God, and the Word was God.

> He was with God in the beginning. Through him all things were made; without him nothing was made that has been made. John 1:1-3

The truth that God is our Creator changes everything. We are the focus of God's intentional plan to have a personal relationship with Him. There is a Divine Order to the universe! We are not a random act of nature. God alone is responsible for our existence. God alone gives our life meaning and purpose. Only through a proper understanding of our Creator God do we have a correct perspective of the meaning of life. Solomon reminds us that God's plan for our life goes beyond this world as he writes,

> He has made everything beautiful in its time. He has also set eternity in the hearts of men; yet they cannot fathom what God has done from beginning to end. Ecclesiastes 3:11

Whether it is under the scrutiny of a microscope or a telescope, more and more scientific discoveries are affirming the creative presence of God. The more we know, the more it shows. In my lifetime, what scientists have learned about the complexity of a single molecule would fill a library. At the same time, we are discovering galaxies we didn't know existed. Let me share some fun facts I learned while doing research for this book.

- Every week, Jethro Gibbs and his NCIS team use the DNA from a strand of hair or a single drop of blood to

---

10   James Houston, *I Believe in the Creator*, (William Eerdmans: Grand Rapid, Michigan, 1980), page 15

identify their killer. The team knows that every human being has 6 feet of 100 trillion cells that are so unique that they can pick the right suspect out of the seven billion people on Earth. We are "fearfully and wonderfully made" (Psalm 139:4).

- Scientists now know that the odds of a molecule coming together on its own is 10 to the 25th power or a hundred thousand trillion, trillion, trillion, trillion, trillion, trillion, trillion, trillion, trillion.[11] If I may translate, "Not a chance in the world" (pun intended).

- I really like this one. If the tilt of the Earth was adjusted *one inch*, gravity would increase a billion fold. The Earth would become a 40-foot cube.[12] That is mind-boggling.

- How about this? While every human being has a personalized DNA, we all share a protein network called Laminin. Scientists believe that Laminin is the key physical element that holds all life together.[13] Guess what? It is formed in the shape of a cross. Look it up!

When my Mom checked into the hospital last year, the admissions person had a small "palm scanner" on her desk. When I inquired about it, the woman said, "Every person's vein pattern is so unique that you can identify any person in the world by scanning their palm." Mom placed her hand over the scanner and the woman replied, "Mildred Schuneman?"

The Simplicity of the Creation Story

The beauty of the Creation Story is found in its *simplicity*. God is writing a love letter, not a science textbook. We could not contain or comprehend all that God knows about the inner workings of the universe. With all of our technology, we are discovering new evidence of God's handprint or should I say "Wordprint?"

---

11   Lee Strobel, *The Case for a Creator*, (Zondervan: Grand Rapids, Michigan, 2004), page 131

12   Ibid. page 132.

13   www.truthorfiction.com/rumors/l/laminin.htm

Although God spoke the universe into existence, He does not say too much or too little. God never intended to explain the *hows* and *whens* we so often seek. God's desire is to tell us *why He created the universe around us.* When we read the Creation Story, it deepens our understanding of who God is and gives us a proper perspective of who we are.

God is saying, "I love you so much that I created you and everything around you." God reveals to us that every detail of the Creation Story is building to the crescendo of the creation of Adam and Eve. Although this thread begins in Genesis 1:1, our Creator God is sewn into every page of the Bible. God did not set the universe in motion and then walk away. The Bible is telling the love story of God's interaction with man throughout the ages.

This first thread of the Bible is the most obvious. It is visible in the intricate details of a newborn baby's hands or the breath-taking view of the Grand Canyon. You can see it in the autumn leaves that look as if God has spilled divine paint all over them. As Max Lucado puts it, "Creation is God's first missionary."[14]

One of my family's favorite activities is to sit outside at dusk and see who spots the first star. A good friend told me, "That sounds boring. The stars appear every night in the same place." Sonja didn't understand how amazing it is to watch the same stars in the same place appear every night. I will always be fascinated when the Big Dipper or North Star appears.

I am not alone in my amazement. When David was a boy tending sheep on the Bethlehem hillside, he had plenty of time to gaze into the star-filled sky. He was amazed the abundant evidence of his Creator all around him. Listen to David's lyrics.

> By the word of the Lord were the heavens made, their starry host by the breath of his mouth. He gathers the waters of the sea into jars; he puts the deep into storehouses. Let all the earth fear the Lord; let all the people of the world revere him. For he spoke, and it came to be; he commanded, and it stood firm. Psalm 33:6

When Peter and John were arrested for healing the lame man by the Beautiful Gate, the disciples knew to turn to their Creator.

---

14   Max Lucado, *In the Grip of Grace*, (Word Publishing: Dallas, Texas, 1996), page 23

When they heard this (*the arrest of Peter and John*), they raised their voices together in prayer to God. "Sovereign Lord," they said, "you made the heaven and the earth and the sea, and everything in them." Acts 4:24

When the Jewish leaders were preparing to stone him, Stephen's prayer included a quotation of Isaiah 66:1-2. Stephen found comfort in the fact that his Creator was more powerful than his enemy. Stephen prays,

Heaven is my throne, and the earth is my footstool. What kind of house will you build for me? says the Lord. Or where will my resting place be? Has not my hand made all these things? Acts 7:49-50

The Significance of the Creation Story

We would love more details, but the one fact we need to know is that *God is the Creator and we are His creation*. However, that truth changes everything! We have hope rather than hopelessness. We look forward to eternity, rather than extinction. We have purpose rather than meaningless existence.

Knowing God is our Creator describes how our relationship works. I first used the phrase, "He is in charge! I'm not!" That certainly is true, but this is a love letter that goes deeper than coming under God's authority. God wants to dance with you. If I weren't so clumsy and lazy, I would love to be a ballroom dancer. How wonderful it would be to glide along the floor with ease and grace. I have only had one lesson and that was while I was standing still.

While I was on a cruise ship with my wife and some friends, I came across some painted footsteps outlining how to do the Waltz. As I looked at the pattern, I realized why the question is always asked, "*Who is going to lead?*" If that question isn't settled, disaster will follow. The Bible clearly settles that issue for us as we walk with God. *God leads, I follow.* Our walk with God only works when we allow Him to lead.

Knowing God is our Creator reminds us of the respect He deserves. The Psalmist reminds us, "The fear of the Lord is the beginning of wisdom; all who follow his precepts have good understanding. To him belongs eternal praise" (Psalm 111:10). If we know God, this fear is not terror. The fear of God means remembering who He is. We can enjoy the majesty of being in the presence of God.

Before Isaiah was called to be God's prophet, he was a priest. While Isaiah is going about the daily tasks of a Temple priest in the Holy Place, he has an experience that only the High Priest experienced in the Holy of Holies on the Day of Atonement. The Temple is filled with smoke and seraphs and cherubim who announce the Holiness of God. (Isaiah 6:1-4) The Shekinah (Divine Light) glory of God fills the room. When Isaiah experiences the presence of God, he sees himself in the light of his Creator. His response is,

> "Woe to me!" I cried. "I am ruined! For I am a man of unclean lips, and I live among a people of unclean lips, and my eyes have seen the King, the Lord Almighty." Isaiah 6:5

Knowing that God is our Creator, describes the reverence we must show for God. When I was pastoring in Bartlesville, Oklahoma, we presented an Easter program entitled *Promise of Hope.* The presentation traced the life of Jesus from Creation to Heaven. It was probably one of the most meaningful experiences I had in my pastoral ministry. Every year, I learned new insights by "walking" from Creation to Heaven. However, I loved the first time the best.

The moment I will most cherish did not come during a public presentation. It was during the first full practice with the portrayal of Jesus being hung on the Cross.

Although the man portraying Jesus had memorized flawlessly every word that Jesus spoke on the Cross, we never got that far. As the soldiers lifted Jesus up on the Cross, the reality of the Crucifixion jolted us all. The whole cast began to cry simultaneously. We had to stop practice and pray together. Wherever we are, true worship takes place when we realize that we are in the presence of the Creator of the universe! When was the last time you stood in awe of God?

When we pray, do we realize that we are praying to the Creator of the universe? Although we may be overwhelmed by our circumstances, God is not. Prayer is not a one-way conversation. How often do we petition God, but forget to listen to His answer? I listened to a discussion on a Christian radio station about how to develop a prayer life. The answers made prayer sound like the hardest task in the world.

If God wanted to spend the day with you, would you talk to Him for fifteen minutes? Of course not! The Creator of the universe desires to have a personal relationship with you. He wants to be with you every hour of every day. It is not a matter of trying to squeeze in fifteen minutes during our personal devotions. Just as Adam and Eve once enjoyed the daily presence of God, that is God's desire for our lives.

Can you imagine what worship must be like in Heaven? The choir raises their voices in heavenly harmony. Everyone has gathered for the same purpose. They have come to worship their Creator. The Apostle John actually experienced it. As he begins to share the revelation of Jesus that he is blessed to see, he writes,

> Whenever the living creatures give glory, honor and thanks to him who sits on the throne and who lives for ever and ever, the twenty-four elders fall down before him who sits on the throne, and worship him who lives for ever and ever. They lay their crowns before the throne and say: "You are worthy, our Lord and God, to receive glory and honor and power, for you created all things, and by your will they were created and have their being." Revelation 4:9-11

I love the saying that my friend Stephen Manley uses, "You can't sing up there until you learn the tune down here." God wants to be in a relationship with you now. We can have a taste of heaven here on earth. This intimate relationship is a gift from God that is not based on our achievement. The price of our salvation has already been paid in full by the Blood of Jesus Christ. What does God expect in return? He wants us to be willing to receive His invitation.

God wants you to trust Him completely with your life. In his classic devotional *My Utmost for His Highest*, Oswald Chambers returns often to one theme. He writes, "The great word of Jesus to His disciples is abandon."[15] Total abandonment to God is the greatest freedom we can know. Knowing that God is in charge of my life means I do not need to handle any circumstances on my own. God does not want to come to us as much as He wants to be with us. Jesus reminded us of the blessing of access to Him when He said,

> Come to me, all you who are weary and burdened, and I will give you rest. Take my yoke upon you and learn from me, for I am gentle and humble in heart, and you will find rest for your souls. For my yoke is easy and my burden is light. Matthew 11:28-30

After all the persecution the Apostle Paul experienced in the Name of Christ, he shares the focus of his life when he writes,

> I want to know Christ and the power of his resurrection and the fellowship of sharing in his sufferings, becoming like him in his death, and so, somehow, to attain to the resurrection from the dead. Philippians 3:10-11

We were not created to live our lives under our own authority. We are too weak and vulnerable by ourselves. The Psalmist David reminds us, "for He knows how we are formed, He remembers that we are dust" (Psalm 103:14). God knows all of our weaknesses and loves us anyway. We are created for communion with God and with each other. When Christ died on the Cross, He provided the means by which we could be restored to the original relationship that God intended for us. God wants us to live under His care.

We can celebrate with the prophet Isaiah when he writes,

> Do you not know? Have you not heard? The Lord is the everlasting God, the Creator of the ends of the earth. He will not grow tired or weary and his understanding no one can fathom. Isaiah 40:28

Are you trying to be in charge? You don't have to be! Why not "Cast all your anxiety on Him because He cares for you? (I Peter 5:7).

---

15   Oswald Chambers, *My Utmost for His Highest*, (Dodd, Mead and Company: New York, 1935), page 144

When my son Robb was four years old, he spent time with my wife's parents. This particular day had been pretty rough for Robb, because he kept getting into trouble. Numerous times, Robb heard Gammy say, "Robb, don't do that!" If he started banging on the piano, he heard, "Robb, don't do that!" If he tossed a ball too close to a lamp, he heard, "Robb, don't do that!"

Sensing that Robb was having a tough time, Baba (my father-in-law) took Robb outside to spend some time with him. The conversation turned to the Creation story. Baba asked, "Robb, who hung the stars in space?"

Defensively, Robb shot back, "I didn't do it!"

What great theology!

If you look at the Seamless Robe Jesus is wearing, you will see stars twinkling and dancing in the background with a picture of you located by Jesus' heart. The Bible is the Story of the Creator of the universe reaching down to save us. The thread of Creation is foundational to our understanding of Jesus. We must never forget we are being invited into a relationship with the Creator of the universe! How amazing!

Do you believe that God is the Creator of the universe? Are you living like it?

ARE YOU BREATHING?

The Holy Spirit

ARE YOU BREATHING? WHAT A SILLY QUESTION! PHYSICAL breathing is an absolute necessity to sustain life. God created an atmosphere on Earth that is perfectly balanced for all living creatures. We inhale oxygen and exhale carbon dioxide while plants use our carbon dioxide to produce oxygen. God created water from the exact combination of two parts hydrogen and one part oxygen so that our bodies can be properly replenished. We know we are healthy when we maintain a 100% oxygen level from our head to our toes. Physically, God created you to breathe.

Spiritually, God created us to breathe as well. God's divine plan was always for us to walk with Him daily and rely upon Him completely for our every need. What if breathing *spiritually* is as vital as breathing *physically*? What if God never intended for us to face each day by our own strength? What if God's divine plan has always been that His Holy Spirit would be the very Breath of Life in us?

Success as a Christian is not based on how busy we are or how hard we are trying, but on how deeply you are breathing in Christ. We were not created to live life without God. He created us with the need to have His Holy Spirit dwelling within us so that we might live our life by God's strength, not our own.

I would propose to you that millions of people on earth are not breathing spiritually. They wake up every morning feeling overwhelmed by the challenges of life and exhausted from trying to "fix" their circumstances. It is even possible for followers of Christ to disconnect what they read in the Bible from their personal walk with Him. They try to be like Jesus without Jesus.

The second thread of the Bible is *the Holy Spirit*. What does the Holy Spirit have to do breathing? Everything! Let me begin with a short Hebrew and Greek lesson. There is only one word for "spirit" in the Old Testament; it's the Hebrew "*ru'ash*," and one word in the New Testament, it is the Greek "*pneuma*" (pneumatic tools are air-driven). In both cases, the words can be defined as *spirit, wind* or *breath*. Please know that I fully believe in the Holy Spirit as the Third Person of the Trinity. However, for the purpose of this chapter, I want to use the word picture of the Holy Spirit as the *Breath of God*.

I want to focus on this metaphor, because it is the picture of the movement of God. The Bible is alive! It is the Story of God's Spirit moving and breathing throughout all of history. God's intention has always been that when you open the Bible, there would be a divine "Whoosh!"[16] When was the last time you asked the Holy Spirit to help you as you did your daily Bible reading? It is the Holy Spirit who illuminates the Bible so it "lights up" for us. The Bible is not a boring record of history. It is the telling of His Story. What a difference!

Timothy emphasizes this fact, when he writes,

> All Scripture is *God-breathed* and useful for teaching, correcting and training in righteousness so that the man of God may be thoroughly equipped for every good work. I Timothy 3:16-17

The Holy Spirit is *how* God communicates with us. The written Word of God (the Bible) envelops the Living Word of God (Jesus Christ). As God breathes through both His written and Living Word, the Holy Spirit enables both Jesus and His Story to work together in harmony. If I can change metaphors for just a moment, the Wind of God's Spirit is blowing throughout the Bible. Every page is moving.[17] Most importantly, the Holy Spirit's purpose is to weave the Word of God into our hearts so that we can know Christ personally.

The Holy Spirit is the Breath of God.

Good news! Because the Holy Spirit is the Breath of God, the Holy Spirit is eternal. From eternity past, present and future, God has always been breathing! Isn't it funny how often we pray as

---

16   I remember getting excited about the book of Lamentations!

17   The genealogies in the book of Numbers remind us that God knows all of us by name. In Christ, we are all a part of His family. Just a thought!

if God was holding His breath? We fear He cannot handle the circumstances we are up against. In spite of what you are facing or how chaotic world events are today, rest assured God is moving and breathing in our world. Today, the power of God is working where persecution is the greatest. Let's trace the thread of the Holy Spirit beginning with the Creation Story. Before the first, "Let there be..." is pronounced, we can hear God breathing. The Father and His Holy Spirit are working in perfect harmony. You can hear God inhaling and exhaling. Listen as God prepares to bring the universe into existence.

> In the beginning God created the heavens and the earth. Now the earth was formless and empty, darkness was over the surface of the deep, and the Spirit (*ru'ash* or Breath) of God was hovering over the waters. Genesis 1:1-2

As God exhales the words, "Let there be light!" (Genesis 1:3), His Breath carries the first Word of Creation throughout the universe. Light drives the darkness out the darkness. With each successive command, God's breath permeates every corner of the universe. From the largest galaxy to the smallest insect, no detail is left undone. Can you imagine a power so great? That is our God! Seeing the force of God's breath makes what happens next even more amazing.

The Holy Spirit is the Breath of Life.

When every detail of the universe is in place, God moves to His ultimate creation, Man. Although God has spoken all things into existence up until now, God kneels down and begins to form Adam out of the dust with His hands. Every part of Adam and Eve's bodies were handcrafted with such intricate detail that the pulmonary, respiratory and nervous systems were set to work in perfect harmony. God exhales once again. We read, "the Lord God formed the man from the dust of the ground and *breathed* into his nostrils the breath of life, and the man became a living being" (Genesis 2:7).

God's heavenly intention from that point forward was to walk with Adam and Eve daily. The desire of God's heart was to be together with Adam and Eve as they enjoyed the beauty of Creation. *We were created to be with God.* The hardest work Adam had to do was naming the animals. God provided the food, the water and even the air. All Adam and Eve had to do was breathe. Michael Green reminds us,

> The Spirit of God is His life-giving breath without which man remains spiritually inert. It is His mysterious wind, which man cannot get under his own tidy control.[18]

In Genesis 3, we find that Adam and Eve chose to break their relationship with God. They chose to try to breathe on their own. Their stubborn disobedience would cost them their relationship with God. Because God loved them, He would not hold Adam and Eve against their will. Even though it broke His heart to let them go, God allowed both of His children to try to *do* something with their life.

For Adam and Eve, the end result would be a brokenness they could never imagine. As they moved out from under God's care, Adam would toil to prepare the ground for food that God had always provided. Eve would experience pain as it accompanied the joy of a new life. Adam and Eve's disobedience would impact their sons as well. The couple would experience the heartache of losing two sons: Abel by the hands of his brother Cain and Cain by the curse of God for his disobedience in killing Abel.

As we will see, Adam and Eve first held their breath in fear and then stopped breathing spiritually all together as they are escorted out of the Garden and out of God's Presence. Every human being from that point forward would be impacted by Adam and Eve's choice to live independent from God. You and I were born in a broken relationship with God. Only God could help us breathe again.

The Holy Spirit is the Breath of God's Presence.

The Holy Spirit did not come into existence on the Day of Pentecost. He has always existed and will continue to exist. God's

---

18   Michael Green, I Believe in the Holy Spirit, (William B. Eerdmans Publishing Company: Grand Rapids, Michigan, 1973), page 19

Eternal Spirit is present and active throughout the Old and New Testament. In the Old Testament, the term *Spirit of God* is used to describe the Holy Spirit. The Spirit of God comes upon an individual to enable them to complete a task. The Holy Spirit provides the power to accomplish that which God wants done.

As God instructs Moses about the building of the Tabernacle, God chooses two men, Bezalel and Oholiab, to oversee the building of each item. God explains, "I have filled him (Bezalel) with *the Spirit of God*, with skill, ability and knowledge in all kinds of crafts" (Exodus 31:3). God was reminding Moses that God would be breathing through the men as they built the Tabernacle.

Job found comfort in the knowledge that "The Spirit of God has made me; the breath of the Almighty gives me life (Job 33:4). After Saul has been anointed King of Israel, we read, "the Spirit of God came upon him in power, and he joined in their prophesying" (I Samuel 10:10). The prophet Ezekiel saw a vision of the exiles in Babylonia and writes, "the vision (was) given by the Spirit of God" (Ezekiel 11:24). Individual people are called to accomplish specific tasks.

In the New Testament, the term Holy Spirit is used to describe the presence of God on a permanent basis through the indwelling or living within the lives of Christ's followers. God's Spirit is given to all believers for the task of evangelizing the world. God never intended the Church to grow based on man-made strategies. The Holy Spirit has come to fill our lives with God's breath.

The Holy Spirit is the Breath of Jesus.

The clearest description of the work of the Holy Spirit is found in John 14-16. Jesus has gathered His disciples into an Upper Room to share the first Lord's Supper (communion) ever. Jesus will begin the evening with the celebration of the greatest event of the Old Testament, the Exodus. Jesus will use the cup and bread from the Passover Meal to transition to the greatest event of the New Testament, the Cross.

Before the storm of events that will lead to the Cross, Jesus will use this oasis moment of calm to prepare His teach His disciples about the coming Holy Spirit. During what is known as the

Upper Room Discourse, Jesus begins His teaching by telling His disciples, "And I will ask the Father, and he will give you another Couselor to be with you forever (John 14:16). There are two Greek words for "another." One of them means *another of a different kind.* For instance, an apple is a fruit and an orange is another type of fruit. The word Jesus uses mean *another of the same kind.*

Jesus Christ and the Holy Spirit are one. The Holy Spirit is the Spirit of Christ. They have the same mission, the same message and are working together to communicate God's message of salvation. Jesus gives an outline of the Holy Spirit's ministry,

- Jesus is the Way, the Truth and the Life (John 14:6). The Holy Spirit is the Spirit (Breath) of truth who communicates the message of Jesus to us (John 14:17).

- Jesus is the Righteous One (Isaiah 24:16). The Holy Spirit comes to convict or make us aware of Jesus' righteousness by showing us our sin, confirming our righteousness or right living and to remind us that we will be held accountable for our response to Christ (John 16:8-10). Jesus is the Way (John 14:6a). The Holy Spirit is the Breath of God that guides us daily (John 16:13).

The Holy Spirit is the Breath of the Resurrection.

I love how the thread of breathing intensifies the Death and Resurrection of Christ. In Mark's account of the Crucifixion, he describes the moment when Jesus dies by writing, "With a loud cry, Jesus breathed his last" (Mark 15:37). God exhales once again. This time, it is not with the breath of life, but with the absence of breath that death brings. Jesus' body is laid in the Tomb and the stone is rolled in place. At the heavily guarded Tomb, it appears Jesus will never breathe again. Death has won.

Jesus has taken His last breath. Now there is divine silence.

But on the Third Day … Let me say it again. On the Third Day, Jesus inhales the Breath of Life and the Victory has been won! Sin, death and the grave have been defeated! Then the Heavenly Choir begins to sing in a loud voice, "Worthy is the Lamb, who was slain to receive power and wealth and wisdom and strength and honor and glory and praise!" (Revelation 5:12). If you are willing to accept Christ's gracious offer of forgiveness, the price for your salvation has been paid in full.

The Holy Spirit is the Breath of Power in the Church.

There was a time when the Church quit breathing or at least held their breath. It is the first Easter Sunday evening. The disciples are all gathered in a room because they fear the Jewish officials will find them and execute them for following Jesus. They are struggling to breath on their own. There have been rumors that Jesus is alive. Mary Magdalene has even testified that she has seen Jesus.

Into that room filled with fear, Jesus comes. John records the event.

> On the evening of that first day of the week, when the disciples were together, with the doors locked for fear of the Jews, Jesus came and stood among them and said, "Peace be with you!" After he said this, he showed them his hands and side. The disciples were overjoyed when they saw the Lord. Again Jesus said, "Peace be with you! As the Father has sent me, I am sending you." And with that he breathed on them and said, "Receive the Holy Spirit." John 20:19-22

I understand how Jesus' bestowment of peace would calm the disciples' fears. Jesus is alive! The Tomb is Empty! I understand how the display of Jesus' nail-scarred hands and sword-scarred side would bring confirmation to the disciples that the events of the Cross had truly happened. What I struggle with is Jesus breathing on His disciples. After Jesus said, "As the Father has sent me, I am sending you." And before He commanded, "Receive the Holy Spirit," Jesus exhales on His disciples.

Why would Jesus breathe on His disciples? When Jesus refers to the Holy Spirit, the word "Spirit" is our old friend "pneuma." The verse could literally say, "Jesus breathed on them and said, 'Receive my Breath.'" Jesus ties the commission of the disciples to go out into their world to evangelize directly to the commandment to receive His Holy Spirit. If this band of disciples are to survive much less succeed, they must rely completely on Christ's Holy Spirit dwelling within them daily.

If we move forward to the Day of Pentecost in Acts 2, we find one hundred and twenty disciples gathered in a room together. They are probably afraid, but they have gathered together in obedience to Jesus' command to wait in the city of Jerusalem so Christ's promise can be fulfilled when He said, "But you will receive power when the Holy Spirit comes on you; and you will be my witnesses in Jerusalem, and in all Judea and Samaria, and to the ends of the earth" (Acts 1:8).

Jesus' Promise of the Holy Spirit is fulfilled ten days later on the Day of Pentecost.

Luke tells us,

> When the day of Pentecost came, they were all together in one place. Suddenly a sound like the blowing of a violent wind came from heaven and filled the whole house where they were sitting. They saw what seemed to be tongues of fire that separated and came to rest on each of them. All of them were filled with the Holy Spirit and began to speak in other tongues as the Spirit enabled them. Acts 2:1-4

By their own strength, the motley crew of disciples would have fallen flat on their face.

With the Holy Spirit breathing within them, this small band of disciples is able to revolutionize their world. They will bring the Roman army to its knees without using any weapon except the love of Christ. There is no explanation for the book of Acts except that the Holy Spirit was empowering believers to do the work God had called them to do.

The Holy Spirit is the Breath in Us.

Do we realize that the same Jesus that the disciples proclaimed is the same Jesus we serve? How can we forget that the same Holy Spirit that breathed into His disciples nearly two thousand years ago is the same Holy Spirit that wants to breathe through us and empower us to be the presence of Christ in our world? If we are honest, we all have to admit that there are many times when we try to deal with our circumstances by our own strength.

Having retired from the pastorate after 33 years, I am very sensitive to the breathing patterns of my fellow pastors. Even pastors can hold their breath. When I talk to fellow pastors and hear them panting from an agenda that is jam-packed with meetings to plan the next event to grow the church, I will usually advise them, "Don't forget to breathe." Let God be in control.

In 2012, I was blessed with an opportunity to be interim pastor at Oklahoma City Trinity Church of the Nazarene in Oklahoma City. During my four months there, it was my privilege to come to know and love Sergio and Gabriela Rodriguez and their children Abigail and Estaban.

I want to close this chapter with an event that happened in their lives that fits perfectly with letting God breathe through us. I am going to share a short summary of the story. I have included Gabby's full account in the Appendix of this book.

On May 20, 2013, a series of F-5 tornadoes broke out across the Moore-Norman area south of Oklahoma City. As heavy rains became filled with hail and the skies grew dark, Sergio called Gabby and advised her to go get the children from school and take them home. Thinking Abigail and Estaban would be safer at school than at home, Gabby reluctantly started towards the school.

When she arrived at Briarwood Elementary School in Moore, Gabby was forced to abandon her car in order to run into the school to pick up her children. Although miraculously she located both children, the tornado hit before any of the family could get home. Gabby made her children lie down on the floor and covered them both with her body. Gabby sustained injuries, but the children were left without a scratch. Sergio was also able to make it home safely.

A few days later, Sergio and Gabby were recounting the events of the tornado with their children. At one point, Gabby asked Abigail, "Were you ever afraid?" Abigail answered, "No, Mommy. I wasn't afraid because I could feel your breath on my neck. I knew I was safe."

God never intended for us to live our life without Him. In His Holy Breath, there is safety?

Let me ask you again. Are you breathing?

GOD GAVE US HIS WORD

Jesus Christ

IN 1985, A FRIEND OF MINE SCHEDULED BASEBALL HALL OF Famer Joe DiMaggio to come to Flint, Michigan for an autograph session. The agent for the Yankee Clipper called to set the date and time for the event. At the end of the conversation, my friend asked when to expect the contracts for signing. The agent answered, "Mr. DiMaggio does *not* sign contracts. When he gives his word, he will keep it. If Mr. DiMaggio says he will be there, he will be there!" The agent knew that if Joltin' Joe gave his word, it *guaranteed his presence*. The person of Joe Dimaggio *could not be separated from the word* he gave.

Before this once-in-a-lifetime event, my friend made sure that everything was ready and then took a two-week vacation. When he got back, he asked his helper "Did anything interesting happen while I was gone?" The helper answered, "No, not really. Oh, a guy called and said he was Joe DiMaggio, but I hung up on him." Joe showed up anyway. He had given his word.

The Bible tells us that God gave us His Word. His Word is Jesus. When you hear the voice of Jesus, you hear the voice of the Father. It is one story. In their book *Jesus: A Theography*, Leonard Sweet and Frank Viola write, "The entire Scriptures, both Old and New Testament, are unified by a common narrative … It's the story of Jesus Christ."[19]

From the beginning of Creation in Genesis 1:1 to the final Amen of Revelation 22:21, every word in the Bible is leading us to Christ. The person of Jesus Christ and the character of God cannot be separated. As Michael Green reminds us, "There is a frequent link in the Bible between 'The Spirit of God" and 'the

---

19   Leonard Sweet and Frank Viola, *Jesus a Theography*, (Thomas Nelson: Nashville, Tennessee, 2012), page x.

Word of the Lord.'" The breath of God and the message of God cannot be divorced."[20]

In the mystery of Jesus' High Priestly prayer found in John 17, Jesus affirms His unity with the Father and prays His disciples will also know that unity with Him. Jesus prays,

> I have given them the glory that you gave me, that they may be one as we are one: I in them and you in me. May they be brought to complete unity to let the world know that you sent me and have loved them even as you have loved me. John 17:22-23

The third thread in the Bible is *Jesus Christ*. Sweet and Viola state it clearly when they write, "Jesus is the thread that holds all Scripture together."[21] Jesus is the central figure of the Bible with the Cross being the central event. The Bible must be read through the lens of Christ. Jesus is the Living Word of God. "*In the beginning was the Word, and the Word was with God, and the Word was God. He was with God in the beginning." John 1:1*

The Apostle John is writing his Gospel account at the end of the first century A.D. Primarily having its roots in Jewish culture, the Church has crossed cultural lines into the Greek world. John faces the challenge of communicating the person and ministry of Jesus Christ to two distinct worlds. What common ground could be found to proclaim the Gospel to both Jews and Greeks? Part of the answer is found in *the concept of the Word* (in Greek, *logos)*[22]. The importance of the word "Word" was an integral part of both Jewish and Greek history.

To the Jewish mind, the Word equated to the vibrant, *active power of God*. William Barclay sheds light on this when he writes, "To the Jew, a word was far more than a mere sound; a word was something which had an active and independent existence and

---

20   Michael Green, *I Believe in the Holy Spirit* (William Eerdmans Publishing Company: Grand Rapids, Michigan, 1975), page 21.

21   Sweet and Viola, page xiv

22   *Logo* is the Greek word for "word." When we see a red checkmark on athletic wear, we know that it is from Nike. The logo and the company are viewed as one.

which actually did things."[23] Words came alive! They took on a life of their own. It was possible to see the Word in action. Jesus is God in action! John Paterson adds, "The spoken word to the Hebrew ... was a unit of energy charged with power."[24]

The power behind the ministry of the Old Testament Prophets was the Word of the Lord. The Prophets' assignment was to speak the Words of God to His people. It was what distinguished them from false prophets. When the Prophets spoke, they did not try to find favor with the people. They spoke from the power and authority of God's lips.

Elijah received the Word of the Lord that directed his path during a great drought (I Kings 17:2-8). It was the Word of the Lord that Samuel received that enabled him to confront King Saul about his disobedience with the Amalekites (I Samuel 15:10). The prophet Isaiah received the Word of the Lord concerning extending Hezekiah's life another 15 years (Isaiah 38:4). It was the Word of the Lord that was the basis for Jeremiah's call (Jeremiah 1:4).

In the New Testament, this Word is the Source of a worldwide revival. We read in Acts 19:20, "In this way the word of the Lord spread widely and grew in power." The Apostles found their authority in the Word of God. The writer to the Hebrews adds to the concept of word as power when he writes,

> For the word of God is alive and active. Sharper than a two-edged sword, it penetrates even to dividing soul and spirit, joints and marrow; it judges the thoughts and attitudes of the heart. Hebrews 4:12

In I Peter 1:25, Peter quotes Isaiah 40:6-8 when he writes, "But the word of the Lord endures forever." When Peter preaches his first sermon (Acts 2:14-41), he traces the Word through Jewish history and then tells the Story of Jesus, the Word of God. As the power of God's Living Word is presented 3,000 people step forward to receive this Word into their life. When Peter preaches a second time, the sermon is the same. The number of believers

---

23   Barclay, William, The Gospel of John, volume 1, (Philadelphia: Westminster Press, 1956), page 3

24   Paterson, William, The Gospel of John, volume 1, (Philadelphia: Westminster Press, 1956), page 7

grows to 5,000! The spiritual revolution that begins that day finds its Source in the active, powerful Word of God. John reminds us that the power of God has a name ... Jesus!

For the Greeks, the Word was directly tied to *Reason*. Again Barclay writes, "Whenever they (intellectual thinkers) used the word *Logos*[25] the twin ideas of the Word of God and the Reason of God were in their minds."[26] For the Greek philosophers, their ultimate quest was to know *Truth*. John will remind the Greeks Jesus *is* "the Way, *the Truth* and the Life" (John 14:6). In the search for Truth, the Answer has been found in the living Word of God! Truth has a name: Jesus!

Jesus is the Eternal Word of God.

"... and the Word was with God and the Word was God" John 1:1b.

I once preached on John 1:1, emphasizing that Jesus is God. Every time I made that statement, a saintly man would call out, "Son of God!" We had a tug of war all the way through that sermon. To make matters worse, I got a phone call from the dear man the next day in which he told me he and his wife were leaving the church. I immediately went to the couple's home to talk with them.

Although I tried to explain that *Son of God* is a title for Jesus, like Savior, Redeemer or the King of Kings, I am pretty sure I failed to convince the man of my point. Fortunately, the precious couple stayed in the church and we became great friends. What my friend did not see was that the Bible clearly declares that Jesus is God. The Apostle John records Jesus' words,

> "I am the Alpha and the Omega," says the Lord God, "who is, and who was, and who is to come, the Almighty." is and has always been." Revelation 1:8

We often think of Bethlehem as the beginning point of Jesus' existence. Speaking of Jesus' eternal existence, Sweet and Viola write, "According to the Second Testament, it (Jesus' story) begins

---

25   Logos is the Greek word for *"word."* When we see a checkmark on an athletic shoe, we know it is from Nike. The logo and the company are inseparable.

26   Ibid. page 7.

long before then (Bethlehem). It begins in the dateless past, before angels or atoms."[27]

The Christmas Story is woven into all Scripture. The Incarnation was a part of God's plan before the foundation of the world. Jesus, God's Word, was spoken on Mount Sinai at the giving of the Ten Commandments (Exodus 20:1-17). God used His Word to outline this foundational covenant of the Old Testament. In Matthew 22:34-40, Jesus is asked to choose the most important commandment. The question was not about choosing from the Ten Commandments, but choosing from the complicated legal system the Pharisees had developed over the previous two hundred years. Because He was at Mount Sinai, Jesus is able to simplify the Ten Commandments down to two. He says,

> Jesus replied: "Love the Lord your God with all your heart and with all your soul and with your entire mind." This is the first and greatest commandment. And the second is like it: "Love your neighbor as yourself. All the Law and the Prophets hang on these two commandments." Matthew 22:34-40

Every time God speaks, it is through the Voice of Jesus. Every time Jesus speaks, it is the Voice of God. Whether it is His presence with the Three Hebrew children at the Fiery Furnace or bringing the Apostle Paul to his knees on the road to Damascus, Jesus is there. Every page of the written Word of God is saturated with the presence of the Living Word of God.

> Jesus is the Creative Word of God. "Nothing was created that was not created by *Him" John 1:2*.

I once thought that the use of Logos, or "word," was simply John's way of reaching two very different cultures. While that is true, there is so much more to John's choice of words. John is taking us back to the Creation Story. With the exception of Adam and Eve, God creates the universe by the power of His Word.

Why would John not even deal with Bethlehem, but start by revisiting the Creation Story? Jesus was not only at the Creation, He is the Creator! Because he wrote his Gospel account thirty

---

27   Sweet and Viola, page 1

years after Matthew, Mark and Luke, John had the freedom to look at the person of Christ throughout eternity.

If the first chapter of John was a symphony, it would begin with a timpani roll and a crescendo as John takes us back to the Creation Story in Genesis 1-2. As John re-enters the majesty, glory and power of Creation, you can almost hear the trumpets beginning to blow. The strings are added as spectacular colors burst into sight! You can hear the French horns as the sounds of Creation fill the universe. Only God could handle the sights and sounds of His Creation. John knows that we were not there, but he wants to remind us that Jesus *was* there! In fact, Jesus is the melody line.

Seeing our Creator God in Genesis 1 is not difficult since He is the opening Truth shared with us. As we have seen already, the Holy Spirit is introduced in Genesis 1:3. *Where is Jesus in the Creation Story?* Jesus is presented to us in each powerful word that is spoken. Except for Man, every part of the universe comes into existence through the Spoken Word. If you are looking for Jesus, open your ears and listen! The Word is interwoven into each day of Creation.

Through my preparation for this writing, I have come to see the Trinity through a new word picture. Imagine a person speaking to you. As they speak, you hear their words as their breath carries them to you. You cannot speak without breathing out. You will also hear their heart. Jesus said, "Out of our words, our heart speaks." Relationally, God is the Father speaking by the Holy Spirit through and about Jesus. Sweet and Viola write,

> Jesus is the Logos. He is the Word or the self-utterance of God. So when God speaks it is Christ who is being spoken about. When God breathes, it is Christ who is being imparted.[28]

A person's breathing pattern can be distinguished from their words, but one cannot function without the other. Likewise, when a person speaks, you can distinguish between them, their breathing and their words. However, all of these three elements function as one.

---

28   Sweet and Viola, page xxi

Jesus is the Word of God Who Became Flesh.

"And the Word became flesh and dwelt among us" John 1:14a.

When we reach John 1:14, the orchestra stops and an oboe begins to quietly play the unbelievable melody of Bethlehem. The Creator of the universe has entered His Creation for the purpose of restoring mankind to fellowship with Himself. The Creative Word of God is preparing to speak Truth to his creation. It will not be a philosophical discourse. The Word of God has come to live and breathe among us. He will reveal the power of God predominantly through His Word.

Although there are exceptions, Jesus performs most of His miracles through speaking to the person. His parables are from the simple examples of life. Jesus drives out demons by demanding that they leave. He brings the dead back to life by calling them by name.(John 11). Jesus' words and His being cannot be separated.

From the Creation, we are escorted to Bethlehem. In this small hometown of David, an event has taken place that has never happened before; God has come to us. Because we were helpless and unworthy to reach God, God reaches down to us! Jesus did not come because of our goodness. He came because we were desperately in need of a Savior. No one else could qualify for this mission.

Over His three and a half years of ministry, the Word of Jesus spread by mouth to mouth communication. There was not any social media or written print, only people telling other people about who Jesus is. At times, Jesus even tells those who have been healed to NOT tell anybody about what He has done (i.e., Mark 1:44). In spite of having only one means of communication, you can hear the revolution growing. A holy "Hallelujah!" begins to be heard as people experience the joy of knowing Jesus. The Army that is forming has no weapons, except the love of God. The Heavenly Choir shouts an affirming "Amen!" as the Word begins to spread that the Messiah has come.

Jesus is the Word of God in the Present Tense.

"Jesus Christ is the same yesterday and today and forever"
Hebrews 13:8.

Now, let's move from John's opening prologue to the story of Moses and the Burning Bush found in Exodus 3-4. Here is Moses; an eighty-year-old man standing bare-foot in the Presence of God. This former prince of Egypt has been on the run for the last forty years as he tries to escape a charge of First Degree Murder. This prince has certainly become a pauper as he now finds himself in the lowly position of being a shepherd. Many of Moses' fellow shepherds were little boys.

As God begins to speak to Moses, He reveals that Moses is His choice to be the leader of the greatest event in the Old Testament, the Exodus! This old man is being called to lead the Israelites out of their Egyptian bondage. Moses begins to spurt out excuses like a fountain. He reminds God of several reasons why he should be disqualified. When it comes to the issue of authority, Moses knows that his name is *mud* in Egypt. The Egyptians AND the Israelites both hold him in contempt. There is no way he can go back to the place that sees him as a fugitive on the run.

Can you hear Moses protesting that he has no authority to do this task? God's answer is, "I know. Isn't that great?" (Exodus 3: 13-14). You will never ever be tempted to use your own name. So let me give you my Name. My name is *I AM (Jehovah or Yahweh)*! In every task I give you, just tell them *I Am that I Am* sent you me." Moses' confidence was not just in what Jehovah would do, but in the confidence of knowing that God would be with him. God's Word would do the work!

As you read John's account of Jesus' ministry, you will find Jesus using the Name given to Moses that day at the Burning Bush. In fact, Jesus using the Name in seven "I Am" statements. Every time Jesus said, "I Am," the Jewish religious leaders burned with anger. They knew that Jesus was claiming to be God when He said,

- I Am the Bread of Life. (6:35)

- I Am the Light of the World (8:12)

- I Am the Door or Gate (10:7)

- I Am the Good Shepherd (10:11)
- I Am the Resurrection and the Life. (11:25)
- I Am the Way, the Truth and the Life. (14:6)
- I Am the True Vine (15:1)

When you combine Genesis 1, Exodus 3 and the I Am statements in John, one thing becomes clear. God is always in the present tense! *"Let there be!"* becomes *the Great I AM!*

As the writer of the book of Hebrews proclaims, "Jesus Christ is the same yesterday, today and forever" (Hebrews 13:4). The option to form Jesus into our likeness is not an option. Jesus has come to form us into His likeness so that we can be a change agent in our culture. The Name of Jesus is just as powerful today as it has ever been!

Jesus is the Word of God in the Heavenly Scroll.

"You are worthy to take the scroll and to open its seals, because you were slain and with your blood you purchased for God persons from every tribe and language and people and nation." Revelation 5:9b

In the beginning of the fifth chapter of Revelation, the choir is preparing to sing the song of the Ages. There is a sealed Scroll that contains His Story. There is only one problem; no one is qualified to break the seals that keep the Words from being read. As far as I know, we find in this passage the only tears shed in Heaven. John records his response,

> I wept and wept because no one was found who was worthy to open the scroll or look inside. Then one of the elders said to me, "Do not weep! See, the Lion of the tribe of Judah, the Root of David, has triumphed. He is able to open the scroll and its seven seals." Then I saw a Lamb, looking as if it had been slain, standing in the center of the throne, encircled by the four living creatures and the elders... He came and took the scroll from the right hand of him who sat on the throne. Revelation 5:4-7

Then, the Heavenly Choir begins to sing the Song of the Ages, "In a loud voice they sang: "Worthy is the Lamb, who was slain, to receive power and wealth and wisdom and strength and honor and glory and praise!" (Revelation 5:12). Jesus not only is the melody line of Scripture, but is the Divine Lyric that is at the heart of God's message to us.

If you look at the Seamless Robe Jesus is wearing, you will notice there is a tinge of red, because our salvation will cost the shedding of Jesus Christ, the very Word of God. He stands with His arms opened wide welcoming you into fellowship with Him. Through the Holy Spirit, the written Word of God will lead you to the Cross. Through the Living Word Jesus Christ, you can experience the power of the Resurrection through a brand new life.

Although the price of our salvation has been paid in full by the Blood of Jesus, we must still accept the gift. It will require admitting we are: sinners who need to *confess* our sins, disobedient children who must *repent* of our sins so God can turn our life around and new creations of God who will accept Jesus by allowing Him to lead our lives daily. Jesus tells us,

> "Here I am! I stand at the door and knock. If anyone hears my voice and opens the door, I will come in and sup with him, and he with me" (Revelation 3:20).

WHO AM I?

The Uniqueness of Man

So God created mankind in his own image, in the image of God He created them; male and female he created them. Genesis 1:27

IF THE BIBLE WAS A SENTENCE, GOD WOULD BE THE SUBJECT (the One who acts) and Man would be the object (the one acted upon).

Recently, I was watching news coverage of the birth of a baby gorilla at the local zoo. I don't know about you, but I think baby gorillas are so ugly they are cute. At the very end of the news clip, a mother was shown holding her newborn baby. The news anchors did not say anything, but the message was clear, *human babies and gorilla babies are a lot alike.*

If you believe that, I dare you to go up to the next Mom pushing a baby cart, look at her baby and say, "Wow! Your baby looks just like a gorilla." See her reaction. The world believes that we are at the top of the food chain. God teaches He created us a little below angels. There is a world of difference between the two perspectives.

After the *power* of God is shown through the Creation of the universe, Creation gets *personal.* By His Voice, God has spent five and a half days painting the sky with galaxies of colors beyond our imagination. By His Word, God has created Earth with every detail in place for it to be a perfect Paradise. Earth and the universe have been set in motion. The orbits of Earth and each star have been perfectly timed. The animals and plants are already enjoying the beauty of God's Creation. The first five and a half days of Creation build to a crescendo as God prepares to create His ultimate Creation: man.

Silently, God kneels down to fill His Hands with the dirt that He has created for this moment. Lovingly, He forms the inner workings of this creature with the five senses that will be necessary to experience God's amazing gift. Every muscle, every blood vessel and every bone are formed to enable Man to enjoy the Earth to the fullest. With water on the Earth and above the Earth, God has created the perfect atmosphere for Man to thrive. Every plant has begun creating the oxygen that Man will need while absorbing the carbon dioxide that man exhales.

The time has come to fulfill the desire of God's Heart. He leans down and performs the first CPR ever! God breathes into the nostrils of Adam the very Breath of Life. Adam's heart begins to circulate the blood to all parts of his body. His nerves begin to feel the ground underneath him. His eyes open and the first thing Adam sees is God. Before he begins to explore the beauty of his surroundings or begins to name the animals, Adam looks into the very Eyes of God and watches God smile. I cannot prove it biblically, but I see in my mind's eye God placing His Arms around Adam and says, "Welcome to my world that I have created for you. Come, let me show you around."

As God and Adam walk together, Adam must have been overwhelmed by the vivid colors of each flower and tree. He was surrounded by a garden that God Himself had designed. Food was available for the picking. Can you imagine tasting a peach or an orange for the first time? Adam's mouth was bursting with flavors of all kinds.

Under God's direction, the animals approach Adam to receive their names. Dogs and cats I imagine were pretty easy, but when a hippopotamus comes before him; it was probably quite a challenge. And now, with every physical need provided for, Adam still lacks one thing: earthly fellowship. God sees the loneliness in Adam's eyes and responds:

> But for Adam no suitable helper was found. So the Lord God caused the man to fall into a deep sleep; and while he was sleeping, he took one of the man's ribs and then closed up the place with flesh. Then the Lord God made a woman from the rib he had taken out of the man, and be brought her to the man. Genesis 2:20b-22

For the first time, Adam finds himself in a social environment. What do you say to the only woman on Earth? If you say the wrong thing, will she ever talk to you again? Immediately, they both realize they were made for each other. Physically, emotionally and spiritually, they were created to be so close that their two lives truly will become one. I have to believe that Adam's concern about silence was soon alleviated as Eve began to talk at a pace twice as fast as he did.[29] The time of loneliness has ended. Now the beauty of God's Creation can be shared.

But what does the Creation of man have to do with how I understand who I am? Well, I have some good news about that and some bad news. Let me share the good news first by telling you how God intended to answer that question.

The Good News: *We Are Created Beings.*

Before Adam took his first breath, God's intention was to take care of him. No problem had to be faced alone. There was no need to worry about anything like food or water. There was an abundant supply of everything that was needed as long as Adam and Eve walked with God. As Creator, God would be in charge of every detail. Every day, Adam and Eve could enjoy each other's company as they relaxed and enjoyed the beauty of a sunrise or sunset. Their agendas were not packed with "Things I Must Do Today." All they had to do was to want to walk with God.

As we have seen in the chapter on God as our Creator, God is the Creator, we are His creation. His role is to lead us. Our role is to follow Him. I realize for many today the thought of God being in charge of our lives seems like a part of the Bad News. We do not want anyone to be in charge of our lives, especially God. However, the truth is that we do not have an option about if someone will be in charge, but only of who will be in charge. As Bob Dylan sang, "it may be the devil or it may be the Lord. But you're gonna have to serve somebody."[30]

---

29   According to the whimsical site funtrivia.com, women use 20,000 words a day while men use 7,000. Adam had already experienced the solitude of being alone. Eve only knew a social environment.

30   *You Gotta Serve Somebody*, Words and Music by Bob Dylan, Copyright © 1979 by Special Rider Music

The Bible teaches that there are only two options from which to choose, God or me. These two choices cannot co-exist in our hearts. Living by the flesh or self is the very definition of sin. It is what caused Adam and Eve to break their fellowship with God. As Jesus said,

"No one can serve two masters. Either he will hate the one and love the other, or he will be devoted to the one and despise the other" (Matthew 6:24).

Paul describes the conflict between these two lifestyles when he writes:

> So I say, walk by the Spirit (God), and you will not gratify the desires of the flesh (me). For the flesh (me) desires what is contrary to the Spirit (God) and the Spirit (God) what is contrary to the flesh (me). They are in conflict with each other, so that you are not to do whatever you want. But if you are led by the Spirit (God), you are not under the law. Galatians 5:16-18

Being under the authority and care of God is wonderful! He knows and wants what is best for us. I will discuss the reason we struggle to live under God's authority in a later chapter. For now, let it be said that there is a spiritual struggle all of us face and a spiritual decision we all must make.

We are the Crown of God's Creation, *created a little lower than angels.*

The Biblical presentation of who we are is vastly different from the modern thought of the day. The Bible affirms the fact that human beings have a unique position in God's Creation. The Psalmist David writes, "What is man that you are mindful of him, the son of man that you care for him? You made him a little lower than the heavenly beings and crowned him with glory and honor" (Psalm 8:4-5).

The writer to the Hebrews picks up on this thread when he writes, "You made them (humans) a little lower than the angels; you crowned them with glory and honor" (Hebrews 2:7). We are held in a place of honor by God and thus should view each other with honor and respect. Every person is important to God. We have dominion over the animal kingdom. We are not part of them.

Since the Fall of Man, the desire of God's heart is to restore us to a right relationship with Him. Jesus Himself shares the reason that He has come to Earth when He says, "For the Son of Man came to seek and to save the lost" (Luke 19:10). The Bible is God's love letter to you telling you that you are so important to Him that He would do anything, including sending His Son to die for you. *Every life is sacred.* Each person is a candidate for God's salvation. The Bible not only tells us of God's desire, but shows us the Way for that desire to be fulfilled in our life.

There is a vast difference between being created a little lower than angels and being a Monkey's Uncle! Animals live based off instinct. They cannot keep themselves from wrong actions or be held responsible for their actions. When my dog Sam chews up my wife's handbag, I do not drop to my knees in prayer. I may discipline the dog, but I honestly know that his love for leather overrode his common sense.

The Bible clearly teaches that we are responsible for our choices. We do not live based on *instinct,* but through *moral choices.* We were created to be in fellowship with God. We are accountable for our response to God's invitation of fellowship. We belittle ourselves and insult God when we think less of ourselves than God intended.

We are created in God's Image.

Genesis 1:27 tells us, "So God created mankind in His own image, in the image of God He created them; male and female He created them." One of the obvious differences between Man and animals is that Man has *a mind, soul and spirit.* We were created to have a relationship with God. We were created to be a reflection of God's character and presence in our lives.

On several occasions, people I have never met have recognized me because they know my dad. I look so much like Dad that people who have never met me have noticed the resemblance. I even had a woman give me a double take when I met her after my father died. I take that as a high compliment. More importantly, I want to remind others of my Heavenly Father through the presence of Christ in my life.

God's design is not that we would look exactly like God physically, but that we would allow Him to reproduce His character
in us *spiritually* so that people see Jesus in our lives. The truth we
must grasp is people can only *see* Jesus in me when Jesus *is* in me.
God's desire for all of us is that His holiness would be reproduced
in our lives, not by self-discipline, but by a miraculous Divine
intervention through the Cross. Listen to these biblical mandates:

> But just as he who called you is holy, so be holy in all you do; for
> it is written: "Be holy, because I am holy." I Peter 1:15-16

> A new command I give you; Love one another. As I have loved
> you, so you must love one another. John 13:34

> Bearing with one another and, if one has a complaint against
> another, forgiving each other; as the Lord has forgiven you, so
> you also must forgive. Colossians 3:24

If these are seen as *comparative* statements, comparing us to
Christ, the situation is hopeless. By our own strength, we cannot fulfill God's call to be like Christ. A few years ago, there was
an emphasis on the phrase, "What would Jesus do?" or WWJD.
There were bracelets, necklaces and other ways that phrase was
promoted. The question comes from the classic Christian novel,
In His Steps by Charles Sheldon. In that novel, a pastor challenges
those in his congregation to make every decision in their life based
on the question, *"What would Jesus do?"* The novel follows the lives
of those who accept the challenge. It is a wonderful story. I have
several copies of the book.

Although the question is a good one, it is not a matter of
deciding what Jesus would do, then doing it. I love to watch Kevin
Durant or Russell Westbrook of the Oklahoma City Thunder as
they dazzle the crowd with their ability to shoot under pressure.
They can make moves that leave their opponents in the dust. I
have watched them play numerous times. However, if you hand
me a basketball and tell me to *do* what Kevin Durant *does*, I would
laugh at you. That is impossible. Dribbling is a challenge for me.

In most cases, we know what Jesus would do. That is not the
problem. Our difficulty is being capable of actually carrying out
His commands on our own. God never intended us to muster up

enough strength and goodness to be like Him. Shortly after Jesus shares the challenge to "love one another as I have loved you." in John 13:34, Jesus spends time in John 15 using the word picture of a vine and its branches. He says, "I am the vine; you are the branches. If you remain in me and I in you, you will bear much fruit; apart from me you can do nothing" (John 15:5). Jesus ties the ability to love as He loves directly to total reliance upon Him to enable us to carry out the command.

If, however, these are relational statements connecting us to Christ, there is more than enough power and grace to make the way possible. Paul writes, "I can do all things through Him (Christ) who strengthens me" (Philippians 4:13). I remember a jewelry store advertisement in which the owner's young sons would always finish the radio spot with the phrase, "I can do all things." It was cute to hear the youngest son quote Philippians 4:13a with a little lisp in his speech. I know the owner was emphasizing his Christian faith, but not quoting the whole verse gives a distorted picture of Paul's message. It is our total reliance upon God that makes the impossible things of this life possible.

We are the Apple of God's eye.

In one of his final speeches to the Israelites, Moses reminds the people of God's care for them throughout their history. He says,

> In a desert land he found him (Jacob), in a barren and howling waste, He shielded him and cared for him; He guarded Him as the apple of His eye, like an eagle stirs up its nest and hovers over it young, that spreads it wings to catch them and carries them on its pinions." Deuteronomy 32: 10-11

Jacob? You mean the scoundrel? The one who stole the birthright from his starving brother when God had already promised it to Jacob? He wasn't even his father's favorite! What kind of role model is that? That is the point! Throughout the Bible, God uses the most unlikely people to carry out His will. Abraham is too old. Moses is a murderer and fugitive shepherd. Jonah is rebelliously stubborn. Peter wants to be the most noticeable disciple. Paul is zealous about destroying the Church. You are not the apple of God's eye because of your perfect character.

Here is a freeing truth: *God loves us, because He loves us!* He sees in us what we could be if we would just trust Him. In the story of the Prodigal Son (Luke 15:11-32), the father sees his son in the distance. This is the son that has wished him dead and broken his heart. This is the son that has wasted all of his inheritance on trying to buy friends and good times. How does the father respond when he sees that son? He runs to him! He wraps his arms around him and calls for a fatted calf and the ring of sonship.

We are not the apple of God's eyes because of our goodness. We are the apple of His eyes because of God's grace! We will never fully comprehend that fact, but all God asks is that we receive it.

We are Hand-made.

The physical body is amazing! Did you know that every human being has a unique tongue-print? Human beings are the only creature on earth to have emotional tears. Everyone has a unique smell, except for twins. Our bones are stronger than some steel. Humans have 60,000 miles of blood vessels in our bodies.

King David saw the miracle that is the human body when he wrote:

> I praise you because I am fearfully and wonderfully made; your works are wonderful, I know that full well. My frame was not hidden from you when I was made in the secret place. When I was woven together in the depths of the earth, your eyes saw my unformed body. All the days ordained for me were written in your book before one of them came to be. Psalm 139:14-16

It is true that God uses His Hands at times to discipline us, but God's ultimate desire is to use His Hands to love us. I love how Isaiah records God's intention. "Behold, I have engraved you on the palms of my hands; your walls are ever before me" (Isaiah 49:16).

Do you remember the first time you fell in love? Do you remember writing that person's name on your notebook or inside your locker? You may have even written on your hand to let everyone know how much you loved that person. We are constantly on God's mind. How should we respond?

The Good News is that God created you to be in fellowship with Him every day. You and I are the crown of His creation. He wants you to know Him here on earth so you can spend eternity with Him. Eternity with Him can be ours if we choose to accept God's offer of restored fellowship.

The Bad News: We Are All Sinners.

With all the blessings that God has bestowed on us by His grace, there is some bad news about Man that the Bible reminds us of. Let's look at a few of them.

We are Sinners.

The Apostle Paul states it concisely when he writes, "All have sinned and fallen short of the glory of God." Romans 3:23 Later in that same letter, Paul reminds us that we are powerless, sinful enemies of God" (Romans 5:6-11). David adds, "Surely I was sinful at birth, sinful from the time my mother conceived me" (Psalm 51:5).

In both our attitude and our actions, we are sinful! I realize that fact offends many people today. I once had a young couple call me because they thought there was a demon in their house. I invited them over to the pastor's study at the church. During the conversation, the girlfriend admitted to lying, stealing and breaking at least six out of the Ten Commandments. Because I knew her boyfriend, I began to talk to him about sin and its consequences. The young lady interrupted me and said, "I may lie and cheat and steal, but I am honest about it. I am not a sinner!"

If we compare ourselves to others, we can always find someone whose lifestyle is worse than ours. That is not the question! The question is, *"Are you in a right relationship with God?"* It is our broken relationship with God that makes us sinners. We are born with a self-centered attitude that demands, "I want my way!" That attitude leads to actions that are displeasing to God. Although we cannot help being born with an *"It's all about me!"* attitude, we are responsible for seeking God's deliverance through the Cross.

We are mortal.

In his celebration of the fact that Christ died once and for all, the writer to the Hebrews also reminds us, *"Just as people are destined to die once, and after that to face judgment" (Hebrews 9:27).* With the exception of Enoch and Elijah, the mortality rate on Earth is 100%! Although some people in the Old Testament lived to be 900 years plus, even Methuselah died after 969 years! Today—or until recently—the oldest person on Earth is 116 years old. Sometime between birth and 116, we will experience death. We are finite beings. On Earth, we have a beginning and an end.

Notice that our mortality is linked to facing judgment. We are not only mortal, but we are accountable for our life. How we live will determine where we spend eternity. You can live anyway you want, but you cannot determine the consequences of your actions. The Bible teaches that it is *not how long* we live, but *how* we live that matters. James reminds us:

> Why, you do not even know what will happen tomorrow. What is your life? You are a mist that appears for a little while and then vanishes. James 4:14

We are unworthy.

Although we are created to have fellowship with God, it is not because we *deserve* it. We are not worthless, but we are unworthy. Nothing we can do will enable us to earn God's love. Since the time of the building of the Tower of Babel, man has attempted to find a man-made way to reach God without God's grace and mercy. No such way exists. Probably the most frequent attempt at this goal is *works*. Surely, I can do something that makes me worthy!

Paul reminds us,

> For it is by grace you have been saved, through faith—and this not from yourselves, it is the gift of God—not by works, so that no one can boast. Ephesians 2:8-9

We are helpless.

We are totally powerless to restore our relationship to God. Although we cannot change our spiritual condition, the Bible reminds us that God can! In fact, the Good News of the Gospel is that Jesus knew us with all of our sin and shortcomings and loved us anyway. Humility is not a natural human character, but as Peter reminds us, everyone must,

> Humble yourselves, therefore, under God's mighty hand, that he may lift you up in due time. I Peter 5:6

God does His best work with those who admit they are helplessly broken. Jesus' most effective ministry was among those people that society looked down upon. Tax collectors and sinners, Samaritans and lepers all experienced the compassionate, healing ministry of Jesus.

> When he saw the crowds, he had compassion on them, because they were harassed and helpless, like sheep without a shepherd. Matthew 9:36

The hardest group for Jesus to reach was those who were self-righteous. The Pharisees and Sadducees believed their pious acts and their bloodline would save them. They did not need Jesus to be their Savior. Nicodemus (John 3:1-15) would be among the rare exceptions to that rule. They would not admit that they needed God's grace and mercy just like all of us do. The bad news is that we are born in a broken relationship with God. Our brokenness cannot be hidden from God and most of the time, from others. We need a Savior!

Who am I? You and I are the very reason that God has provided reconciliation to the world to Himself. From Creation to Bethlehem, from Calvary to the Empty Tomb, we are the focus of God's love. If you look at Jesus' Seamless Robe, you will see your picture over His heart. You're on the heart and mind of Christ every day! He is reaching out to you. Why not reach out to Him?

THE TWO SHALL BECOME ONE

The Marriage Language of the Bible

THE CANDLES ARE NOW FLICKERING, CAUSING A GENTLE GLOW IN the darkened sanctuary. The mothers have been seated and have begun quietly crying. The groom and his groomsmen have taken their place in front of the sanctuary. As the music begins to play, the bridesmaids come in and take their place on stage. Hopefully, the flower girl and ring bearer will make it down the aisle without crying.

Finally, the moment we have all been waiting for! The organist stops for a brief moment before she begins playing the Bridal March. With the opening chords, the mother of the bride motions everyone to stand, because *Here Comes the Bride!* She is more beautiful than she has ever been before! Her Father proudly escorts his daughter down the aisle knowing that everyone is focused on her. The groom even gasps as he sees her radiant beauty.

Over the next thirty minutes, these two young people will make a commitment to spend their life together as husband and wife. They exchange not only all they have, but all that they are. The bride even accepts the name of her husband. There is a change from *mine* to *ours*. From this moment forward, everything will change. The couple is married!

Did you know that the Bible begins and ends with a wedding? As the recounting of the Creation Story comes to an end, the last detail given is about a wedding. After describing the wonder of Creation, God concludes His recording of Creation with the statement, "And a man shall leave his father and mother and cleave only to his wife. And the two shall become one" (Genesis 2:24).

Why would God's design for marriage be the last thing He mentions before He takes His first Sabbath Rest? It is because God's love letter is all about His Divine Plan for His relationship with us spilling over into our relationship with each other. The

Creation Story is never meant to be a scientific manifesto on the mechanics of the Creation process. It is all about relationships. You cannot diagram love.

In the book of Revelation, we are drawn back to a wedding. The Bride of Christ (all believers) is welcomed to the Marriage Supper of the Lamb. This wedding has been paid in full by the Blood of Jesus Christ. No one at this wedding is there by their own merit. Each one has a story to tell of how the Groom changed their lives. The Apostle John writes,

> Let us rejoice and be glad and give him glory! For the wedding of the Lamb has come, and his Bride has made herself ready. Fine linen, bright and clean, was given her to wear. Then the angel said to me, "Write: Blessed are those who are invited to the wedding supper of the Lamb!" Revelation 19:7-9a

Marriage (i.e., Groom/Bride or Husband/Wife) is another thread that is sewn into the Bible from Genesis to Revelation. Most frequently, it is the picture of a Bride and Groom on or near their wedding day. The Bride's heart palpitates when she sees her groom. The groom finds it hard to speak in his bride's presence. There is no relationship on Earth that comes closer to exemplifying the relationship God wants to have with us than the love that a husband and wife should have for each other. In the Bible, God is the Groom and the Church is His Bride.

The Stages of a Wedding. In Jesus' day, a Jewish wedding included three stages: the *betrothal* (formal engagement), the *preparation* of the new home by the groom and the *wedding* itself. Each of these stages plays an important role in understanding the Bible. They especially serve as a backdrop for the life and ministry of Jesus. Let's look at each stage and how it is woven into the Scripture.

The Betrothal

The Betrothal was a very formal event. The fathers of the prospective bride and groom arranged the marriage. Meticulous details were addressed from the negotiation of the dowries to the gifts that would be given to the bride and groom. This process was more of a business transaction than an act of love. There was a set time for this official engagement to take place.

At the conclusion of the betrothal ceremony, a marriage license was signed. Although the date of the actual wedding was always uncertain, the groom and his betrothed would be considered bound for life to each other. Breaking the betrothal required a divorce. The marriage was not to be consummated until the wedding had taken place. For the bride to become pregnant during the betrothal period would be a social and spiritual disgrace because it was proof either of unfaithfulness on the bride's part or of sexual sin on the couple's part.

The Nativity Story in Matthew's gospel account opens with Mary and Joseph in what appears to be an unthinkable relationship. From all outward appearances, Mary had become pregnant by Joseph prior to their wedding. Matthew explains,

> This is how the birth of Jesus came about: His mother Mary was pledged to be married to Joseph, but before they came together, she was found to be with child through the Holy Spirit. Because Joseph her husband was a righteous man and did not want to expose her to public disgrace, he had in mind to divorce her quietly. Matthew 1:18-19

In Matthew 1:20-21, we find God revealing to Joseph through a dream that Mary's pregnancy is not an act of her unfaithfulness, but of the faithfulness of God to bring salvation. This child who was miraculously conceived is the long-awaited Messiah. The child is given the name Jesus, because He will be living proof that "Jehovah saves." The King of Kings will not be born in a palace, but placed in a lowly manger. Paul declares the reason for Jesus' humble start. "For you know the grace of our Lord Jesus Christ, that though he was rich, yet for your sakes he became poor, so that you through his poverty might become rich" (II Corinthians 8:9).

After the dream, Joseph immediately marries Mary, but for those who only saw outward appearances, there had to be judgmental looks cast at Joseph and Mary as Mary's pregnancy became more apparent. Only Mary and Joseph knew that, "he (Joseph) had no union with her (Mary) until she gave birth to a son (Matthew 1:25).

The Cup of Acceptance

There was only one romantic moment during the betrothal ceremony. At the conclusion of the ceremony, the groom's father would hand his son a cup of wine. The groom would then offer the cup of wine to his bride. The Cup of Acceptance was the groom's way of saying, "I love you. Do you love me?" By accepting this special cup, the bride was responding, "I do love you too."

Using the word picture of the Cup of Acceptance, let's look back as Jesus moves from the Upper Room to the Garden of Gethsemane just before His arrest. During the Passover Meal in the Upper Room, there were four cups of wine that were passed. The four cups symbolized the four promises in Exodus 6:6-7 that God made to the Israelites concerning the Exodus from Egyptian bondage.

- The Cup of Deliverance (verse 6) "I will bring you out…"
- The Cup of Blessing (verse 6), "I will free you from being slaves…"
- The Cup of Redemption (verse 6), "I will redeem you…"
- The Cup of Acceptance (verse 7), "I will take you as my own…"

The first two cups would be received during the first part of the meal. There would be an informal break and then the third and fourth cup would be received. It is the Cup of Redemption that Christ lifts when we read, "In the same way, after the supper he (Jesus) took the cup, saying, 'This cup is the new covenant in my blood, which is poured out for you" (Luke 22:20).

Jesus and His disciples will make their way to the Garden of Gethsemane singing the Hallel (Psalms 118-120). At Gethsemane, Jesus comes face-to-face with the cup of God's wrath. The only way we can be redeemed is if someone pays the price for our lives to be "bought back."

As Jesus prepares to have our iniquities laid on His shoulders (Isaiah 53:6), Jesus struggles to the point that He sweats drops like blood under the heavy load. Does Jesus love us enough to drink from this cup? Is He willing take on sin, death and the grave? As the battle rages, we read,

> Going a little farther, he fell with his face to the ground and prayed, "My Father, if it is possible, may this cup be taken from me. Yet not as I will, but as you will. Matthew 26:39

In triumphal surrender, Jesus prays, "My Father, if it is not possible for this cup to be taken away unless I drink it, may your will be done" (Matthew 26:42). Do you see the picture? Jesus loved us so much that He accepted the Cup of Wrath. He took the cup from us and drank it for us. How could Christ love us that much?

Building the Room

Before the wedding could take place, the groom was responsible to go to his father's house and build a room onto the house where he and his wife would live. The process could take weeks or months. Only after the father gave his approval that the room was ready was the groom allowed to get his bride. Finally, his bride would be where he was.

Does that remind you of anything Jesus said? In the Upper Room, Jesus uses marriage language to comfort His disciples before He goes to the Cross. Jesus says,

> In my Father's house are many rooms; if it were not so, I would have told you. I am going there to prepare a place for you. And if I go and prepare a place for you, I will come back and take you to be with me that you also may be where I am. John 14:2-3

Did you hear that? Jesus wants us to be where He is. One of the key ingredients in a good marriage is wanting to *be* together. One of my very favorite moments of the day is drinking a cup of coffee with my wife. Bonnie fixes my one cup of the day just perfectly. What makes that moment my favorite is that we get to *be* together. I love being in her presence. Jesus feels the same way about you!

The Wedding Preparation

When the father placed his stamp of approval on the completion of the room, the groom was free to go retrieve his wife. As the groom approached his bride's hometown, he would blow a trumpet sound on a shofar (an instrument made out of an animal's horn) announcing that he was approaching. Because the bride never knew when her groom would come back, she always needed to be ready.

Preparation for the bride meant having her wedding dress by her bed and her lamp filled with oil in case her groom was coming. The wedding itself would happen spontaneously as everyone gathered to celebrate the joyous occasion. Because the brides never knew if the groom approaching was their groom, the brides had to be ready every time the trumpet was blown.

Based on this wedding custom, Jesus tells the Parable of the Ten Virgins (Matthew 25:1-13). Five virgins have properly prepared with adequate oil (a symbol of the Holy Spirit) and five virgins have failed to store enough oil. When the bridegroom comes, the five virgins are not prepared to attend the wedding. In Matthew 25:13, Jesus leaves no question about his message when he concludes, "Therefore keep watch, because you do not know the day or the hour (of Christ's return)." In light of Christ's return, we must remain spiritually ready at all times.

The Singleness of Marriage

To me, one of the miracles that God performs in marriage is molding two lives into one. Through my years in ministry, I have been blessed to meet numerous couples who have celebrated fifty years of marriage or more. In a few years, my wife and I will celebrate that milestone ourselves. Couples who have been married for a half century are able to finish each other's sentences. When a young couple is first married, they hold hands to express their love. When an older couple holds hands, it serves a dual purpose: it is an expression of love and a necessity so neither will fall. In the state of Oklahoma, the witnesses who sign a marriage certificate cannot be a husband and his wife. Why? Because a husband and wife are considered one person. Ironic as it may sound, there is singleness to marriage that God makes very clear.

The Single Definition

God only has one definition of marriage. Biblically, *marriage is a covenant or commitment made between a man and his wife*. God's intended for marriage to be an exclusive, life-long commitment. That is not a statement of judgment or hate. It is simply a biblical fact. As we have seen, the Creation Story ends with, "For this reason a man will leave his father and mother and be united to his wife, and they will become one flesh" (Genesis 2:24). Paul quotes Genesis 2:24 in Ephesians 5:31 as part of his teaching about marriage.

It is important to note that Jesus also quoted Genesis 2:24 in His discussion with the Pharisees concerning divorce. When confronted with the legality of divorce, Jesus goes back to the Creation Story.

> "Haven't you read," he replied, "that at the beginning the Creator 'made them male and female,' and said, 'For this reason a man will leave his father and mother and be united to his wife, and the two will become one flesh'? Matthew 19:4-6

Physically, God beautifully designed the human body to enable a husband and wife to become one during sexual intercourse. In this face-to-face encounter, two hearts are meshed together in love. This is not an act of instinct, but an intentional act of the will for procreation and pleasure. *Emotionally*, God's design was for a man and his wife to form an emotional bond that would not be broken. *Spiritually*, a husband and wife are to walk together in spiritual harmony. Marriage is more than a legal action. It is the making of a spiritual covenant.

Like it is true in marriage, God intended there to be an oneness in our relationship with Him. As Jesus prepares for His arrest, He prays a prayer for unity for all believers when He prays, "that all of them will be one, Father, just as I am in you and you are in me. May they also be in us so that the world may believe that you have sent them" (John 17:20-21). His thoughts are to become our thoughts. His strength is to become our strength. His love is to become our love to the point that when people see us, they see Him in us.

The Single Commitment

God created marriage to be an *exclusive* relationship. A part of the commitment in marriage is "forsaking all others." Faithfulness is absolutely necessary if a marriage is going to survive. No one other than your spouse can be the object of your affection. We were not created to have a divided heart. Jesus explains,

> No one can serve two masters. Either he will hate the one and love the other, or he will be devoted to the one and despise the other. You cannot serve both God and Money. Matthew 6:24

I realize that many of the Old Testament characters had multiple wives, but it was never by God's directions. Although he only loved Rachel, Jacob ends up with two wives; two handmaidens and a "blended" family of thirteen children (Don't forget Dinah). The result is the first recorded dysfunctional family. For political gain and personal pleasure, Solomon had 300 hundred wives and 700 concubines. As he reflects on his life, Solomon writes, "I found one upright man among a thousand, but not one upright woman among them all" (Ecclesiastes 7:28).

Because marriage is an exclusive relationship, God gave sex as a gift to be experienced only within the covenant of marriage. The writer to the Hebrews states, "Marriage should be honored by all and the marriage bed kept pure, for God will judge the adulterer and all the sexually immoral" (Hebrew 13:4). The emotional and physical bonding that is experienced in sexual intercourse was meant to be a spiritual renewal of the marriage covenant.

I realize that many find the concept of "sin" offensive today. We want God to be changed into our likeness rather for us be changed into His likeness. What was meant to be experienced within the bounds of marriage has become an expectation for a second date. What is of equally great concern is how we justify our actions by using a distorted picture of Jesus as our affirmation.

While it is true that Jesus did not come into the world to *condemn* us in our sins (John 3:17), He did not come to *condone* our sins either. Christ came to radically *change* our lives. Through the Holy Spirit, Jesus convicts (convinces) us of both our obedience and our disobedience. God's motive is not to belittle us, but to keep us from the scars and brokenness that comes from not listening to God's voice. The Psalmist David expresses the Heart of God when he writes, "He (Christ) heals the brokenhearted and binds up their wounds (Psalm 147:3).

God does not want to share our affections with someone or something else. Just as is true of marriage, our relationship with God was meant to be exclusive too. That is why He says, "You shall not bow down to them or worship them; for I, the Lord your God, am a jealous God" (Ex 20:5). Jealousy here does not mean uncontrollable outrage. It simply means that God does not want to share our love with other "gods" that might steal our heart.

The Wedding Dance

Marriage is more than a *legal contract*; it is a *spiritual covenant*. Marriage was never meant to be an act of *self-discipline*. With Christ as the Third Party, a couple learns how to become *selfless* with their spouse. Just like our relationship with Christ, there must be a yielding of our lives in marriage.

It wasn't unusual when I did pre-marital counseling for the prospective bride to begin by saying, "Now, before we get started, I want to make something perfectly clear. I am not going to say that I will 'honor and obey' my husband." I always knew that the woman was struggling with Ephesians 5:22-33, which reads,

> Wives, *submit* to your husbands as to the Lord. For the husband is the head of the wife as Christ is the head of the church, his body of which he is the Savior. Now as the church *submits* to Christ, so also wives should *submit* to their husbands in everything.

The dirty word was the word "submit." The woman was saying, "I do not want to be controlled by my husband." When we first got married, Bonnie and I purchased t-shirts that said "Master" on my shirt and "Slave" on hers. We wore them because it was funny. If I had ever tried to *be* the Master in the relationship, it would not have been a laughing matter. To understand the passage, we have to back-up to Ephesians 5:21 which says, "Submit to one another out of reverence for Christ." Marriage requires a mutual yielding of the heart by both the husband and the wife.

God intended marriage to be like ballroom dancing.

Just as is true in our relationship with Christ, a bride and groom have to settle the question *"Who is going to lead?"* Otherwise, marriage becomes a tug-of-war. God has chosen the husband to be the *spiritual* leader. He is to set the spiritual example for his wife and children can follow. The absence of a husband's spiritual leadership will always have a ripple effect on his family.

The husband's spiritual leadership is not an act of controlling his wife or children, but of leading them in their walk with God. While the music is playing, all the couple should know is the joy of being together. Sometimes, the partners dance freely through times of joy. At other times, they hold each other tightly when challenges come. Through it all, the couple will learn how to move in sync.

God is planning a great reception. Jesus is preparing a reception for all believers that will outshine anything we can imagine. In fact, it is the grandest reception of all. Every believer will have a place at the Marriage Supper of the Lamb. Listen to the Apostle John as he describes what he sees.

> Let us rejoice and be glad and give him glory! For the wedding of the Lamb has come, and his bride has made herself ready. Revelation 19:7

> I saw the Holy City, the new Jerusalem, coming down out of heaven from God, prepared as a bride beautifully dressed for her husband. Revelation 21:2

> Then the angel said to me, "Write this: Blessed are those who are invited to the wedding supper of the Lamb." And he added, "These are the true words of God." Revelation 19:9

The marriage language throughout the Bible reminds us of the depth of God's love for us. God wants to bring us into an intimate relationship with Him where every day we become more like Him. Yes, it does require us to yield our lives to Him. In return, we have the blessing of His Presence and Protection. The longer we walk with Christ, the more we look like Him. The Christian walk is a journey of love. We can celebrate the unbelievable truth that God knows us and loves us anyway!

As you look at the Seamless Robe of Jesus, can you hear the wedding music playing? Throughout the Bible there is a wedding invitation being extended to those who would accept it.

I HAVE FALLEN AND I CAN'T GET UP!

Sin

POOR MRS. FLETCHER FINDS HERSELF ON THE FLOOR WITH HER walker between herself and the telephone. What is she to do? She reaches for the device hanging around her neck, pushes the button and calls out those immortal words, *"I've fallen and I can't get up!"* Although Mrs. Fletcher's condition is serious, the dispatcher calmly says, "We have help on the way, Mrs. Fletcher.[31]" Family, neighbors, policemen, firemen and the LifeCall emergency team show up in seconds.

Unfortunately, because of really poor acting and the disclaimer that the commercial is a dramatization, the phrase, *"I've fallen and I can't get up?"* became a catchphrase used for almost every comedic situation since 1989. Because I work as a hospice chaplain, I realize how dangerous and real the threat of falling is for elderly people. In real life, it is no joke. However, I have to also admit that I have used that line to get a laugh hundreds of times.

There was a young couple whose fall was no laughing matter. What they did broke the very heart of God. Adam and Eve's decision to break their relationship with God was the biggest spiritual disaster that has ever happened. Because of their intentional rejection of God's promise of an eternal relationship, we have experienced unbelievable atrocities of people against people in our world. The sacredness of life has been replaced by self-centered gain. What man has done to man goes beyond our comprehension.

It has infected your life, the life of your family and every human being that has ever lived on Planet Earth, except Jesus Christ. The decision that Adam and Eve made to take their lives into their own hands is the source of broken homes, abused children, murder as

---

31   It also worked for Mr. Miller's heart attack later in the commercial.

well as every other example of sin. The greatest problem facing our world today is not economic, ecological or political. As has always been true from Genesis 3 forward, our greatest problem today is spiritual. The evening news is filled every day with tragedies that have happened because someone was even willing to murder in order to have their way. From a pair of expensive basketball shoes to the overtaking of a country, people are willing do to whatever it takes, because they believe life is "all about me!"

The effect of Adam and Eve's decision shows up clearly in the life of a two-year-old when they throw a fit for not getting their way. It raises its ugly head every time a teenager says, *"Whatever!"* You can easily spot the problem in adults when they only talk about themselves. The desire to be in control has caused wars, murder and deceit. It is the most dangerous problem in the world today! Spiritually, *we have fallen and we can't get up!*

The thread of *Sin* is also interwoven through the Bible. Paul describes it in Romans 1:21, "For although they knew, God, they neither glorified him as God nor gave thanks to him, but their thinking became futile and their foolish hearts were darkened."

Paul goes on to describe the results of this attitude. He writes,

> Therefore God gave them over in the sinful desires of their hearts to sexual impurity for the degrading of their bodies with one another. They exchanged the truth about God for a lie, and worshipped and served created things rather than the Creator—who is forever praised. Amen! Romans 1:24-25

Paul then describes the sinful actions that are by-products of a sinful attitude. Because Adam and Eve rejected who God is, they also rejected how He wanted them to live.

> Because of this, God gave them over to shameful lusts. Even their women exchanged natural relations for unnatural ones. In the same way the men also abandoned natural relations with women and were inflamed with lust for one another. Men committed indecent acts with other men, and received in themselves the due penalty for their perversion.

> Furthermore, since they did not think it worthwhile to retain the knowledge of God, he gave them over to a depraved mind, to do what ought not to be done. They have become filled with every kind of wickedness, evil, greed and depravity. They are full

of envy, murder, strife, deceit and malice. They are gossips, slan-
derers, God-haters, insolent, arrogant and boastful; they invent
ways of doing evil; they disobey their parents; they are senseless,
faithless, heartless, and ruthless. Romans 1:26-31

The third chapter of Genesis describes the greatest spiritual
disaster in human history. With the partaking of the forbidden
fruit, Adam and Eve deliberately chose to break fellowship with
God. What started out in the Garden as God's perfect intention
for mankind ends up shattered by one fatal choice by Adam and
Eve. They deliberately came out from under God's authority and
set out on their own. Although Adam and Eve could choose to
walk away from God, they would never have the power to return
to Him by their own strength.

The Origin of Sin. Things could not have been more perfect
for Adam and Eve. Their days were filled with being with God
on their daily walks, being with each other as they explored the
beauty of this God-crafted Garden and being with the animals,
watching them play without any fear of a "cat fight." There was
only one restriction: they could not eat of the fruit of the Tree
of the Knowledge of Good and Evil. *That Tree was one that only
God had the right to eat from.* God alone determined good from
evil. Everything else was available for their pleasure. There was a
choice, but there was no valid reason to cross that line. God provided for their every need.

Then one day, a conversation started between Eve and the Serpent. The underlining issue was *trust.* Could God be trusted? Was
God really who He presents Himself to be? What if He is not our
Creator? Maybe God was lying to them. What if God is no different than me?

When the conversation begins between Eve and the Serpent,
the Serpent begins by questioning God's *instructions.* He says,
"Did God really say, 'You must not eat from *any* tree in the garden'? (Genesis 3:1). Did Eve really hear God correctly? Of course,
the Serpent globalizes God's requirement by included all the trees,
not just the one.

Eve responds by repeating God's warning verbatim. "You
must not eat fruit from the tree in the middle of the garden, and

you must not touch it, or you will die" (Genesis 3:3). Eve knew that only one tree that was off limits. She knew she had access to every other fruit in the Garden. God's instructions are clear and are motivated by His love for us. God has proven He is worthy of trust.

If the conversation had ended there, things would have been fine. However, Eve allows the Serpent to continue the conversation. Satan tries to make Eve question God's *intention*. Why would He withhold that one tree? Surely, God had an ulterior motive. For the first and last time in the Bible, Satan tells the truth. He says, "For God knows that when you eat from it your eyes will be opened, and *you will be like God*, knowing good and evil" (Genesis 3:5). The Serpent's ploy was, "God has been withholding the truth from you! You should be in charge of your own life. Take the lead! God is afraid of a little competition. Eat the fruit and taste independence!"

Actually, it was a half-truth. Adam and Eve would usurp God's leadership in their lives, thus becoming "like God." The part the Serpent left out was that by determining for themselves what was right and wrong their relationship with God would be broken. They were not created or prepared to take matters into their own hands. By deciding in their hearts that they would usurp God's place as Leader in their life, Adam and Eve would lose everything. The right to partake of the fruit of the Tree of the Knowledge of Good and Evil belonged to God and God alone.

The reason that God established the restriction concerning the Tree of the Knowledge of Good and Evil was because He created us with free will, the ability to choose whether or not we *wanted* to be in relationship with Him. God could have created us to do only what He said. We could have been His puppets, but God wanted us to choose to love Him. God risked the experience of having His heart broken in order to allow us to respond to His love.

As long as Adam and Eve were obedient to God's command, they were saying, "God, I want to be with you!" The partaking of the fruit was a clear statement that their desire to be with God was over. Adam and Eve chose to reverse God's desire in Creation, by saying, "I want to be in charge! From this point forward, *it is all about ME!*"

The Outcome of Sin. As the juices of the forbidden fruit trickled down Adam and Eve's throat, life as they have known was over. Their eyes are open not to whom God is, but who they are apart from Him. For the first time, their nakedness was awkward and embarrassing. They tried to cover their sin with fig leaves. They began to find it hard to breathe.

Then they heard the sound of the Lord God coming. Their Creator had come for his daily walk with them. Adam and Eve's response is to try to hide from God. Had it not been so serious, Adam and Eve's plan would have almost been comical (Genesis 3:8). How could the only two human beings on Earth think they could hide from their Creator? Would He not hear the unusual rustling of the trees? Would He not hear them panting for air as they hid in fear?

God had come for His daily walk. When Adam and Eve are not quickly visible, "the Lord God called to the man, "Where are you?" (Genesis 3:9). Adam's answer gives both him and his wife away. Their cover has been blown! Adam answered, "I heard you in the garden, and I was afraid because I was *naked*; so I hid" (Genesis 3:10). The awareness of their nakedness and their fear of God gave away their disobedience. God confronts Adam and Eve with the obvious issue, "Have you eaten from the tree that I commanded you not to eat from?" (Genesis 3:11).

What follows next is the recording of the first time someone threw someone else "under the bus." Instead of confessing his disobedience, Adam passes the buck to Eve. Adam replies, "The man said, 'The woman you put here with me—she gave me some fruit from the tree, and I ate it' (Genesis 3:12).

Adam is blaming God first and Eve second. Adam does not take responsibility for his actions. What a great moment to admit your guilt and ask for forgiveness! Instead, Adam almost demands God apologize for setting him up with "the woman."

When Eve is confronted by what she has done, she shows no remorse, but instead says, "The serpent deceived me, and I ate" (Genesis 3:13). The devil made her do it. Although it is obvious both people have made a deliberate choice to disobey, they decide to stick to their story.

I cannot prove it biblically, but I have to believe that both Adam and Eve were unable to look God in the eyes. What Adam and Eve needed is a spiritual "facelift" where once again they can walk with God unashamed. They needed to be restored to a relationship based on total honesty and trust. Adam and Eve chose to break their relationship with God and will be escorted out of the Garden unable to ever return again.

When He evaluates the situation, God uses the same words the Serpent used to describe what would happen if they chose to eat of the fruit. God concludes what has happened when He says,

> And the Lord God said, "The man has now *become like one of us, knowing good and evil.* He must not be allowed to reach out his hand and take also from the tree of life and eat, and live forever." Genesis 5:22

The difference between Genesis 5:3 and Genesis 5:22 is *who* made the statement. The first statement is made by the Father of Lies. The second statement is made by the Creator of the universe, who never lies. Satan made it sound as if Man being in charge was a good thing. In fact, it is the worst thing that has ever happened to us! As consequences of Adam and Eve's decision, all of us are born with what Martin Luther called, *"A bent towards sin."* We are born with an attitude that is *self-centered*.

It is possible to summarize the Bible by following the thread of *sin*.

- Genesis 1-2—God's Divine Intention to create a perfect environment for Man (both male and female) to live with Him in perfect harmony.

- Genesis 3—Man's rejection of God, thus breaking the relations with God.

- Genesis 4-Revelation 22—God's Intervention to restore our relationship with Him through the Cross.

No one needs to go to Seminary to find evidence of the existence of sin. I was in a Christian bookstore a few years ago when a Mom and her young daughter came into the store. The little girl could not have been cuter. Her hair was tightly curled, her frilly dress was perfectly ironed and her shoes were white patent with frilly socks with a bow in her hair.

Near the window of the store, there was a display of $5 plastic Noah Ark sets. The little girl walked over to examine the cheap little set of animals. She looked at her Mom and said, "I want one of those Noah Ark sets."

Her Mom gently told her, "No."

Apparently thinking that her Mom had not heard her, the little girl increased her volume by a few decibels and said, "I Want One of Those Noah's Ark sets!"

The mom again gently answered, "No!"

For a moment, I thought the little girl's head was going to start spinning around. She stomped her feet and yelled at the top of her voice, "I WANT ONE OF THOSE NOAH'S ARK SETS!"

Thinking it would calm her daughter down; the Mom finally gave in by saying, "Okay. Okay. Okay. I will get one...*for your cousin.*" Needless to say, the mom ended up dragging the little girl out of the store without a Noah's Ark set.

There is a spiritual explanation for the little girl's action. That sweet little girl is driven by a desire to always have her way. It is all about me. As long as it is not your child, such an evident may be funny. Unless sin is dealt with, it is no laughing matter.

The Overflow of Sin. Sin is a social disease. Disobedient acts will become contagious as other's lives are impacted. Like the plague, Adam and Eve's disobedience infected the attitudes and actions of those who came after them. Separated from God, Adam and Eve will experience the heartache of the murder of their son Abel at the hands of his brother Cain. Under the curse of a broken covenant, Cain will depart from the presence of God and live apart from his family in the land of Nod.

The birth of Adam and Eve's third son Seth brings hope for a new beginning. The genealogy of Adam in Genesis 5 begins with an affirmation of God's original intent for man. "When God created man, he made him in the likeness of God. He created them male and female and blessed them. And when they were created, he (God) called them 'man'" (Genesis 5:1b-2).

As we examine the genealogy, we find a man named Enoch who "walked with God; then he was no more, because God took him away" (Genesis 5:24). Enoch and later Elijah are the only two people who did not experience death, but were taken directly into Heaven. Three generations after Enoch, Noah is born. The Bible tells us, "Noah was a righteous man, blameless among the people of his time, and he walked with God" (Genesis 6:9b).

The problem is that Noah was the exception, not the rule. The depth of the perversion of sin mankind reaches before the Flood requires God's judgment to come. Many have trouble with "the God of the Old Testament" carrying out such judgment. We must remember that it took 120 years for Noah to build the Ark. Three generations saw the evidence of God's coming wrath. The Flood was not a knee-jerk reaction to sin. There was plenty of time for repentance.

What caused the sinful condition of man to become so bad that God would have no choice but to begin again? In the unusual passage found in Genesis 6:1-2, we find an explanation of how sin reached that point when we read,

> When men began to increase in number on the earth and daughters were born to them, the *sons of God* saw that the *daughters of men* were beautiful, and they married any of them they chose. Genesis 6:1

I cannot count how many times complete strangers have called my office and asked about the meaning of this verse. Were there angels having children with humans? Let me propose a much simpler explanation. Prior to the Flood, there were men and women, like Enoch and Noah who were walking with God. They had chosen to follow God in the midst of a world filled with sinful temptations. They chose God's *presence* over the world's *perversion*. The righteous (sons of *God*) began to marry into unrighteous families (daughters of *men*).

This was more than the change of a marital status. It was the entry point for sin to infect those who had once followed God. What was God's response? "Then the Lord said, "My Spirit will not contend with man forever, for he is mortal; his days will be a hundred and twenty years" (Genesis 6:3).

During the forty years of wandering in the wilderness, the Israelites engaged in a similar spiritual compromise. Their willingness to forsake God for the local god, Baal, will be the reason that a whole generation must die before God's people are spiritually ready to enter the Promised Land. We read,

> While Israel was staying in Shittim, the men began to indulge in sexual immorality with the Moabite women who invited them to the sacrifices to their gods. The people (Israelites) ate and bowed down before these gods. So Israel joined in worshiping the Baal of Peor. And the Lord's anger burned against them. Numbers 25:1-3

Because of the pagan worship of his three hundred wives, Solomon allowed their pagan temples to be built outside the walls of Jerusalem. Because every pagan religion in the Old Testament (Baal and Asheroth, Marduk, Dagon, etc) included temple prostitutes and child sacrifice, the sound of babies crying as they were burned to death could be heard inside the Temple. Those worship centers would stand until their destruction by Josiah shortly before the fall of Judah to the Babylonians. The need for Elijah to challenge the priests of Baal on Mount Carmel was the result of Ahaz's marriage to the foreigner Jezebel. It was Jezebel who aided in the spread of Baal worship in Judah.

There was never a time in the Old Testament when the Israelites totally forsook God. Their sinfulness always arose from trying to serve both "God and…" A perfect example of this behavior can be found in II Kings 16:1-18. While seeking help from the Assyrian king Tiglath-Pileser to battle the armies of Aram and Israel, Ahaz sees an altar in Assyria and has a replicate built near the Temple. The pagan altar is placed where the bronze altar has been. However, Ahaz does not demolish God's altar. Listen to what Ahaz did,

> The bronze altar that stood before the Lord he brought from the front of the temple—from between the new altar and the temple of the Lord—and put it on the north side of the new altar. II Kings 16:14

Ahaz kept God's altar just in case the new altar did not work. He wanted to keep God "on the sidelines." Satan seldom attacks us directly. In the same way he approached Eve, Satan presents small compromises that will lead to a life we would never have chosen if we had been shown the "bigger picture." When we choose to yield to temptation, it amazing how far away from God sin will carry us.

The Overcoming of Sin

Fortunately, the Bible does not end with the Fall of Man. Jesus came to defeat sin by dying on the Cross. Although man cannot save himself, Jesus came to redeem us by His grace. Even through the Old Testament God is weaving the thread of salvation. The sacrificial system was built on the faithfulness of God. When the blood of animals was poured on the horns of the altar, the people were crying out for God to keep His promise to be faithful.

The ultimate act of God's faithfulness was to send His Son to be the final Sacrifice for our sins. Jesus' death on the Cross paid the price for our sins, once and for all. The prophet Isaiah writes, "We all, like sheep, have gone astray, each of us has turned to his own way; and the Lord has laid on him the iniquity of us all" (Isaiah 53:6). I love how Paul describes the victory that Christ has won for us.

> When you were dead in your sins and in the uncircumcision of your sinful nature, God made you alive with Christ. He forgave us all our sins, having canceled the written code, with its regulations, that was against us and that stood opposed to us; he (Jesus) took it away, nailing it to the Cross. Colossians 2:13-14

Jesus paid the price for your salvation and mine. Sin no longer has to be the driving force of your life. You can be set free! Sin is not the end of the story. While it is true that "all have sinned and fall short of the glory of God (Romans 3:23), there is a greater truth. The Bible celebrates the fact that, "The death he (Jesus) died, he died to sin once for all; but the life he lives, he lives to God."(Romans 6:10).

If you look at Jesus as He wears the Seamless Robe, you will see that His arms are opened wide, welcoming us to receive His forgiveness. The blood stains on His Robe remind us that He paid the price in full for our salvation. All we must do is accept His gracious gift of salvation. Hallelujah!

BLOOD BROTHERS (AND SISTERS)

The Blood Covenant

WERE YOU EVER SOMEONE'S *BLOOD BROTHER*? IN ORDER FOR THE relationship to be official, two parties had to prick their fingers enough to draw blood. Then, both parties would place their fingers together, letting the blood intermingle. From that moment forward, the blood brothers would vow to be friends for life. If anyone came against you, your blood brother was committed to be on your side.

By the shedding of your blood, you and your blood brother made a *covenant*, which is *a contract or commitment of relationship*. Just as the shed blood could not be separated one from the other, so the identity of the two parties could not be separated. Just as we have seen in the word picture of marriage, two lives became one. Every covenant in the Bible is a *blood covenant*. Each covenant required the shedding of blood.

One of the major threads of the Bible is the *Blood Covenant*. Malcolm Smith writes, "Studying the Bible by its covenants gives us a whole Bible—one that is woven together as the unfolding, revealing of the one purpose of God."[32] If you want to follow the storyline of Scripture, tracing the covenants is one of the most effective ways.

As James Garlow writes,

> In many ways the covenant is the foundation of our faith and the epicenter of what we understand about our relationship with God. Upon it is based our understanding of salvation, holiness, healing, worship, deliverance, and sanctification.[33]

---

32   Malcolm Smith, The Blood Covenant: A Study on the Faithfulness of God, (Unconditional Love: San Antonio, Texas, 1998), page 2

33   James Garlow, The Covenant: A Study of God's Extraordinary Love for You, (Beacon Hill Press, Kansas City, Missouri, 2007), page 13

In fact, the Bible is divided into two major covenants, the Old Testament (Covenant) and the New Testament (Covenant). Smith writes, "It (covenant) is the common denominator of the Old Testament and the New Testament people of faith."[34] The covenants that are initiated in the Old Testament are fulfilled in Christ in the New Testament. Each of God's Covenants is still "active" today and plays a role in God's Divine Purpose. From the Covenant of Creation forward, the faithfulness of God is revealed.

The Definition

The word *covenant* literally means, *"to cut."* Malcolm Smith defines a blood covenant as, *a blood bond, for life or death, made between two parties, always with shedding of blood and the taking of oaths."*[35] A Covenant is different than a business contract in that a Covenant is based on the *relationship* of the parties involved more than on their *resources*. Although there may be financial advantages to a covenant, the purpose is to establish a life-long relationship together. Our best example today is the Marriage Covenant.

The most obvious "cutting" in the Old Testament is found in Genesis 22. God commands Abraham to take Isaac to the top of Mount Moriah and sacrifice him there. When He sees the depth of Abraham's obedience, God provides a ram to be slain on the rock where Isaac was to be sacrificed. In the New Testament, "Jesus' death is the 'cutting' of the New Covenant."[36]

The Demand

A covenant always required the shedding of blood, because "the blood is the life" (Deuteronomy 12:23b). The two parties of the covenant were putting their life on the line to insure this covenant was kept. One of the ten necessary steps for completing a covenant was called "the walk of blood." One writer describes the process. "The walk of blood: Each participant walks a path in the

---

34   Ibid., page 1 (Smith)

35   Ibid, page 1 (Smith)

36   Ibid., page 38 (Smith)

shape of a 'figure 8' between the halves of the slain animal, then stops in the middle in the midst of the pool of blood to pronounce the blessings and the curses of the covenant."[37] This walk served two purposes: to remind both parties that breaking the covenant would cost them their lives and to affirm that both parties would be willing to die to save each other.

The clearest picture of this process is found in Genesis 15:1-21. As God prepares to make a covenant with Abraham, He instructs Abraham,

> Bring me a heifer, a goat and a ram, each three years old, along with a dove and a young pigeon. Abram brought all these to him, cut them in two and arranged the halves opposite each other; the birds, however, he did not cut in half. Genesis 15:9-10

Blood plays an important role in each of the major covenants of the Bible. For the covenant with *Adam and Eve*, the blood of an animal is shed to make the garments God clothes them in (Genesis 3:21). For the covenant with *Noah*, clean animals and clean birds are sacrificed as a burnt offering (Genesis 8:20). We have already seen the sacrifice made for the covenant with Abraham (Genesis 15:9-10).

For the covenant with *Moses*, Moses built an altar of the foot of Mount Sinai and offered burnt offerings and sacrificed young bulls (Exodus 24:4-6). For the covenant with *David*, God explained the reason to David why he would not be allowed to build the Temple explaining, "You have shed much blood and have fought many wars. You are not to build a house for my Name, because you have shed much blood on the earth in my sight" (1 Chronicles 22:8).

For the *New Covenant*, the blood shed will be from the very veins of Jesus. As Jesus initiates the New Covenant meal in the Upper Room, He tells His disciples, "This is the blood of the covenant, which is poured out for many for the forgiveness of sins" (Matthew 26:28). Jesus' blood that was shed on Calvary becomes a cleansing stream for all our sins.

---

37   http://www.rockofoffence.com/myst4.html

The Desire

Covenants could be made for a variety of reasons. For instance, the main reason behind most of Solomon's marriages was to create a *military alliance* that would protect him from attacks from the South. Marrying into Egyptian royalty assured Solomon that the key North-South road (the Via Maris) would be safe-guarded in times of war. Financial gain, control of land and protection of the peace would be other examples of motivation for a covenant.

Every Covenant God made has one motivation, His love. God does not need Abraham's wealth or David's military prowess. Most of the time, God calls into Covenant some of the most unlikely characters. Adam defied God by eating the forbidden fruit, Abraham was too old, Jacob was a schemer, Moses had a criminal record and David was the "runt" of the family.

The Covenant that God extends to us is not based on anything we are or have accomplished. Our relationship with Christ is based solely on God's grace and mercy. No one has earned this relationship. Like paupers, we come into this covenant with nothing. We are not worthless in God's eyes, but we are unworthy.

The Distinction

Although covenants can be between equal parties, God's covenants are always *lop-sided*. It is the offer of a King to a pauper. God has everything to offer and we come to Him completely empty-handed. We have everything to gain and nothing to lose. God has nothing to gain, except a relationship with us. Here is the amazing Good News of the Bible; God has acted in Christ to reconcile us to Himself, even though we have nothing to offer in return.

This is known as a *suzerainty* covenant. This is the only type of covenant God can make. It is also a covenant that God alone can and must bring to us. He has chosen us. As one author writes,

> The inequality between the parties (Creator and creatures) is absolute. It is always made clear that the initiative is God's—that He makes covenants with his people and not vice versa. God ini-

tiates, confirms and even fulfills (ultimately in Christ, both sides of) the covenant.[38]

Through Christ, the Creator of the universe has come to offer us a relationship of which we all are totally unworthy. As the Prophet Isaiah reminds us,

> All of us have become like one who is unclean, and all our righteous acts are like filthy rags; we all shrivel up like a leaf, and like the wind our sins sweep us away. Isaiah 64:6

Because the purpose of this book is to serve as a primer, it would be impossible to present a thorough overview of the richness and depth of the Covenant Concept. Instead, we will examine some of aspects of the covenant making process. I have included an article on all ten covenant steps in the Appendix. If you want to, you can flip back to that page now to get a fuller picture.

The Seven Covenants

There are seven major covenants in the Bible. These are not seven disconnected covenants. The first six covenants are all woven into the fabric of the Ultimate Covenant: the New Covenant of grace through Christ. Like the background of a painting, each covenant provides depth and dimension to their fulfillment in Christ.

1. The *Creation Covenant* (Genesis 1-2)

This is the covenant of Perfection. The Creation Story describes God's sole intent for creation of man. Just as is true of Adam and Eve, you and I were created to be in a relationship with God. His desire was and is to guide us and protect us. We find the beginning of the Creation Covenant in Genesis 1:26-27.

> Then God said, "Let us make man in our image, in our likeness, and let them rule over the fish of the sea and the birds of the air, over the livestock, over all the earth, and over all the creatures that move along the ground." So God created man in his own image, in the image of God he created him. Genesis 1:26-27

---

38   theopedia.com/Covenant

As we saw in the chapter on Creation, God's plan is built on a Creator-creation basis. Adam and Eve lived under the authority and protection of God. The authority they had on earth was based on a right relationship with God. Their nakedness symbolized the transparency of the relationship with God. There was nothing to hide. There is the daily blessing of walking and talking with God. The only agenda items were enjoying the presence of God and the beauty of His creation. The hardest job was naming the animals.

The return to this Original Covenant is the ultimate goal of God's Word. The Christ Event (Jesus' Birth, Death and Resurrection) paves the way for man to be restored to this perfect relationship. In Heaven, believers will live in a sinless world where,

> Nothing impure will ever enter it (heaven), nor will anyone who does what is shameful or deceitful, but only those whose names are written in the Lamb's book of life. Revelation 21:27

2. The Covenant with Adam (Genesis 3)

This is the covenant of Mercy. How will God respond to sin? Because Adam and Eve broke the Creation covenant, God has every right to carry out the curse of death. By their act of disobedience, Adam and Eve have rejected God. Justice requires the Death Sentence be carried out swiftly. God does punish Adam and Eve for their actions. However, in Genesis 3:15, we find hope in God's response Adam and Eve's disobedience.

> And I will put enmity between you and the woman, and between your offspring and hers: he will crush your head, and you will strike his heel. Genesis 3:15

In the opening scene of the movie *The Passion of the Christ*, Jesus is agonizing on the ground in the Garden of Gethsemane. A snake slithers down from inside the black robe of Satan onto the ground and towards Jesus. Suddenly, Jesus' sandal crushes the head of the snake. This is Mel Gibson's weaving of Genesis 3:15 to the Garden of Gethsemane. Instead of justice, God provides *mercy*. Adam and Eve do not get the punishment they deserved.

We all know John 3:16, but John 3:17 is an important verses in understanding God's mercy. In that verse we read, "For God did not send his Son into the world to condemn the world, but to save the world through him" (John 3:17). Mercy is always God's first response to sin. Mercy is not a sign of weakness, but a revelation of the very heart of God. In every story in the Bible, mercy is shown. There is punishment pronounced, but Judgment is always God's last resort. Although Adam and Eve could not come back to God, God will come to them. The biblical message of *a seeking God* (i.e., Luke 15) cannot be found in any other religious teaching.

Jesus' earthly ministry was a mission of Mercy. Christ's Death and Resurrection will provide the mercy we need to be saved. The Apostle Peter states it beautifully when he writes,

> Praise be to the God and Father of our Lord Jesus Christ! In his great mercy he has given us new birth into a living hope through the resurrection of Jesus Christ from the dead, and into an inheritance that can never perish, spoil or fade—kept in heaven for you, who through faith are shielded by God's power until the coming of the salvation that is ready to be revealed in the last time. I Peter 1:3-5

3. The Covenant with Noah (Genesis 6-9)

This is the covenant of New Beginnings. As we have already seen, mankind had reached a point of such blatant disobedience that God's judgment must fall. God's justice cannot allow such animosity to continue. Although God forewarned all the people of the impending judgment through the Flood, all except Noah and his family failed to heed God's call.

God's plan to destroy all living creatures by the Flood is irrevocable. God's plan for a new beginning is found in the safety of the Ark. Noah is given specific dimensions and material with which to build the Ark. God's Covenant is established with Noah in Genesis 6:

> But I will establish my covenant with you, and you will enter the ark—you and your sons and your wife and your sons' wives with you. You are to bring into the ark two of all living creatures, male and female, to keep them alive with you. Genesis 6:18-19

Although the Flood is an act of judgment, there is mercy in this Covenant as well. The Ark will be built before rain has ever fallen on the earth. Curiosity alone should have drawn the people to ask Noah for an explanation. No one can deny seeing this large boat out in the middle of the desert. Those who will perish do not die because of ignorance. Unwilling to repent, those who die will perish because of an intentional rejection of God's plan of salvation. When Mercy has been exhausted, Judgment will come!

Through the Flood, there is a physical and spiritual new beginning. The righteous family of Noah is given the mission of replenishing the earth. For the first time, God gives permission for Noah and his family to eat the meat of animals. They are not permitted to eat the blood of animals. God also gave a Rainbow as a covenant sign that He will never flood the earth again.[39]

Jesus will fulfill this Covenant by replacing the Flood with His Blood. The New Beginnings will be found at the Cross. As Paul states it,

> Therefore, if anyone is in Christ, he is a new creation; the old has gone, the new has come! II Corinthians 5:17

4. The Covenant with Abraham (Genesis 12-22)

This is the covenant of Blessing. Even after the impact of the Flood, the rebellious spirit of Man is shown in the building of the Tower of Babel (Genesis 11:1-9). Man attempts to reach God by his own strength. However, like a prism, God takes the one common language and breaks it into various languages. The people are unable to speak to each other much less to God. Through the genealogy of Abram (Genesis 11:10-32), we are led to the moment when God will make the foundational covenant of the Old Testament.

Beginning in Genesis 12, God calls a 75-year-old pagan named Abram (later Abraham) to leave his home in the Ur of Chaldees and go where God will lead him. The key to understanding the covenant is found in the three promises God will make to Abraham:

- A Promised Son (Genesis 15:4)—fulfilled in Genesis 21:1-7

---

39   Since the Flood is the first rain ever, the rainbow is also the first rainbow.

- A Promised Nation (Genesis 12:2)—fulfilled in Exodus 1:6
- A Promised Land (Genesis 15:7)—fulfilled beginning in Joshua 1.

If you follow these three promises, you can find their fulfillments are a helpful thread in understanding Genesis 12 through the book of Joshua. The covenant is expressed in the phrase; "the God of Abraham, Isaac and Jacob" which is repeated as a reminder of God's faithfulness at:

- The Exodus (Exodus 2:24)
- The Call of Moses (Exodus 3:6)
- The Levitical Law (Leviticus 26:42)
- The Final Speech of Joshua (Joshua 24: 3-4)
- Elijah and Mount Carmel (I Kings 18:36)
- The Second Sermon of Peter (Acts 3:13)

The Israelites' rejection of this Covenant will also cause God to keep the older generation of Israelites out of the Promised Land (Numbers 32:11). We often focus on the faith of Abraham; the emphasis of the covenant with Abraham is *God's faithfulness.* The existence of the state of Israel can only be explained through God's faithfulness to His covenant. The Promised Land will be center stage in the last days.

5. The Covenant with Moses (Exodus 19-40)

This is the covenant of *Deliverance.* At the end of Genesis, God's promise of a Promised Nation has been fulfilled. The small family of 70 has become a nation of 600,000 fighting men plus their families (between 1.5 million to 2 million people). Before Joseph dies, life is good for all of his family. They have the blessings of Pharaoh and are living in the Land of Goshen, Egypt's choicest location.

However, Joseph knows that God must fulfill His third promise of bringing this nation into the Promised Land. Joseph's last words serve as a reminder the Abrahamic Covenant continues.

> Then Joseph said to his brothers, "I am about to die. But God will surely come to your aid and take you up out of this land to the land he promised on oath to Abraham, Isaac and Jacob." Genesis 50:24

The fact that God is faithful to His Covenant with Abraham is not surprising. However, how God chooses to fulfill the promise of the Promised Land is unique. In Exodus 3, we find God calling an 80-year-old former prince-turned-shepherd as His leader for the central event of the Old Testament, the Exodus. The Exodus will become the central event of the Old Testament. The Exodus will be the ultimate proof that God is our Deliverer. God is worthy of our trust.

Although Moses is a reluctant leader, God works through him to bring the Israelite people to the very verge of possessing the land God intended for the seed of Abraham. Throughout the journey from Egypt to Canaan, God proves His faithfulness over and over again. He patiently works with a critical people that are never satisfied.

The question now becomes, "What does the Covenant look like in community?" Dealing with Abraham was one thing, but now there are millions of people who are living side-by-side. Although the constantly see God work miracles in their presence, they tend to want to go back to the slavery of Egypt rather than trust God. In Exodus 20, God gives Moses the Ten Commandments as a description of what life among God's people should look like.

As Smith reminds us, "The Mosaic Covenant was doomed from the very beginning. After intelligently swearing to keep the covenant, the people of Israel broke it within a few weeks."[40] The disobedience of the Israelites over the next forty years will cause God to exclude all people 40 years and older from entering the Promised Land.[41]

The Law was never meant to be the means of our of salvation. Paul writes, "Therefore no one will be declared righteous in his (God's) by observing the law; rather, through the law we become

---

40   Smith, page 36

41   Caleb and Joshua being the exceptions

conscious of sin" (Romans 3:20). Jesus' Death and Resurrection will fulfill the Mosaic Law by making the way possible for His people to fulfill the heart of the Mosaic Law, which is found in two commandments.

When asked what the greatest commandment was, Jesus will summarize the Ten Commandments into two by saying.

> Jesus replied: "Love the Lord your God with all your heart and with all your soul and with all your mind.[42] This is the first and greatest commandment. And the second is like it: 'Love your neighbor as yourself.[43] All the Law and the Prophets hang on these two commandments." Matthew 22:37-40

Jesus fulfills this Covenant by becoming, "The Way, the Truth and the Life" (John 14:6) by which this relationship with God is made possible. The Ten Commandments are not nullified. However, this covenant written on stone cannot be fulfilled by human effort. It is through the Law that we see our need for Jesus in our life.

6. The Covenant with David (II Samuel 7; Psalm 89, 132)

This is the covenant of Faithfulness. In II Samuel 7:1-6, God makes David aware through Nathan that David will not build the Temple. God does promise David that his descendants will always sit on the throne of Judah. When Israel becomes a Divided Kingdom, the kings of Judah are all descendants of David. Through Nathan, God promises,

> Your house and your kingdom will endure forever before me; your throne will be established forever. II Samuel 7:16

The history of the Northern Kingdom of Israel is filled with assassinations and intrigue. However, the lineage of David is nothing to brag about. While there are no "good kings" in the Northern Kingdom, it is difficult to find righteous kings in Judah as well. Of the twenty kings of Judah, only eight are considered good, or mostly good. On the other hand, Manasseh served 55 years and

---

42   Deuteronomy 6:4

43   Leviticus 19:18b

among other things, sacrificed his children. Ahaz built an altar to a foreign god and only used the altar of God when he was desperate.

Reading through the Major Prophets (Isaiah, Jeremiah, Ezekiel and Daniel), one will find the struggle God goes through to keep His promise to David. Why did God stay faithful to David until the fall of Judah? David saw the answer when he wrote, "But you, O Lord, are a compassionate gracious God, slow to anger, abounding in love and faithfulness" (Psalm 86:15). When judgment does come, we must take responsibility. God's mercy must never be mistaken for weakness.

7. The New Covenant (Jeremiah 31; Hebrews 8)

This is the covenant of Salvation and Grace in Christ. Let's begin with a short history lesson. When Solomon died (931 B.C.), his son Rehoboam became King of the United Kingdom of Israel. Instead of listening to his older advisors, Rehoboam chooses to raise taxes as his peers suggested. An uprising occurred ending with the ten northern tribes breaking away and establishing the Northern Kingdom with Jeroboam as their King.

The Northern Kingdom is missing one thing, the Temple in Jerusalem. If people stay in Jerusalem, Jeroboam could lose his kingdom by default. His solution was to build worship centers in Dan in the north and Bethel in the south. Along with the convenience of location, Jeroboam also added an eclectic variety of worship. People could choose their own god—Yahweh was just one option among many. The golden calf returns to prominence in worship.

Needless to say, the history of the Northern Kingdom is filled with murder and intrigue. Because of their disobedience, the Northern Kingdom falls to the Assyrian army in 721 B.C. The Assyrians will nearly wipe out the Northern Tribes until they are referred to as "the Lost Tribes of Israel."

Just as God promised, the Davidic line continues from Rehoboam to the fall of Jerusalem to the Babylonians starting in 597 B.C. Unfortunately, the Kings of Judah did not learn the spiritual lessons from the fall of the Northern Kingdom.[44] The captivity in Babylon will be completed in 586 B.C. when the Temple is destroyed. Babylon is kinder in its treatment of the captives, but the captives find themselves without a home, without a Temple and worst of all, without a Covenant with God.

The ministries of the Major Prophets (Isaiah, Jeremiah, Ezekiel and Daniel) coincide with the events leading up to and during the fall to Babylonia. Isaiah prophesizes right before the end of Judah, Jeremiah's ministry is during the takeover by Babylon, Ezekiel is a street preacher during the exile and Daniel is employed by King Nebuchadnezzar during the exile.

Jeremiah finds himself imprisoned in a courtyard while Jerusalem is falling. In the midst of all the chaos, Jeremiah receives a confusing request from God to buy his cousin's land in Benjamin (Jeremiah 18:8-16). Why would God command Jeremiah to buy property that will be in his enemy's hands soon? It is because God is establishing a new covenant with His people. In the midst of a hopeless situation, God provides hope when He states,

> The time is coming," declares the Lord, "when I will make a new covenant with the house of Israel and with the house of Judah. It will not be like the covenant I made with their forefathers when I took them by the hand to lead them out of Egypt, because they broke my covenant, though I was a husband to them," declares the Lord. "This is the covenant I will make with the house of Israel after that time," declares the Lord. "I will put my law in their minds and write it on their hearts. I will be their God, and they will be my people." Jeremiah 31:31-33 (quoted in Hebrews 8:8-13).

How can God write His Law on our minds and hearts? Only through the atoning Blood of Jesus! The fulfillment of the New Covenant is Jesus Christ. All the previous covenants lead us to Calvary. In the New Covenant, "all the forms and rituals of the Law have faded into the realities they represented.[45]

---

44   For example, Manasseh's reign of 55 years is marked by worship of Baal and even the sacrifice of some of his children.

45   Smith, page 64.

While the Mosaic Law provided *covering* of sin, the New Covenant provides *cleansing* from sin. The Ten Commandments were not intended to be the *means* of salvation, but a *mirror* of our sinful condition. Salvation is no longer based on rituals, but a personal relationship with Christ. We rely on God's grace, not our own works.

The Sacrificial System with all of its complex details has been fulfilled through Christ, as He becomes the Final Sacrificial Lamb. Through the Cross, Christ has satisfied the requirements for holy justice. When God forgives our sins, our sin will be remembered no more. What has been *external* now becomes *internal*.

The New Covenant celebrates that what we could not do for ourselves, Christ has done for us. The price has been paid in full by the Blood of Jesus. The Cross changes everything! If you look at the Seamless Robe that Jesus is wearing, you will see all the covenants woven into one thread. It is through the Cross that we all can become blood brothers and sisters.

WOOF THREADS

WHAT ARE WOOF THREADS?

WHEN A JEWELER SHOWS A DIAMOND, THEY USUALLY PLACE THE stone on a black cloth. The dark cloth serves as a backdrop to enhance the beauty of the diamond. The buyer is able to see more clearly the brilliance of the cut and quality of the precious stone they are considering. Every quality diamond store uses this technique as common practice.

My wife's original wedding ring only had diamond "chips" in it. Forty years later, I was able to buy Bonnie a *real* diamond wedding ring. We were able to find a ring that looked similar to the wedding band her mom wore. The sewing together of those two rings made the diamond even more beautiful. There was a story in the detail.

Woof threads serve a similar purpose as the black cloth. It is amazing how detailed God is in telling His Story. God intentionally added details that show the depth of His love. For the purpose of this book, we will define woof threads as *threads that tie the Old Testament to the New Testament.* Personally, I have come to realize that I have glossed over many of these threads without realizing it. What difference does it make that the High Priest's robe was blue? Why do so many events take place on mountains? Why is the number seven used so often? Once you notice these backdrop threads, the beauty of the Gospel stands out more clearly. Identifying Woof threads has helped me see familiar stories in a brand new light.

Just as we looked at seven Warp threads, we will limit our study to seven Woof threads. My purpose in this section is not to exhaust the list of Woof Threads. That would be impossible. My hope is that you will begin to take notice of the details in each passage as well as the obvious story going on. I think you will be amazed at how much deeper and richer the message of the Bible will become.

THE SEARCH FOR INNOCENT BLOOD

The Virgin Birth

In his book *VELVET ELVIS*, Rob Bell presents a new perspective on how to view the doctrines of the Church. Using the word picture of trampoline springs, Bell suggests that doctrine can be examined independently of each other. If a spring was taken out from around the trampoline, removing one spring would not disable the trampoline from working. Therefore, if one doctrine were removed, would it change things? One of the examples Bell uses is the Virgin Birth. He asks a very intriguing question.

> What if tomorrow someone digs up definitive proof that Jesus had a real, earthly, biological father named Larry, and archaeologists find Larry's tomb and do DNA samples and prove beyond a shadow of a doubt that the virgin birth was really just a bit of mythologizing the Gospel writers threw in to appeal to the followers of Mithra and Dionysian religious cults that were hugely popular at the time of Jesus, whose gods had a virgin birth?[46]

Bell adds several questions which are also fascinating. He asks:

- What if that spring (the Virgin Birth) was seriously questioned?

- Could a person keep jumping?

- Could a person still love God?

- Could you still be a Christian?

- Is the way of Jesus still the best possible way to live?

- Or does the whole thing fall apart?[47]

Bell compares examining doctrines as interdependent of each other to removing a brick from a brick wall. If the brick is taken

---

46   Rob Bell, Velvet Elvis: Repainting the Christian Faith (Harper Collins Publishers: New York, 2005), page 11.

47   Ibid.

out, the whole wall falls down. His example is someone believing that the days of Creation were seven, twenty-four hour days (which is not a doctrine, by the way). So if it can be proven that the Virgin Birth is a myth, does that really impact the message of the Bible? Do you have to believe in the Virgin Birth to be a Christian? Isn't Jesus still Jesus and His way if He had a biological earthly father?

Although Bell affirms that he believes in the Virgin Birth just a few sentences later, he does leave a series of imposing questions unanswered. What difference would it make if the second chapter of Luke was actually the recording of the birth of Joseph's (or Larry's) biological son? It is fine to ask the question, but there *is* an answer to the question, "Or does the whole thing fall apart?" The answer is "Absolutely!" If it could be proven beyond a shadow of a doubt that Jesus was merely a man, *everything changes.*

The Virgin Birth is an essential thread in understanding the Bible. Without the Virgin Birth, Jesus becomes nothing more than a great religious teacher and an unreachable example of righteous living. His earthly ministry and teaching would set a high standard for living, but nothing more. If Jesus is only human, the Cross is emptied of its meaning. The shedding of Jesus' blood would be meaningless if His blood is like yours and mine.

I would like to suggest a third word picture. Like three strands interwoven together, the threads of Jesus' birth, His death and His resurrection are totally interdependent on each other. They cannot be separated and cannot be broken. You cannot understand the Gospel without realizing that the baby lying in a manger in Bethlehem is God in human flesh (John 14). You cannot understand the power of the Cross until you realize that the Babe of Bethlehem has become the Crucified Christ. The Resurrection of this same Jesus has won a victory for us on Easter Sunday morning over sin, death and the grave!

I realize that doctrinal statements can become like pieces of a theological puzzle. We can and do argue over different stances all day long. However, as Leonard Sweet and Frank Viola remind us, "to deny Jesus as divine Messiah is to negate the entire gospel story, the purpose of His ministry, the reason for His death and the magnitude of His resurrection."[48] Jesus was "conceived by the Holy Spirit, born of the Virgin Mary, suffered under Pontius Pilate, was crucified, died, and was buried,"[49] but on the Thirrrd Day He rose again from the dead!

Bell's question about the Virgin Birth is not new. In the second century (144 A.D.), a man named Marcion began to teach that the wrathful Hebrew God of the Old Testament was a separate and lower entity than the all-forgiving God of the New Testament. Marcion taught that Jesus was the Savior sent by God with the Apostle Paul being His chief Apostle. He rejected the Hebrew Bible and the God of Israel. His teaching disconnected the Old Testament from the New Testament, thus distorting the biblical picture of who Jesus is. In response to his teaching, Marcion became the first heretic of the Church.

In the second and third century, Arius, a Christian presbyter in Alexandria, Egypt, asserted that Jesus was a *subordinate entity* to God the Father. By rejecting the unity between God the Father to God the Son, Jesus becomes disconnected from the Father. The Child born in Bethlehem is not God, but was created by God to be the Savior of the world. Arius was denounced as the second heretic of the Church.

One other distortion of the Virgin Birth is docetism. Docetism is the belief that Jesus only *seemed* to be human, and that his human form was just an illusion. The Babe born in Bethlehem was not human. Jesus felt no pain at the Cross, he only *seemed* to suffer. Jesus felt no pain or agony on the Cross. The problem with all three false teachings is that they distort the biblical presentation of who Jesus is. If Jesus was just a man, he cannot die for my sins. He is one of us. If Jesus was only a subordinate of God, the Cross is just an illusion.

In Christ, we see the union of the two natures, human and divine. Jesus is the perfect and only Mediator we have because He as both God and man can serve as the bridge between God and man. He is the Messiah (Savior) that makes the way possible back

48   Leonard Sweet and Frank Viola, Jesus A Theography (Thomas Nelson: Nashville, Tennessee, 2012), page 82.

49   The Apostle's Creed

to God. The heart of the Gospel message is that Jesus who is fully God, emptied Himself of all His heavenly glory and became fully man. Paul writes,

> Who, being in very nature God, did not consider equality with God something to be grasped, but made himself nothing, taking the very nature of a servant, being made in human likeness. And being found in appearance as a man, he humbled himself and became obedient to death—even death on a cross! Philippians 2:6-8.

The reversal of the man's sin is the very reason Christ was born, why He died and why we celebrate His Resurrection. There are no religions that present a god who comes to us. Like man's attempt to reach God at the Tower of Babel (Genesis 11:1-9), religion forces man to reach their god. Mankind must do something to earn their god's approval. The end result is always failure and frustration.

The Details of Scripture

The first foreshadowing of the Virgin Birth is found in Genesis 3:15. There God tells the serpent, "And I will put enmity between you and the woman, and between your offspring and hers; he will crush your head, and you will strike his heel" (Genesis 3:15). God's punishment for Adam and Eve is immediate. Although the serpent is punished by having to crawl on the ground, the serpent's ultimate punishment will come later through "her offspring" (or her "seed" in some translations). The fulfillment of this promise will come through Jesus.

There are two Old Testament prophesies that are directly tied to the Virgin Birth of Jesus in the New Testament. Both of the Old Testament passages are in the book of Isaiah. Let me give a little background of events. The nation of Judah is under attack from King Resin of Aram and King Pekah of Israel. King Ahaz of Judah and the people of Judah are terrified (Isaiah 7:1-2). Although the armies of Israel and Aram have tried to take the city of Jerusalem, they have not been able to win the battle (Isaiah 7:1).

In spite of the overwhelming circumstances, God sends Isaiah and his son Shear-Jashub to reassure Ahaz of ultimate victory against the combined armies. God promises, "Yet this is what the Sovereign Lord says: It will not take place, it will not happen'" (Isaiah 7:7). In the midst of a hopeless situation, God brings a message of hope about the future of His people. In Isaiah 9:1, God gives more detailed insight into the future ministry of Jesus. Isaiah writes,

> Nevertheless, there will be no more gloom for those who were in distress. In the past he humbled the land of Zebulun and the land of Naphtali, but *in the future* he will honor Galilee of the Gentiles, by the way of the sea, along the Jordan. Isaiah 9:1

In addition to the promise of victory and protection, God offers a sign. Although Ahaz refuses God's sign, God remains faithful. God promises,

> Therefore the Lord himself will give you a sign: The *virgin will be with child and will give birth to a son, and will call him Immanuel.* He will eat curds and honey when he knows enough to reject the wrong and choose the right. *But before the boy knows enough to reject the wrong and choose the right, the land of the two kings you dread will be laid waste* Isaiah 7:14-16.

The identity of the boy referred to for Ahaz's day is a point of discussion. Some have suggested it was Ahaz's son, Hezekiah. However, as one commentator points out, "This is not to be understood of Hezekiah, the son of Ahaz, by his wife…Hezekiah was nine years old when he began to reign." he must be at this time thirteen years of age."[50] The fact is, we cannot be sure who God chose or how the promise was fulfilled. What we do know is that Isaiah 7:14 is fulfilled in the birth of Christ.

The account of Jesus' birth in Bethlehem is recorded in both Matthew and Luke. Matthew gives us some very specific details about the Virgin Birth when he tells us, "His (Jesus') mother Mary was pledged (betrothed) to be married to Joseph, but *before they came together*, she was found to be with child through the Holy Spirit" (Matthew 1:18).

---

50 www.biblestudytools.com/commentaries/gills-exposition-of-the-bible/isaiah-7-14.html

Although it is true that the word *virgin* in the Old Testament can refer to a young woman who is of the age to have a child, Matthew makes clear that this was not the result of the sexual union of Joseph and Mary.

After considering divorcing Mary quietly for her apparent unfaithfulness, the Lord speaks to Joseph through a dream. God reveals, "Joseph, son of David, do not be afraid to take Mary home as your wife, because what is conceived in her is from the Holy Spirit" (Matthew 1:20b). God's promise in Genesis 1:15 is fulfilled.

Luke's account of the Nativity also affirms the Virgin Birth. First, Luke tells us of the angel's announcement to Mary that she would be the mother of the Messiah. The angels tells her, "You will be with child and give birth to a son, and you are to give him the name Jesus" (Luke 1:31). Mary asks the obvious question, "'How will this be,' Mary asked the angel, 'since I am a virgin' (Luke 1:34)?" The angel explains, "The Holy Spirit will come upon you, and the power of the Most High will overshadow you" (Luke 1:35).

Luke also records what appears to be a scandalous circumstance, "He (Joseph) went to register with Mary, who was pledged (betrothed) to be married to him and expecting a child (Luke 2:5). For a woman to be pregnant while betrothed was disgraceful. Luke adds an interesting face, "She (Mary) gave birth to her firstborn, a son" (Luke 2:7a). In a male-dominated world, Jesus is described as Mary's son with no mention of Joseph.

The Dangling Question: Why is the Virgin Birth so intertwined in the story of salvation? Let's go back to the Garden of Eden for a moment. As we have seen, God gave very clear instructions to Adam and Eve about the covenant they had together.

> And the God commanded the man, "You are free to eat from any tree in the garden; but you must not eat from the tree of the knowledge of good and evil, for when you eat of it *you will surely die*. Genesis 2:16-17

Adam and Eve do partake of the fruit of the forbidden tree. Surely, when God sees them next, He will strike them dead, right? Most assuredly, Adam and Eve are punished. Adam will have to work the ground from which he gets his food. Thistles and thorns will add to his labor.

Eve will experience pain with the birth of every child. Wait a minute! Isn't someone supposed to die? It is possible that God's plan never included physical death. Still Adam and Eve live long lives and enjoy numerous children.

Adam and Eve did *spiritually* die that day. They have chosen to separate themselves from God. By their actions, they have told God that they no longer want to be with Him. They are escorted outside of the Garden of Eden and cherubim armed with flaming swords are placed to guard the entrance to the Garden. The cherubim walk back and forth to guard the way to the tree of life (Genesis 3:24b).

Adam and Eve leave the presence of God and their perfect life with no way back. They cannot do anything that would correct their actions. Their lives are now hopeless. They are going to experience heartaches that were the consequences of their sins. Since they broke a blood covenant with God, the only hope they have is for innocent blood to be shed. Adam and Eve's blood is now tainted by sin. *Where can innocent blood be found?*

God's answer in the Old Testament is the *Sacrificial System*. Since animals were not created as spiritual beings, they cannot sin. Animals are driven by instinct. They cannot be held accountable morally for their actions. Thus, the Levitical law is built on the shedding of the blood of animals, because, "the law requires that nearly everything be cleansed with blood, and without the shedding of blood there is no forgiveness (Hebrews 9:22).

Unfortunately, the shedding of animal's blood was very tedious and did not have any permanent effect. Sacrifices had to be made daily plus a sacrifice for the sins of the nation was required on the Day of Atonement. "Those sacrifices are an annual reminder of sins, because it is impossible for the blood of bulls and goats to take away sins" (Hebrews 10:3-4). The Sacrificial System served the purpose of showing us our sinfulness and our need to totally rely on God's faithfulness.

As Malcolm Smith writes, "If the covenant is to be achieved between God and man, there must be a representative; one who can stand for both God and man."[51] Praise God, we find that representative in Jesus Christ. Jesus alone has innocent blood. The blood of Jesus is the *cleansing agent* that can wash away our sins. Paul proclaims, "God made him who had no sin to be sin for us, so that in him we might become the righteousness of God" (I Corinthians 5:21).

There truly is power in the blood of Jesus Christ. No matter what we have done, the blood of Christ can cleanse our sins if we would but sincerely ask for forgiveness.

As the writer to the Hebrews states,

> How much more, then, will the blood of Christ, who through the eternal Spirit offered himself unblemished to God, cleanse our consciences from acts that lead to death, so that we may serve the living God. Hebrews 9:14

The Dinner: A part of every blood covenant was a covenant meal. This meal celebrated that the covenant was now in effect. Our closest parallel today would be a wedding reception.

After the wedding ceremony has been completed and the marriage license signed, the bride and groom are able to share a meal with their family and friends. The couple is now husband and wife. It is reason for celebrating! More than likely, there will be dancing and toasts, but everyone will enjoy a great meal together.

On Thursday evening before the events begin that led up to the Cross, Jesus gathers His disciples together in an Upper Room to partake of the Passover Meal. The Passover Meal was the covenant meal that celebrated the central event of the Old Testament, the Exodus. Each item of food served was symbolic of different parts of the Exodus story. Along with the meal, the story of God's deliverance of the children of Israel from Egyptian bondage was re-told. How do we know that God can deliver us? He delivered us from the Egyptians.

One of the things to note is that Jesus had the sacred meal prepared one day earlier than usual. It is Thursday evening when the disciples gather with Jesus. Everyone else will be having their

---

51   Malcolm Smith, The Blood Covenant: A Study on the Faithfulness of God, (Unconditional Love: San Antonio, Texas, 1998), page 42.

Passover Meal beginning on Friday evening. Jesus knows that He will die at the exact moment the shofar blows to announce it is time to kill the sacrificial lamb. He knows that when the meal is being partaken of, He will be lying in a tomb. Tonight is the night to celebrate His victory.

There are three distinct times within a Passover Meal. The first part is the beginning of the meal. Through a series of questions and answers, the story of Moses and God's deliverance is told. Along with the breaking of bread and sharing of the meal, there are two cups of wine partaken of in the first part of the meal. This formal time in the meal is then followed by an informal time where people can talk freely. It is more than likely that it is during this time that Jesus shared His teaching about the Holy Spirit in John 14-16.

The meal was concluded with a second formal time in which bread was broken and two cups of wine were shared. When Jesus broke the covenant bread, He ushers in the New Covenant by giving thanks over the bread, breaking it[52] and saying, "This is my body given for you; do this in remembrance of me" (Luke 22:19). Jesus will deliberately lay His body down for us experiencing the brutality of the Crucifixion.

When the third cup of wine (the cup of Redemption) is passed, Jesus holds the cup before His disciples and says, "This cup is the new covenant in my blood, which is poured out for you" (Luke 22:20b). The innocent blood of Jesus will be spilled out on our behalf in just a matter of hours. The institution of the Lord's Supper is the turning point between the Old Covenant and the New Covenant. The blood of Jesus has disarmed Satan of his weaponry of sin, death and the grave. We have reason to celebrate!

Who is going to die for us? Jesus Christ! He loves you and me so much that He shed His precious blood on the Cross so that He could cleanse our hearts from sin. The Babe in Bethlehem has become our Crucified Christ and thanks be to God He is now our Risen Lord! Have you received His amazing gift of salvation?

---

52   During the feeding of the five thousand and the four thousand, Jesus the Father thanks for the bread, breaks it and shares it. Jesus will use fish and bread when He reinstates Peter in John 21:15-18.

If you look at the Seamless Robe of Jesus, you will notice that the blood stains from the Cross are not setting in, but are moving towards those who are seeking a new life in Christ.

LET GOD BE THE JUDGE

Judgment

WHEN MY SISTER JUDY WAS A FRESHMAN AT BETHANY NAZArene College (now Southern Nazarene University), she was a member of the Gospel Team, a travelling group for the college. I remember very clearly the weekend the group came to my home church for both Sunday services. They sang and testified in the morning service with one of the religion majors doing the preaching.

At the beginning of the Sunday evening service, the members of the team presented a skit about standing before God at the Judgment.

Because the students were now into their second semester together, I have to imagine these same people had done this same skit several times. The script was fairly simple. Three or four members were chosen to portray individuals coming before the Lord on Judgment Day. The first person had accepted Christ early into their life and heard Jesus say, "Well done thou good and faithful servant" (Matthew 25:21). The group clapped and shouted praises as they celebrated the person's acceptance into heaven.

As the next person's life was reviewed, it was obvious that he had rejected Christ throughout his life. He had chosen to live a life of disobedience and self-sufficiency. Obviously, the person was going to go to hell. I know it was only a skit, but when Jesus said, "Depart from me, I know you not" (Matthew 25:41), the college students all began weeping. It wasn't because the script called for it. They truly felt the emotions of watching someone going to Hell.

How would we react if we saw that presentation today? I am pretty sure someone would leave the service and call the pastor on Monday to say, "If that is the kind of God you worship, I don't want anything to do with it. I will never come back to your church again." Someone else would surely call a television station to tell the reporter, "This church believes that God condemns people to hell. Can you believe it?" Worst of all, too many people would come out of the service *laughing* at the possibility of hell. The thought of standing accountable for how we live isn't a popular topic these days. However, what do we do with verses like Hebrews 9:27? "Just as man is destined to die once, and after that to face *judgment?*"

One of the threads of the Bible is *judgment*. I have lived through a full pendulum swing by the Church on their view of God's Judgment. When I was growing up, the evangelists made us pretty sure that *everyone was going to Hell*. I was convinced that God was just waiting for me to slip up so He could *zap* me with His Divine Finger. Even if a person did the right things, did they do them *long enough*: fifteen minutes for Bible reading and one hour for prayer.

It appears that we have swung back to the other extreme of believing that *everyone is going to Heaven*. We question the character of God for even the thought of punishing someone for their disobedience. If He knew we were going to sin, isn't it His fault if we disobey. Maybe "the God of the Old Testament" would consider it, but Jesus is all about love, isn't He? Some even have *downgraded* Hell to be more like a garbage dump.[53] In a culture where our moral code has nearly disintegrated, a recent poll showed that 85% of the Americans polled believed they were going to Heaven.

One of the questions that Pontius Pilate asked during Jesus' final trial is crucial for today. Thinking he could use the Jewish custom of releasing a prisoner at Passover, Pilate offers the crowd an opportunity to choose to free Jesus and crucify a notorious criminal named Barabbas. Much to Pilate's surprise, the crowd chooses to set Barabbas free. Pontius Pilate then asks an eternal question, *"What shall I do, then, with Jesus who is called the Christ"* (Matthew 27:22)? Everyone of us must answer that question. Unlike any other religious figure, Jesus demands a decision! Choosing to accept Christ or reject Him is our choice. We will be held accountable for the choice we make and the life we live.

---

53   The first reference to a town dump was made by Rabbi David Kimhi in a commentary in 1200 A.D. This is over eleven hundred years after the ministry of Jesus.

The Desire of God's Heart

Doesn't God want all of us to be saved? Didn't Jesus say, "For the Son of Man came to seek and to save what was lost" (Luke 19:10)? What did Paul mean in Philippians 2:10-11 when he wrote, "*Every* knee should bow ... and *every* tongue confess that Jesus Christ is Lord?"

In his book *Erasing Hell*, Frances Chan writes, "While it is true that God desires that every person would choose to accept Him as their Savior, it is also true that *not all people will be saved.*"[54] Chan adds, "Some things may be part of God's desire for the world, and yet be *resisted.*"[55]

Through the Cross, Christ has provided the means through which we can have restored fellowship with God. That truth is at the heart of the good news of the Bible. However, we have to respond. You and I must personally choose between accepting or rejecting God's offer of forgiveness and fellowship. No one else can make that choice for us. Our salvation is not based on our *goodness*, but on *God's grace*.

I have a friend named Bill. Bill faithfully attended church services, did handiwork for those who were in need and was the *nicest* guy in the world. Bill was the epitome of *goodness*. That was the problem. Bill's biggest excuse for not accepting Christ was that he was nicer and kinder than most of the people in the congregation. You know what? He was right! If niceness was the requirement to be a Christian, Bill would have been at the front of the line. When I left that pastorate, my heart was broken that I had not seen Bill accept Christ.

It was a few years later that I got a phone call from Bill's wife. With joy in her voice, she said, "I have a new husband!" I was shocked at first, but Carolyn put Bill on the phone and he told me, "You remember when I told you that someday I wanted you to be able to talk about how I accepted Christ? Well, I did today!" I wish I could have been at that service when the Holy Spirit convinced

---

54   Francis Chan and Preston Sprinkle, Erasing Hell (David C. Cook: Colorado Springs, Colorado, 2011), page 12

55   Ibid. page 12.

Bill that entrance into Heaven is not about our goodness. I understand Bill almost ran to the altar!

The desire of God's heart is that each of us would make a decision to follow Christ. However, it is our choice. Whether we spend eternity in Heaven or in Hell will depend on our response to God's grace. The evidence that Christ loves us fills the pages of the Bible. However, there are also clear warnings of the consequences of rejecting Christ. Christ loves us too much not to warn us of the dangers of turning our backs on Him.

The Description

The Bible gives a description of both Heaven and Hell. The two destinies could not be further apart. When the Apostle John explains his vision of Heaven, he struggles to find earthly words adequate enough to describe it. Listen to his description,

> The wall was made of jasper, and the city of pure gold, as pure as glass.

> The foundations of the city walls were decorated with every kind of precious stone. The first foundation was jasper, the second sapphire, the third chalcedony, the fourth emerald, the fifth sardonyx, the sixth carnelian, the seventh chrysolite, the eighth beryl, the ninth topaz, the tenth chrysoprase, the eleventh jacinth, and the twelfth amethyst.[56]

> The twelve gates were twelve pearls, each gate made of a single pearl. The great street of the city was of pure gold, like transparent glass.

> I did not see a temple in the city, because the Lord God Almighty and the Lamb are its temple. The city does not need the sun or the moon to shine on it, for the glory of God gives it light, and the Lamb is its lamp. Revelation 21:18-23

The place that Jesus has prepared for us (John 14:2) is more beautiful than our human minds can imagine. We only get a glimpse of what Heaven looks like in John's vision. It is the Pres-

---

56   The list of precious stones is almost identical to the stones worn on the High Priest's Breastpiece in Exodus 39:10-13.

ence of Christ that makes Heaven so glorious. All the suffering of earth will be gone. John reminds us, "He will wipe every tear from their eyes. There will be no more death or mourning or crying or pain, for the old order of things has passed away" (Revelation 21:4).

I have been working as a hospice chaplain since September 2012. During this time of ministering to the dying, I have come to believe in Heaven more than ever before. There are numerous stories I have experienced and heard from my co-workers that affirm the reality of Heaven.

One of my favorite stories was about a man whose wife was our patient. The man was in great health, but since his wife was dying, he chose to move into the same room to be with her. A short time after his wife died, the man had a massive heart attack. While the nurses were caring for him, one of the nurses asked if he had signed a DNR (do not resuscitate) form. He had not. The nurse placed the form before the man and gave him a pen. As he put the pen up to sign, the man looked at the nurses and said, "I am so sorry, but my wife says I have to come right now." He fell back on the bed and died.

The last thing my daughter Jennie did before she died in June 2010 was to look up and smile. Just before my Father passed away, he began looking above the family members in the hospital room. At one point, my Mother asked Dad if he knew who she was. Dad actually had to look down at Mom and said, "Of course, I do Millie. We have been married for sixty-six years." Then he returned to looking above us.

Even if they don't believe in Heaven, most people don't mind hearing descriptions or stories about it. No one usually gets offended by the reality of Heaven. It is the description of Hell that bothers us. The truth is that Jesus taught more about Hell and Judgment than He did about Heaven. The imagery that Jesus uses is of fire, darkness and suffering. At the end of the Parable of the Talents (25:14-20), the Master (who always represents God), rewards the faithful servants by doubling their talents (two become four and five become ten). We have no problem with blessings, right?

However, when the servant with one talent blamed his actions on the Master's harshness, the Master sentences the unfaithful servant by saying, "And throw that worthless servant outside, into the darkness, *where there will be weeping and gnashing of teeth*" (Matthew 25:30). God addresses the servant's disobedience. If we deliberately choose to live our life without God, there are eternal consequences.

In the Parable of the Sheep and the Goats, the Master pronounces judgment on those who have not cared for the needy, "Then he will say to those on his left, 'Depart from me, you who are cursed, *into the eternal fire prepared for the devil and his angels*'" (Matthew 25:14).

Because of His very character, God cannot and will not leave sin unchecked. Christ did not die on the Cross to *wink* at sin. He died to deliver us from our sins and set us free.

As much as we dislike it, the Bible teaches that there are people *who will go to Hell.* That truth should do two things for us: keep us from being casual in our walk with God and bring urgency to us about reaching the lost. This is not about a doctrinal debate, but the lives and destinies of real people. Just as Heaven is not about our abundant good deeds, Hell is not about being excessively evil. Some of the hardest people to reach for Christ are "good people," people who are relying on themselves rather than God.

The Dividing Line

In the Old Testament, God draws some very distinct lines of judgment. The most obvious moment is when God brings judgment on all mankind through the Flood. God actually says,

> I will wipe mankind, whom I have created, from the face of the earth—men and animals, and creatures that move along the ground, and birds of the air—for I am grieved that I have made them. Genesis 6:7

How could a loving God wipe out men, women and children, except for Noah and seven family members? What right does God have to do that? God has every right in the world! God is the Creator of the universe. God had every right to bring the Flood, but

He also had every reason in the world to do it. What is surprising is not that God brings judgment on us, but that He extends mercy to us through Christ. God warns us of the consequences of sin, because He wants to deliver us from sin.

The Flood was not a knee-jerk reaction by God to an innocent people. As I have already said, God's first reaction is *mercy*, but there comes a time when *judgment* must come. It took Noah one hundred and twenty years to build the Ark. No one was ignorant of the judgment that was coming. These are not innocent people, but those who defiantly chose to live their life without God.

In the Parable of the Wheat and the Tares (Matthew 13:24-30), Jesus reminds us that there God will extend His mercy to us as long as we are alive. When the owner of a wheat field realizes that the enemy has sown weeds into his wheat, he gives these instructions, "Let both grow together until the harvest. At that time I will tell the harvesters: First collect the weeds and tie them in bundles to be burned; then gather the wheat and bring it into my barn."

The Deliverance that Has Been Provided

The good news is that through the Cross, God has provided a means of delivery from condemnation. In Romans 8:1, Paul rejoices that in Christ, "Therefore, there is now no condemnation for those who are in Christ Jesus, because through Christ Jesus the law of the Spirit of life set me free from the law of sin and death."

I love this statement from Francis Chan, "The Cross is where *righteousness* and *wrath* kiss."[57] Remember, the thread of the story of Jesus runs from Genesis 1 all the way to Revelation 22. Although we are unworthy, God has chosen to provide a means of salvation. We cannot make our way back to God, but "All this is from God, who reconciled us to himself through Christ and gave us the ministry of reconciliation" (II Corinthians 5:18).

---

57   Ibid., page 106

The Decision That Must Be Made

We live in a day of eclectic religious beliefs. We feel free to mix all religions together, because no matter which one we choose; we are all going to end up in the same place. Nothing will start an emotional religious debate quicker that to quote John 14:6 where Jesus states, "I am the *way* and the *truth* and the *life*. No one comes to the Father *except through me*."

The only time I have ever been cursed at during a Bible Perspectives class was when I quoted John 14:6. One student was so outraged at the suggestion that you have to choose Christ to get to Heaven that she unleashed a tirade that would make a sailor blush. It was offensive to her that Jesus would be that exclusive. Jesus can be one of many ways of salvation, but to be the only way was unacceptable. The means of our salvation is not a multiple-choice question.

In one of his final speeches to the Israelites, Moses prepares to hand his leadership role over to Joshua. Because he will not be going with the Israelites into Canaan, he reviews the blessings and curses of God's covenant with His people. Moses challenges his people, "Now choose life, so that you and your children may live" (Deuteronomy 30:19). That choice will be before the Israelite people every day.

When the Israelites moved into the land of Canaan, they find themselves in a culture filled with religious options. One of the major reasons for the Israelites failure to take possession of the land was their unwillingness to serve God with their whole heart. As he concludes his final speech to his fellow Israelites before he dies, Joshua challenges his people by saying,

> But if serving the Lord seems undesirable to you, then choose for yourselves this day whom you will serve, whether the gods your forefathers served beyond the River, or the gods of the Amorites, in whose land you are living. But as for me and my household, we will serve the Lord. Joshua 24:15

Although the Israelites vow to stay faithful to God, the time of the Judges that follows will be marked by a vicious cycle of *prosperity, sin, bondage* and *repentance* that would last for nearly 350 years (around 1380 to 1050 BC). When God blessed them, the Israelites always turned back to a time of self-reliance.

You have to decide what you are going to do with Jesus! In one of the most familiar passages of Scripture in the Bible, Jesus says, "For God so loved the world that he gave his one and only Son, that whoever *believes* in him shall not perish but have eternal life" (John 3:16). Believing in Christ is more than head knowledge of who Jesus is. You must be willing to stake your life on the fact that Jesus is the Savior of the world. It will require *believing* in Him in your heart to the point you rely upon Him daily.

It will require *repentance*. In Mark 1:15, Jesus is beginning His earthly ministry. Jesus clearly states His message when He declares, "The time has come," he said. "The kingdom of God is near. *Repent* and believe the good news!" There must be a willingness to let Jesus *turn our life around*. Christ has come to re-create your life. Paul writes, "Therefore, if anyone is in Christ, he is a new creation; the old has gone, the new has come!"

Finally, accepting Christ will require *contrition*, true sorrow for our sins. The Psalmist/King David writes, "The sacrifices of God are a broken spirit; *a broken and contrite heart* O God, you will not despise" (Psalm 51:17).

We will see Jesus in His Seamless Robe someday. I urge you to accept Christ today.

COLOUR MY WORD

The Significance of Colors

IF YOU BOUGHT RED AND GREEN STORAGE TUBS IN WALMART, what holiday decorations would you store in them? If the store display was black and orange, would that scare you? What color are the hearts on Valentine's Day? What color represents St. Patrick's Day? What color does a bride wear at a traditional wedding? If you were going to a formal party, what color would you most likely wear? When you are shopping for baby clothes, what is the purpose of pink or blue designs?

Of course, red and green are Christmas colors. When the store changes displays to black and orange, Halloween is just around the corner. It would be strange to receive a green Valentine's Day card, right? When February 14th arrives, everyone expects cards with red hearts. We know we will get pinched on St. Patrick's Day if we don't want to wear green. Wedding dresses should be white for purity. Black is the most popular formal color. Pink or blue baby clothes symbolize a baby girl (pink) or a baby boy (blue).

Colors play an important part in our lives. As Americans, our hearts fill with emotions when the "old red, white and blue" is lifted in the air. If you are driving a red car, you have to watch your speed, because you are more likely to get stopped for speeding. We use interior designers to help choose the colors we are going to use in our home. In our daily lives, there are many times when colors send a message.

In the Bible, colors *always* have significance. Colors are threaded throughout the Bible with a message behind each one. When you are studying a passage of Scripture, it is important to look for the thread of colors. Whatever colors are included in the text are there for a reason. It will add a deeper dimension to the passage.

The Meaning of Colors in the Bible

Let me give you a short list of some frequently used biblical colors and their meaning.

- *Black* signifies the *negative aspects of human experience—including death, disease, famine, and sorrow*—all of which are the results of sin. Hell is the place of "blackest darkness" reserved for the godless (2 Peter 2:17).

- *Red* symbolizes *blood*. The images of red, blood-soaked garments of God as an avenging warrior (Isaiah 63:1-6) and the fiery red horse bringing slaughter through warfare (Zechariah). Red also describes divine retribution against evildoers. (Revelations 6:12).

- *White* signifies *purity* and *holiness*. It can represent the complete forgiveness of sin (Isaiah 1:18) and the certainty of God's conquest and victory over evil (Revelation 19:11).

- *Purple* signifies *wealth* and *royalty* (Esther 8:15). Before his crucifixion, Jesus was robed in purple in mockery of him as "king of the Jews" (Mark 15:17). Purple was the royal color of a king.

- *Blue* signifies *holiness* and *heavenly things* (Exodus 26:31-33). Blue is the color of the high priest's seamless robe (Exodus 28:31). The veil in the Tabernacle and the Temple use blue in their patterns (Exodus 26:4). Blue also represents the priesthood.

- *Scarlet* signifies *sin*. Scarlet yarn was used to deal with infectious diseases (Leviticus 14:49). The Lord describes "your sins are like scarlet" (Isaiah 1:18). The woman in Revelation 17:3 is sitting on a scarlet beast.

- *Gold* signifies the *glory of God*. In Exodus 25, gold is used to cover everything related to the Ark of the Covenant plus the furniture in the Tabernacle. When Solomon builds the Temple, he uses gold throughout this magnificent building (II Kings 6). When he describes heaven, John tells us that the city is covered in gold (Rev 21:18).

- *Gray* signifies *old age*[58] (Genesis 42:38), the beauty of old age (Proverbs 20:29) or weakness (Hosea 7:9).

The Obvious Threads.

Identifying colors in some Scripture is easy. When God tells Isaiah, "Though your sins are like scarlet, they shall be as white as snow; though they are red as crimson, they shall be like wool" (Isaiah 1:18b), we know that scarlet, red and crimson are used to describe sin while white is used as a symbol of the purity of God's forgiveness.

The meaning of colors is even explained in the context of some passages. The imagery of the Four Horseman of the Apocalypse is described and defined in Revelation 6:2-8. Although this passage may still make us uncomfortable, there is no question about the significance of the four horses. As the first four seals are opened, a new color of horse and its rider are invited to come. Seal by seal, the forces of evil are unleashed. Let's look at the significance of each horse.

- *White* (verse 2) the rider is a conqueror with a crown, bent on conquest *(the Antichrist)*.
- *Fiery Red* (verse 4) the rider is given power to take peace from the earth *(Lawlessness)*.
- *Black* (verse 5) the rider holds a pair of scales in his hand *(Judgment)*.
- *Pale* (verse 8) the rider's name is Death and Hades *(Punishment)*.

There is one twist in the plot. The lead rider of this quartet of evil is riding a white horse, has a crown and is hungry for conquest. In Revelation 19, Jesus is riding a white horse in victory. It would seem that everything about the rider of the white horse in chapter six looks like Jesus in chapter 19. Why would Jesus be running with this hellish crowd in chapter six? The answer is that the first rider is *not* Jesus! The rider of the white horse in Revelation 6 may look like Christ, but he is actually the Antichrist!

---

58   Some things never change!

T. W. Willingham once said in a sermon, "Jesus and Satan must look an awful lot alike. Why else would we have trouble telling them apart?" When you read the book of Revelation, you find Satan mirroring Jesus. There is a Holy Trinity (Father, Son and Holy Spirit), but there is also an Unholy Trinity (the Beast, the Antichrist and the False Prophet). The Antichrist will appear to be wounded like Jesus, but is faking his injury (Revelation 13:14). This shows that Satan is crafty, but he is not creative.

The Combined Colors

How about those prominent colors that we may have missed? Once you identify them, it is amazing how many times you find them throughout Scripture. Let me give you an example of one combination of colors that describes Jesus' ministry to us.

As God explains the plans for the Tabernacle to Moses, a combination of three colors are used throughout the design of this magnificent and portable building. When materials are being gathered for the project, *scarlet, blue* and *purple* thread are requested. These tri-color threads are used in the design of the ten curtains that will surround the Tabernacle (Exodus 26:1).

They are also used in the creation of the veil that divides the Holy Place from the Holy of Holies (Exodus 26:31) and the entrance to the tent of the Tabernacle. We find it embroidered into the entrance to the Courtyard (Exodus 27:1-6). Scarlet, blue and purple thread are also used for the priestly garments (Exodus 28:5) and the Ephod of the High Priest (Exodus 28:6). An abundant supply of these yarns was plundered by the Israelites from the Egyptians at the beginning of the Exodus (Exodus 3:22).

When the Temple is built, Solomon once again uses scarlet, blue and purple threads in embroidering of the Veil. Why would these three colors combined be so important? What does this mean? All the details of the design of the Tabernacle and Temple tell a story about Jesus. The Tables of Showbread tell us that Jesus is the Bread of Life. The candlesticks speak to the fact that Jesus is the Light of the World. The veil represents Jesus as the only means to be ushered into the Presence of God.

And the scarlet, blue and purple threads tell us about Jesus as well. As John Notter Jr. explains, "The red color points to the prophetic, sacrificial death of Jesus."[59] He goes on, "The blue color speaks of heaven and it is the color used for priests since they are heaven's voice."[60] Of course, purple is the color for kings.

In these threads, we are reminded that Jesus is our Prophet, Priest and King. Notter concludes, "The very colors of the tabernacle show His ministry. Jesus Christ our prophet, priest and king."[61] Jesus is the Sacrifice for our sins, the Bridge to God and our reigning King.

The Red Heifer

During my trip to Israel in 2008, our guide began to share the significance of the Jewish search for a red heifer. I had read Numbers 19:1-22 before, but it did not register as something so important. Moses and Aaron are receiving God's instructions for the building of the Tabernacle and implementing of the sacrificial system. God gives the command,

> This is a requirement of the law that the Lord has commanded: Tell the Israelites to bring you a red heifer without defect or blemish and that has never been under a yoke. Number 19:2

The purpose of the red heifer's sacrifice was to be used for the water of cleansing which represented purification from sin. How the sacrifice was to be carried out is given in great detail. Let me share two applications of this passage.

First, the sacrifice of the Red Heifer parallels the sacrifice of Christ on the Cross. As Gary Collett writes,

> The imagery of the blood of the heifer without blemish being sacrificed and its blood cleansing from sin is a foreshadowing of the blood of Christ shed on the cross for believers' sin. He was "without blemish" just as the red heifer was to be. As the heifer was sacrificed "outside the camp" (Number 19:3) in the same way Jesus was crucified outside of Jerusalem: "And so Jesus also suf-

---

59 From the Soon2Come website: bit.ly/1CRC8nM

60 Ibid.

61 Ibid.

fered outside the city gate to make the people holy through his own blood."

Second, the search for the Red Heifer is in preparation for the re-establishment of the Temple and the Sacrificial System during the Tribulation. The Temple built by Herod the Great was destroyed in A.D. 70 by the Romans. Before that time, the Passover meal would have included a leg of lamb which represented the Sacrificial System.

After the destruction of the Temple, the Passover meal only includes a shank of lamb, representing that the Jews have nowhere to make sacrifices. Each Passover, the phrase "next year in Jerusalem" is repeated in hope that the Temple will be rebuilt and the Sacrificial System will be re-implemented. Remember that the color red represents sin. Instead of trusting the blood of Jesus, the search is on for yet another sacrificial animal.

There is only one recording of the sacrifice of a red heifer in the Bible. However, according to Jewish tradition, there have been nine red heifers sacrificed altogether. Today, there is an intense search for a new red heifer that can be sacrificed so that the Sacrificial System can be restored when the future Temple is built. There is a present-day Sanhedrin. There are several websites that are dedicated to keeping a twenty-four hour watch on the Temple Mount.

Our hope is not in the return of a red heifer, but in the return of Jesus as He triumphantly comes to us on the White Horse of Victory.

If you look at the Seamless Robe that Jesus is wearing, you will see that the Bible was written in Technicolor! Don't forget, God colored His Word for a reason.

READING BY THE NUMBERS

Numbers in the Scripture

I<small>F YOU SAW THE NUMERICAL SEQUENCE</small>, "3, 4, 5 ... 7, 8, 9" <small>HOW</small> would you respond?

If you were an algebra teacher, you might examine the pattern of the numbers. If you were a kindergarten teacher, you might think you have your work cut out for you. If you are three years old, your parents probably would applaud you for counting! As a Yankees fan, those are the retired numbers of Babe Ruth, Lou Gehrig, Joe DiMaggio, Mickey Mantle, Yogi Berra (and Mickey Cochrane) and Roger Maris.

One of the threads that we tend to gloss over is the *numbers* in the Bible. Numbers in the Bible always have significance. For instance, there is a reason that Jesus waited two days to respond to the news that His friend Lazarus had died (John 11:1-44). Jesus arrived on the *fourth* day after Lazarus died. Jewish thought was that a person was not truly dead until the fourth day following their death. When Jesus arrived, Lazarus was *dead, dead*. Jesus was too late! That detail makes John 11:43 even more powerful when Jesus commands, "Lazarus, come out!"

Let's look at some of the key numbers in the Bible.

One

The number one represents *unity* and *primacy*. At the very heart of the most important Jewish prayer (the Shema) is the statement, "Hear, O Israel: The Lord our God, the Lord is one" (Deuteronomy 6:4). As the Israelites prepare to go into the Promised Land, Moses reminds them that God is the only true God. Because God is One, He deserves our complete attention. Our response must be, "Love the Lord your God with all your heart and with all your soul and with all your strength" (Deuteronomy 6:5).

In John's account of the Garden of Gethsemane (John 17), Jesus prays what we refer to as the High Priestly Prayer. At the heart of this prayer, Jesus prays for an intimacy and unity with those who are and will be His disciples. As He is preparing to go to the Calvary, Jesus explains His goal in going to the Cross. Jesus prays,

> I have given them the glory that you gave me, that they may be one as we are *one*: I in them and you in me. May they be brought to complete unity to let the world know that you sent me and have loved them even as you have loved me. John 17:22-23

The Apostle Paul reminds Timothy that there is no other means to salvation except through Jesus by stating,

> For there is *one* God and *one* mediator between God and men, the man Christ Jesus, who gave himself as a ransom for all men—the testimony given in its proper time. I Timothy 2:5-6

As the Apostle Paul writes to the Ephesians from a prison cell, he reminds them to stay united in Christ.

> Be completely humble and gentle; be patient, bearing with *one* another in love. Make every effort to keep the unity of the Spirit through the bond of peace. There is *one* body and *one* Spirit—just as you were called to *one* hope when you were called—*one* Lord, *one* faith, one baptism; *one* God and Father of all, who is over all and through all and in all. Ephesians 4:2-6

Three

Three is the number of *resurrection*. Three is the first of four spiritually perfect numbers (the others being 7, 10 and 12). The third day of Creation was the day God created living things (Genesis 1:11-13). As Abraham prepared to sacrifice Isaac, he saw Mount Moriah (Genesis 22:4) on the third day. Moses and the Israelites arrived at Mount Sinai in the third month of the Exodus. It is on the third day that God appears to Moses on Mount Sinai (Exodus 19: 10-11). Jonah spent three days in the belly of the whale (Jonah 1:17). To begin His earthly ministry, Jesus and His disciples attended a wedding on the third day (John 2:1).

My favorite use of the number three is found in Jesus' use of the phrase, "on the third day." As I like to use it, *"on the thirrrd day!"* Jesus' predictions of His Death and Resurrection are recorded three times in the Gospels: at Caesarea Philippi (Matthew 16:21); shortly after the Mount of Transfiguration (Matthew 17:23); and on the Road to Jerusalem as He enters the city for the last time (Luke 18:33). Each time, Jesus shares more details about his Crucifixion, but He always ends the prediction with the affirmation of the Resurrection, "on the *third* day (the Son of Man) will be raised to life."

On Good Friday, Jesus is crucified, wrapped up by Joseph of Arimathea and Nicodemus, and then placed in Joseph's new tomb. Witnessing the reality of Jesus' death, it is no wonder the disciples are confused and afraid. Satan begins to laugh as he celebrates the defeat of Jesus once and for all. If only the Enemy can hold Him in the Tomb until the fourth day, Jesus will be finished. Saturday seems to go by quietly, but ...*on the thirrrd day*, the Stone is rolled away and the Tomb is Empty! Sin, death and the grave have been defeated! All of history has been redeemed by the Blood of the Lamb of God. All the third day events have been building to the crescendo of the Resurrection.

Seven

Seven symbolizes *perfection* and *completion*. It derives its meaning from its direct tie to God's creation of all things. The seventh day is the day of Sabbath rest. There are seven annual Holy Days or Feasts. Noah was to take seven of every kind of bird onto the Ark. The lampstand in the Temple had seven candles. The Apostle John shared seven signs or miracles of Jesus in his Gospel account. In the book of Revelation, there are seven churches, angels to the seven churches, seven seals, seven trumpet plagues, seven thunders and the last seven plagues. The Holy Spirit is referred to as the seven-fold Spirit.

One of the unusual uses of the number seven is found in Jesus' Feeding of the Four Thousand. The Feeding of the *Five* Thousand takes place outside of Bethsaida on the northeast corner of the Sea of Galilee. The five thousand men plus women and children were predominantly, if not totally, Jewish. Because of the importance of the Twelve Tribes of Israel, it is not surprising that the twelve disciples collect twelve baskets of bread after the miracle.

However, when Jesus feeds the *four* thousand, he has traveled along the eastside of the Sea of Galilee into the region known as the Decapolis. This was enemy territory. It was in the Decapolis on the southeast side of the Sea of Galilee that Jesus delivered a demon-possessed man from the region of the Gerasenes (Luke 8:26-39).

The audience for the Feeding of the Four Thousand is made up of the tribes of Canaanites who were driven out of the Promised Land. When He feeds this crowd, Jesus has seven loaves and a few small fish to use. Once the crowd has been satisfied, the disciples gather up seven baskets of bread. Do you know why seven baskets? There were seven tribes who lived in Canaan.[62] Jesus' message through this miracle is that the Gospel is for all people. The completion of Jesus' ministry includes those who have been the enemies of God.

Twelve

The number twelve is the number of God's *power* and *authority*. Twelve is also considered a perfect number. It also can represent the nation of Israel (twelve tribes of Israel) and/or the church (twelve disciples). God specifies that twelve unleavened cakes of bread be placed every week in the Temple, with new bread being placed in the Temple every Sabbath.

The number twelve can be found 22 times alone in Revelation. In Revelation 7, we find twelve thousand from each tribe of Israel (144,000) who will receive salvation during the Great Tribulation.[63]

---

62   Hittites, Girgashites, Amorites, Canaanites, Perizzites, Hivites and Jebusites (Deuteronomy 7:1)

63   In his book *The Most Revealing Book in the Bible*, Mark Lowe sees the number 144,000 as 12 times 12 times a thousand. Thus, the number is not limiting, but freeing. One thousand symbolizes abundance.

There are twelve stones on the breast piece of the High Priest. Each of the stones represents one of the tribes of Israel (Exodus 28: 17-20). There is a very similar list of stones mentioned in God's message to Tyre through the prophet Ezekiel. (Ezekiel 28:13). Out of the twelve stones mentioned in the description of Heaven in Revelation 21:14-20, nine of the stones are the same as the High Priest's breast piece.

Each manned by an angel, New Jerusalem contains twelve gates made of pearl which represent the tribes of Israel. The walls of New Jerusalem will be 144 cubits high (12 times 12) with the city being 12,000 furlongs square. In Revelation 12, Christ's Bride wears a crown with twelve stars. From the establishment of the Sacrificial System to the construction of Heaven itself, God's power and authority shines through.

Forty

The number forty symbolizes a *period of testing, trial or probation*. During the Flood, it rained for forty days and forty nights. During the giving of the Ten Commandments, Moses was on Mount Sinai for forty days on two separate occasions. For forty years, the Israelites wandered in the wilderness in order that the original generation (forty years) who left Egypt could pass away. The prophet Ezekiel laid on his side for forty days as a symbol of Judah's sins. Elijah went without food or water for forty days. Jonah warned Nineveh that they had forty days to repent.

In the New Testament, forty comes into play in the ministry of Jesus during His Temptations. As recorded in Matthew 4:1-11, Jesus begins His ministry by experiencing the Temptation in the Wilderness. After forty days and nights of fasting, Jesus is near the point of starvation. When Jesus is most vulnerable, Satan comes to tempt Him.

The first temptation is *physical* (Matthew 4:3), when Satan challenges Jesus to use His divine powers to turn stone into bread. At the point of death, it must have been tempting for the Bread of Life to produce bread to satisfy His hunger. No one would have to know. Jesus defends Himself by quoting Deuteronomy 8:3 which reads, "It is written: 'Man does not live on bread alone, but on every word that comes from the mouth of God.'"

The second temptation was *social* (Matthew 4:5) as Satan tempts Jesus with acceptability. Satan takes Jesus to the Pinnacle of the Temple and challenges Him to throw Himself off, so that the angels will catch Him. Jesus would have instant celebrity. Satan even quotes the Psalmist David when he uses the words of Psalm 91:11-12 as a part of this temptation. "He will command his angels concerning you and they will lift you up in their hands so that you will not strike your foot against a stone." Jesus once again refuses to give into temptation by quoting Deuteronomy 6:16, "It is also written: 'Do not put the Lord Your God to the test.'"

The final temptation was *spiritual* (Matthew 4:9), as Satan offers Jesus all of the kingdoms of the world if Jesus will bow down to Satan. Satan tempts the Creator of the universe with the kingdoms that belonged to Jesus already. Jesus responds by quoting Deuteronomy 6:13, "For it is written: 'Worship the Lord your God, and serve him only.'"

If you look at the Seamless Robe that Jesus is wearing, you will notice numbers sewn into it. Whenever you are reading a passage of Scripture, be sure and look for any numbers that are included. They are there for a reason. God never does anything unintentionally!

WHERE AM I?

The Geography of the Bible

THE HOUSE HAS 1,400 SQUARE FEET OF LIVING SPACE, THREE bedrooms, an eating area and one and a half baths. How much would you pay for it? Oh, by the way, it is on the Hawaiian Island of Maui with a beautiful ocean view! Did that change your level of interest? What if it was located in the center of the Bowery in New York City? Every real estate agent has a mantra that goes "Location! Location! Location!" Knowing the location of a property is vital to understanding its value.

The same is true of the locations where biblical events take place. God never randomly chooses where events happen. One of the interesting threads of the Bible is *geographical settings*. Often, God weaves His love story through the same location at different times in history. Knowing the location of a biblical event adds a dimension of richness to the story that might otherwise be missed.

For instance, the major focus of biblical geography is on a tiny tract of land that would seem insignificant if based on size. The whole area would be about the size of New Jersey. Most of the significant locations in the Bible are located in and around the present State of Israel. Today, the state of Israel is about 170 miles long and is as narrow as 9.3 miles at one point. Of those 170 miles, the majority of land is barren desert.

Throughout history, more wars have been fought to control this strip of land than anywhere else in the world! Since the establishment of the state of Israel in 1948, there have been major Arab-Israeli wars in 1948, 1956, 1967 and 1973. Although Israel is one of the safest places on earth, there is always a sense of tension in the air. As small as Israel is today, the events that happen in Jerusalem, Tel Aviv and the surrounding areas often end up making world news.

The Significance of the Location

Why would such a small area of land be so important to world history? *Spiritually*, this land is important because it is the covenant land God promised to Abraham. The present-day state of Israel includes the heart of the land promised to Abraham, but God's Promised Land is actually much larger than the borders of Israel today. From Genesis 12 to today, God has been weaving this land into a story of His faithfulness.

This is also *spiritually sacred* land, because this is the location of the ministry of Jesus. Besides being carried into Egypt by Mary and Joseph for a short time, Jesus spent His whole life within this general area. His birth in Bethlehem is separated from His Death and His Resurrection in Jerusalem by less than five miles. The majority of Jesus' miracles take place in three small cities (Capernaum, Bethsaida and Chorazin) on the northern shore of the Sea of Galilee. Although Jesus made limited trips to Jerusalem, it was in the city of David that the history of the world would be changed.

Financially, it has been vital for trade, because the only north-south trade route,[64] the Via Maris, runs along the western boundary of this area. The Via Maris (the Way of the Sea) runs along the western shore of Israel by the Mediterranean Sea. The road does run towards the east around Capernaum, but if you were going to do any trade between Egypt and the northern empires of the day, you had to use the Via Maris. The Via Maris was the *only main north-south road* between Egypt and the rest of the world.

As you move east from the Mediterranean coastline of Israel, the topography of the land changes dramatically. The coastal plains quickly elevate into hillsides and then into the Judean Mountains. The elevation then drops into the Rift Valley. Due to the topography, there were not any other options for travel. Even today, the main highway going north and south in Israel is along the route of the Via Maris.

Militarily, the Via Maris was needed for military dominance. Whoever controlled the Via Maris controlled the world. During the reign of King Josiah, Egypt wanted to peacefully pass through

---

64

Judah on the Via Maris. We read of Josiah's foolish decision to fight Egypt:

> While Josiah was king, Pharaoh Neco king of Egypt went up to the Euphrates River to help the king of Assyria. King Josiah marched out to meet him in battle, but Neco faced him and killed him at Megiddo. II Kings 23:29

The Story of Bethlehem

Nestled on the hillside five miles from Jerusalem, in the Judean Mountains, is the little town of Bethlehem. It is believed to have been a community of around 200 people at the time of Jesus' ministry. As small as the town was, it still had a rich past even before the birth of Christ. Here are some of the stories that take place there.

The Love Story of Ruth and Boaz

During the time period of the book of Judges, Bethlehem becomes the background for one of the greatest love stories of the Bible (Ruth 1:1). Because of a famine in the Bethlehem area, a man named Elimelech and his wife Naomi move to the land of Moab with their two sons. The Moabites were descendants of Lot through an incestuous relationship with his oldest daughter (Genesis 19:37). Needless to say, the Moabites were looked down upon by the Israelites.

While Naomi's family is living in Moab, the two sons marry Moabite women. First, Naomi's husband Elimelech dies, and then both her sons die. This is not only an emotional loss, but a financial one as well. The loss of her husband and sons leave Naomi and her daughters-in-law in dire financial straits. Naomi decides to leave Moab and return to Bethlehem to the protection of her family.

Naomi gives her daughters-in-law permission to stay in their homeland of Moab. One of the daughters-in-law, Orpah, decides to remain in Moab, but Ruth chooses to follow Naomi to the unfamiliar land of Judah and the little town of Bethlehem. Ruth has three strikes against her: she is a Moabite, she is poor and she is a widow. In order to financially survive, Ruth begins to gather leftover grain from the fields of Boaz.

As Boaz arrives from Bethlehem to oversee the harvest, he notices Ruth and is told of the family connections through Naomi. Boaz tells his workers to leave extra grain for Ruth and even let her pick from the sheaves. Here's where the love story begins! Before it's over, Boaz has become Naomi and Ruth's *go'el,* their kinsman-redeemer. Boaz redeems Naomi's estate and takes Ruth as his wife. The poor foreigner widow becomes the wife of a rich man!

The story ends with the birth of the couple's first-born son, Obed. The genealogy of Obed leads directly to King David. In that way, this love story is woven into Matthew's genealogy in Matthew 1. Can you imagine how many times the citizens of Bethlehem retold this love story?

Bethlehem—the home of the greatest love story ever!

The Reign of David

If you fast-forward to I Samuel 16, we are brought back to Bethlehem for the anointing of the greatest King of Israel, King David. The Prophet Samuel is sent to Bethlehem to anoint the future King, because King Saul has failed to completely destroy the Amalekites and has built a monument to himself (I Samuel 15). Samuel is told by God to go to Jesse's house, because it will be one of his sons that will be chosen as Saul's successor.

During a sacrificial meal, Samuel is introduced to seven of Jesse's sons. All of them look like the perfect choice to become the next King. They are young, handsome and strong. However, when the seven sons come before him, Samuel is told by God that none of these men are His choice. Almost as an afterthought, Jesse remembers that his youngest son is out on the Bethlehem hillside tending the family sheep. When Samuel meets this young shepherd boy who carries a slingshot and a lyre, he must have wondered what God was thinking! David was handsome and healthy, but how could a little shepherd-boy become a King?

David received his training for becoming King by using his musical ability to sooth King Saul's nerves with his music. David was able to watch the inner-workings of government daily from the inside. From his victory over Goliath to his reign as the great-est King of Israel, David's story is one of God's grace, David was not the biggest or strongest, but he was "a man after God's own heart" (I Samuel 16:8).

If there had been a sign at Bethlehem's city limits, it could have read, "Bethlehem—home of King David." The story of this great king would have been shared frequently by the Bethlehem citizens. What a great heritage! What a great place for the Messiah to be born!

The Birth of Jesus

In this small town where romance and royalty have lived, Jesus is born. The location for the Messiah's birth had been predicted by the prophet Micah when he wrote, "But you, Bethlehem Ephra-thath, though you are small among the clans of Judah, out of you will come for me one who will be ruler over Israel, whose origins are from of old, from ancient times" (Micah 5:2).

On the same hillsides where Ruth and Boaz fell in love and David tended his father's sheep, angels appear before a group of shepherds to announce the birth of the Messiah. Luke tells us,

> But the angel said to them, 'Do not be afraid. I bring you good news that will cause great joy for all the people. Today in the town of David, a Savior has been born to you; he is the Messiah, the Lord. This will be a sign to you: You will find a baby wrapped in cloths and lying in a manger.' Suddenly a great company of the heavenly host appeared with the angel, praising God and saying, "Glory to God in the highest heaven, and on earth peace to those on whom his favor rests." Luke 2:10-14

What a perfect place for Jesus to be born! In this small town, God had chosen unlikely people and circumstances to fulfill His plan. Ruth has three strikes against her when she came to Beth-lehem with Naomi, because she is young, a Moabite and a widow. But because of her faithfulness to her former mother-in-law, Ruth marries Boaz and becomes the great-grandmother to King David! Ruth becomes a part of the royal bloodline of Jesus.

We have already talked about David's humble beginnings. However, when our Savior was born in Bethlehem, it was in even lowlier settings. There was no place to stay, except a lonely stable. The only warmth for baby Jesus was the body heat of the animals around him. None of the luxuries reserved for a King! What a perfect place for Jesus to be born, because as the Apostle Paul reminds us,

> For you know the grace of our Lord Jesus Christ, that though he was rich, yet for your sakes he became poor, so that you through his poverty might become rich. II Corinthians 8:9

The Sacrificial Lambs

There was one more thing that made Bethlehem such an important location. The sheep that grazed the pastures outside of Bethlehem were no ordinary sheep. From these flocks, the sacrificial lambs would be chosen. The flocks were born to die. Their blood would be shed for the people of Israel. It is so fitting that Jesus was born in Bethlehem. When the Lamb of God died, He died once and for all *of us*. The blood of Jesus paid the price for your salvation and mine.

Caesarea Philippi

As Jesus prepares for His final trip to Jerusalem, He leads His disciples to the most unlikely retreat spot imaginable. With His final destination being south, where Jerusalem is, Jesus leads His disciples to a location twenty-five miles north of Galilee! Not only is Caesarea Philippi located in the opposite direction of Jerusalem, but it was enemy territory.

William Barclay writes, "The area was scattered with temples of the ancient Syrian Baal worship. Here was an area where the very breath of ancient religion breathed in the very air and atmosphere."[65] The landscape was cluttered with the ruins of Baal temples where sexual orgies had taken place to awaken Baal and his female counterpart Ashtoreth. By the thousands, children were placed in the fire of the Tophet in exchange for these fertility gods

---

65   William Barclay, The Gospel of Matthew, Volume 2, (Westminster: Philadelphia, 1958), page 147.

to bring rain. Why did Jesus come here to ask His disciples such a key question about His identity?

Carved into the hillside were statues of the god Pan, a half-goat, half-man god of nature. The statues were displayed in frame-like settings in the hillside. In front of these idols, children had been sacrificed in honor of Pan. Barclay explains the reason when he writes,

> Hard by Caesarea Philippi there rose a great hill, and in it was a deep cavern; and that cavern was said to be the birthplace of the great god Pan, the god of nature. So much was Caesarea Philippi identified with that god that its original name was Panias, and to this day the place is known as Banias.[66]

The large opening in the side of Mount Hermon was believed to mark the source of the Jordan River. Because it was believed to also be the place where Baal and Ashtoreth entered for sleep for winter, the opening was called the Gates of Hell. As if that were not enough, Herod the Great had built a great temple of white marble in Caesarea Philippi to honor the deity of Caesar.

So why would Jesus choose such a location to ask the eternal question, "But what about you?" he asked. "Who do you say I am?" (Matthew 16:15). Caesarea Philippi is the perfect location for Jesus' question, because the rubble of pagan temples serves as a fitting backdrop to Jesus' deity. Like a black cloth placed behind a diamond, the setting enhances Jesus' question and Peter's answer, "You are the Christ, the Son of the living God." (Matthew 16:16). I have to agree with Barclay when he writes, "There are few scenes where Jesus' consciousness of His own divinity shines out with more dazzling light."[67]

If you look at the Seamless Robe of Jesus, you will see some maps woven into it. That's because the thread of *Location* is always an important part of understanding a passage of Scripture.

---

66   Ibid.

67   Ibid. page 149.

DON'T TRY SO HARD

Relationship, not Religion

WHEN I WAS FOURTEEN, MY DAD PURCHASED TWO STATE-OF-the-art tractors. They were 930 Case tractors with air-conditioned cabs and an AM radio! I know that may sound ancient in today's world of high-tech tractors with GPS tracking and Sirius radio. However, when you were used to a tractor umbrella and nothing but the sound of the tractor engine, this was heaven. I spent my day rocking to the music on WKY 930.

The only thing I didn't like about that 930 Case was the hydraulic system. Each piece of equipment had a lift on it so the disc or plow could be lifted out of the ground. That lift was connected to the tractor by hydraulic hoses. It seemed simple: *push the hose into the holder and you were done.* If the pressure in the holder was not right, the hoses would kick back out. When this happened, Dad would simply adjust the levers by the holders until the hoses connected properly. He made it seem so easy.

My problem was that if the hose(s) came out while Dad was away, I could not get the hose(s) back in. Every time I tried, the hoses jumped back at me. I don't know if I didn't watch closely enough or I didn't hold my mouth just right, but it never worked. I remember one day when I turned too quickly and one hose popped free. For about an hour, I worked as hard as I could to fix the problem.

Dad drove up, came over to where I was and offered to help. I refused his help. I told him, "I am going to do this thing myself. Just stand back and watch." Patiently Dad watched me struggle for another ten minutes before he said, "Randy, let me do it for you." A couple of adjustments with the levers and the hose went right in! I was trying too hard. My father did something for me that I couldn't do for myself. That's grace!

We live in a performance-based culture where what we *do* is more important than who we *are*. I realize that when we first greet each other we do ask, "How *are* you?" However, we really do not expect the person to actually answer. Nothing will make a person walk away more quickly than a report on your last doctor visit or the financial trouble you are experiencing. We expect the response to be, "Just fine."

The question we want answered is, "What *do* you *do* for a living?" or "What *do* your kids *do* for a living?" We like to brag about how successful we are at our job, the success of our children or how many hours we work each week. The thought is that the more you *do*, the more successful you are. The truth is that the more you *do*, the more exhausted you become. Our agendas are full with work, school and family activities. Even in our leisure time, it is hard to just relax.

This attitude of busyness equaling success has even crept into the church. A common buzzword these days is "*doing* church." While it is important to find new ways to reach people for Christ, the tendency is to measure success by how many people came. We will turn off the lights, replace the pulpit with a music stand or round table, replace the pews with padded chairs and even remove the Cross, if necessary. We will *do* whatever it takes to "get our number up." The end result is that most pastors and staff are exhausted from trying to figure out what they must do next in order for their church to grow. If you listen carefully, you can hear pastors gasping for air.

When it comes to our personal walk with Christ, we tend to measure our Christian walk by how disciplined we are to *do* what a Christian should *do*. We dutifully discipline ourselves to set aside thirty minutes a day to *do* our daily devotions. We try hard to work Christ into our busy schedules. We may have time to talk to God, but we have little time to listen to Him. Our walk with God becomes trying to *do* what Christians should *do*. We think we are to perform for God.

The Bible is not about *religion*. It is about *relationship*. Although the Bible is a religious book, it is not a book of religion. The message is not about what we must *do* to earn our salvation. Christ has already *done* what was necessary to pay for our salvation. By His death on the Cross, Jesus *did* for us what we could not *do* for ourselves. As Max Lucado writes, "Every other approach to God is a bartering system; if I *do* this, God will *do* that."[68]

God's grace also extends to our daily life. It is especially hard in American culture for us to grasp that we *do* not "*do* something" to earn God's favor. Surely, if I read my Bible enough and pray long enough, God will have to love me. In his letter to the churches of Galatia, the Apostle Paul opens his letter without any positive comments about the churches. This is the only time it happens. Paul begins the letter by scolding the congregations. He writes,

> I am astonished that you are so quickly deserting the one who called you by the grace of Christ and are turning to a different gospel—which is really no gospel at all? Evidently some people are throwing you into confusion and are trying to pervert the gospel of Christ. Galatians 1:6-7

Although the Galatians realize they were saved by God's grace, they are now trying to *be* like Christ by doing righteous acts. After calling them "foolish," Paul asks the key question that separates our relationship with Christ from a religion about Christ. Paul asked,

> Did you receive the Spirit by observing the law, or by believing what you heard? Are you so foolish? After beginning with the Spirit, are you not trying to attain your goal by human effort? Galatians 3:2b-3

John MacArthur defines the sharp line between relationship and religion when he writes,

> As far as the way of salvation is concerned, there are only two religions the world has ever known or will ever know—the religion of divine accomplishment, which is biblical Christianity, and the religion of human achievement, which includes all other kinds of religion, by whatever names they may go by.[69]

Religion is the enemy of our soul. Religion was the greatest enemy of the Israelites both during the Exodus and in their battle to possess the Promised Land. Religion leads to self-righteousness. Religion does not need the Cross.

---

68   Max Lucado, *In the Grip of Grace* (Dallas: Word Publishing, 1996), page 71.

69   John MacArthur, The New Testament Commentary on Romans (Chicago: Moody, 1991), page 199

Before we go any further, let me define what I mean by *religion*. It is thinking that my *doing* will produce Christ *being* in my life. We tell ourselves we can make God move by our actions. But *performance* is not the basis of being a Christian; it is the problem that keeps us from enjoying our walk with Jesus. Christ did not come to establish a new *religion*. To compare Jesus to Buddha or Mohammed is an insult to God's character.

As a teenager, I had a good case of religion. I had long list of things I *did* to deserve my salvation (read my Bible, prayed, attended church[70]) and an even longer list of what I *did* not *do* (drink, smoke, curse, do drugs and go to movies). When I became a pastor, my list got even longer. At one time, I preached three times a week, taught two discipleship classes, led two Bible studies at a nursing home, taught a Sunday School class, led music, sang specials, held Board Meetings and prepared the church bulletin on a mimeograph machine! Somehow, I thought my many activities would impress God into loving me.

I remember the day that God disarmed me from *doing* anything. I had no options, except to *be* with God. For the first time in my life, I realized what the writer to the Hebrews meant in Hebrews 4:11 when he wrote, "Let us, therefore, make every effort to enter that rest, so that no one will fall by following their example of disobedience." My friend and mentor Stephen Manley interprets that verse as "work to quit working."

How freeing it was the day I finally realized that God loves me because He loves me! I cannot *earn* His love, but can *receive* it. For the first time in my life, I realized that I needed grace. Self-righteousness blinds us from seeing our need for God's help.

Living without Christ is much more difficult than living with Him. Christ came to pay the price for us to have an intimate *relationship* with God. By relationship, I mean that *God's being in my life produces my doing*. Whether at work, school or home, God is present with me. My prayer life is not a 15-minute discipline, but a daily ongoing conversation with God. My Bible reading is not 15-minutes of duty, but allowing God to speak to me constantly

---

70   I had a 14-year perfect attendance Cross and Crown pin with bars that hung down on my sports jacket very impressively.

through His written Word. I realize that God is with me 24/7, not just when I am in a tough spot.

Do you know how God sees you? He is not a hard taskmaster that is waiting for you to make a mistake. Like a loving parent, God enjoys being with us. There will be times of failure, but like a father teaching his child to walk, God helps us to our feet and begins to teach us once again. God does not expect you to be flawless, just useable. In fact, God wants us to do nothing except trust Him. Let's look at some examples.

While You Were Sleeping

When God officially "cuts" His covenant with Abram (later renamed Abraham) in Genesis 15: 1-21, God reassures Abram that He will provide a Promised Son (Genesis 15:4), a Promised Nation (Genesis 15:5) and the possession of the Promised Land (Genesis 15:7). In answer to Abram's request for tangible evidence, God gives instructions to Abram to prepare a sacrifice.

> So the Lord said to him, "Bring me a heifer, a goat and a ram, each three years old, along with a dove and a young pigeon." Abram brought all these to him, cut them in two and arranged the halves opposite each other; the birds, however, he did not cut in half. Genesis 15:9-10

It was not unusual that God asked Abram to prepare for the walk of death which concluded the covenant ceremony. You would have found this preparation as a part of every covenant ritual. God's covenant with Abram, the greatest covenant of the Old Testament, is about to be finalized. When the sacrifices are prepared, God adds a special twist to the story. "As the sun was setting, Abram fell into a *deep sleep*, and a thick and dreadful darkness came over him" (Genesis 15:12). Abram slept through the history-changing covenant! It is like a groom sleeping through his wedding.

Abram was asleep, "When the sun had set and darkness had fallen, a smoking firepot with a blazing torch appeared and passed between the pieces" (Genesis 15:17). Abram never saw God walk through the blood twice, once for Himself and once for Abram. By His actions, God was saying, "If *I* break this Covenant, you can put me to death. If *you* break this Covenant, you can put me to death." This covenant was not about Abram's great faith or goodness. It was because, "Abram believed the Lord, and he credited it to him as righteousness" (Genesis 15:6).

If you had interviewed Abram after the Covenant Ceremony, he would have made sure you knew it was God's doing, not his. What *did* you *do* Abram? *"Nothing, except trust God."*

And the Walls Came Tumblin' Down

It was Joshua's very first battle as the leader of the Israelite army. Joshua, along with Caleb, was one of two spies sent to the land of Canaan who came back with a positive report. The other ten spies thought it would be impossible to possess the land. After crossing the Jordan River, Joshua's first military test was taking the fortified city of Jericho. Jericho prided itself in its impenetrable walls.

With such limited weaponry and with their hands full of the materials for the Tabernacle, Joshua receives instructions from God that must have sounded almost silly,

> March around the city once with all the armed men. Do this for six days.
>
> Have seven priests carry trumpets of rams' horns in front of the ark. On the seventh day, march around the city seven times, with the priests blowing the trumpets.
>
> When you hear them sound a long blast on the trumpets, have all the people give a loud shout; then the wall of the city will collapse and the people will go up, every man straight in. Joshua 6:3-5

Can you imagine Joshua coming back from talking to God and being asked, "Joshua, what are we going to *do*?" Joshua begins to stammer a little as he shared God's instructions. "Well, guys we are going to march once around the city for six days." The Israelites had to be thinking, "What are we going to *do* next?" Joshua finishes by adding, "Then on the seventh day we will have seven priests blowing shofars (ram's horn trumpets) in front of the ark. We will march around the city seven times. When we hear a long trumpet blast, we will all shout loudly and the walls will collapse."

The Israelites had to be thinking, "That is the dumbest thing I have ever heard!"

But that is exactly what happened! This untouchable, fortified city crumbles before the eyes of the Israelites. They march into Jericho and plunder the city without firing a shot. If you had interviewed Joshua right after the taking of Jericho and asked him, "What *did* you *do* Joshua to bring about this great victory?" He would have answered, *"Nothing, except trust God."*

I've Got My Ai on You

The next battle will be at the small city of Ai (Ay-eye). Having seen Jericho fall, Ai looked like a piece of cake! The spies come back and basically say, "Give us two or three thousand soldiers and the rest of you take the day off. No problem." Because of their wrongly placed self-confidence, the special-ops team loses 36 men and end up running for their life!

Joshua's response was to get mad at God! In Joshua 7:6-15, God and Joshua have a conversation. Joshua sounds just like the grumbling Israelites Moses had to work with. Joshua's response was to get angry at God and blame God for the failure. God tells Joshua to stand up and quit drowning in self-pity.

The problem wasn't with God. The people had broken the covenant by relying on themselves. The post-defeat interview would have ended with someone asking, "Joshua, what *did* you *do* wrong?" Joshua would have to answer, *"Something, without trusting God."*

Chariots of Fire

Can you imagine being surrounding on all sides by the mightiest army in the world? It is just you and your servant against the army of Aram. You have no weapons and no way of escape. What is a person supposed to *do*? *Nothing, except trust God.*

In II Kings 6:8-23, the Aramean army has been trying to hunt down the army of Israel. Every time the Aramean army moves, the Prophet Elisha is able to get word to the King of Israel and keep the army of Israel one step ahead of the Aramean forces.

When the king of Aram finds out that Elisha is the informant, he musters a strong force of soldiers with horses and chariots to go to Dothan at night to kill Elisha. Imagine the terror that struck the heart of Elisha's servant the next morning to see that they are surrounded on all sides by enemy forces. Elisha's servant asks the obvious question, "Oh, my lord, what shall we *do?*" the servant asked (II Kings 6:18b). It seems like a fair question considering the circumstances! Elijah answers, *"Nothing, except what God tells us to do."* Elisha was not afraid, because he could see something his servant could not. Elisha could see God's presence. Calmly, Elisha responds,

> Don't be afraid," the prophet answered. "Those who are with us are more than those who are with them." And Elisha prayed, "O Lord, open his eyes so he may see." Then the Lord opened the servant's eyes, and he looked and saw the hills full of horses and chariots of fire all around Elisha. II Kings 6:16-17

In response to Elisha's prayer, God blinds the Aramean forces and allows Elisha to march the mightiest army of the day into the presence of the King of Israel! Elisha advises the King of Israel not to kill the enemy soldiers, but to feed them and send them home. The story ends with the King of Israel providing a feast for his enemy. The conflict is over.

If you interviewed Elisha's servant after this ordeal, he would have made it clear that it was God, not him who won the battle. What *did* you *do?* The servant would have answered, *"Nothing, except pray and trust God."*

The Invitation of Jesus

Everything about Jesus' ministry was personal. Although there are often large crowds around Jesus, the majority of the recorded ministry of Christ consists of personal conversations. Jesus is the personal, touchable Savior. From the demon-possessed men of the Gadarenes (Matthew 8:28-34) to the Pharisee Nicodemus (John 3:1-16), Jesus communicated directly to those in need.

Jesus enjoyed *being* with the despised tax collector Zacchaeus and his friends for a meal (Matthew 19:2-10) and takes time to be with the scorned Samaritan woman at the well (John 4:1-26).

Jesus hears the cry of Bartimaeus over the noisy crowd (Luke 8: 35-43). To each life He touched, Jesus' message was the same.

> Come to me, all you who are weary and burdened, and I will give you rest. Take my Yoke upon you and learn from me, for I am gentle and humble in heart, and you will find rest for your souls. For my yoke is easy and my burden is light. Matthew 11:28-30

Jesus has big shoulders. He created us to rely upon Him, especially with the burdens we carry. Christ's love for us is not based on our *performance*. What we *do* is an extension of *being with Christ*. Why is it that we so often find ourselves trying to work out our problems without His help? Why is *being* with Jesus something we try to work into our schedule of *doing*?

In the quiet oasis moments of the Upper Room, Jesus teaches His disciples the importance of being with Him. Using the word picture of vine and branches, Jesus shares the heart of how our relationship must work. He reminds the disciples,

> *Remain* in me, and I will *remain* in you. No branch can bear fruit by itself; it must remain in the vine. Neither can you bear fruit unless you remain in me. "I am the vine; you are the branches. If a man remains in me and I in him, he will bear much fruit; *apart from me you can do nothing.*
>
> If anyone *does not remain* in me, he is like a branch that *is thrown away* and *withers;* such branches are picked up, thrown into the fire and burned.
>
> If you *remain* in me and my words *remain* in you, ask whatever you wish, and it will be given you. John 15:4-7

Jesus was not afraid to address self-righteous people, like the Pharisees. In His confrontation with the Pharisees recorded in Matthew 23: 13-39, Jesus proceeds to call the powerful religious leaders *hypocrites* (vs. 13), *blind guides* (vs. 15), *dirty cups* (vs. 25), *white-washed tombs* (vs. 27) and *snakes* (vs. 33). Jesus spoke harshly as a wake-up call to the self-righteous, because self-righteousness is deadly. With a broken heart Jesus concludes,

> "O Jerusalem, Jerusalem, you who kill the prophets and stone those sent to you, how often I have longed to gather your children together, as a hen gathers her chicks under her wings, but you were not willing. Matthew 23:37

The Choice

While it's not our *performance* that defines our faith, being a Christian *does* demand a deliberate *decision* on our part. You cannot be in fellowship with Christ without knowing it. We must choose what we are going to *do* with Christ's offer of salvation. Christ wants to *be* with you, but *do* you want to *be* with Him? I fear we have customized our definition of being a Christian so that it fits any present lifestyle. In the age of cellphones, we communicate more than ever before, but find it hard to *be* together. We are busy texting, tweeting and talking on the phone to enjoy the company of the people around us. Jesus came to transform you! Zacchaeus gave back to those he had stolen from five times what he had taken. The Samaritan woman became an evangelist in her hometown. Christ's death on the Cross was an act of deliverance from sin. It is not a matter of self-discipline, but total reliance upon the power and presence of Christ.

There is a distinct line between living for God and not living for Him. In Galatians 5:16-26, the Apostle Paul describes the vast difference between living by the *Spirit* (by relying on Christ) and living by the *Flesh* or sinful nature (relying on ourselves). The two lifestyles cannot co-exist. Paul reminds us,

> For the sinful nature desires what is contrary to the Spirit, and the Spirit what is contrary to the sinful nature. They are in conflict with each other, so that you *do not do* what you want. Galatians 5:17

When you compare the results of living by the Spirit or living by the Flesh, the two lifestyles produce radically different results. Living by the Flesh produces,

> sexual immorality, impurity and debauchery; idolatry and witchcraft; hatred, discord, jealousy, fits of rage, selfish ambition, dissensions, factions and envy; drunkenness, orgies, and the like. I warn you, as I did before, that those who live like this will not inherit the kingdom of God. Galatians 5:19-21

Compare those results to living by the Spirit. Paul says,

> But the fruit of the Spirit is love, joy, peace, patience, kindness, goodness, faithfulness, gentleness and self-control. Against such things there is no law. Galatians 5:22-23

The Apostle Paul certainly knew about trying to please God by the things he *did*. It was not until Paul had his encounter with Christ on the Damascus Road (Acts 9:1-19) that Paul's life was changed. If anyone could have gotten to Heaven by what they did, Paul would be first in line. Listen to his list of accomplishments:

> circumcised on the eighth day, of the people of Israel, of the tribe of Benjamin, a Hebrew of Hebrew; in regard to the law, a Pharisee, as for zeal, persecuting the church; as for legalistic righteousness, faultless. Philippians 3:5-6

What changed Paul's life? Paul died to his self-righteousness. In Galatians 2:20, Paul testifies, "I have been crucified with Christ and I no longer live, but Christ lives in me. The life I live in the body, I live by faith in the Son of God ..."

Are you trying too hard to make yourself worthy of God? It is impossible! The amazing news of the Bible is that we will never completely understand why God wants to be with us, but He does. The band Casting Crowns recorded a song entitled "Who Am I?" For me, it has the most concise explanation of how God wants our relationship with Him to work,

> Not because of who I am
> But because of what You've done
> Not because of what I've done
> But because of who You are
> I am Yours![71]

When you look at Jesus as He wears the Seamless Robe, you will notice that His arms are opened wide. Christ is not asking you to *do* anything. He just wants to wrap His arms around you and let you feel the warmth of His presence. Jesus wants to be with you so that you will never be alone again.

---

71 Pip Williams, Peter Hutchins, John Mark Hall, from the album Casting Crowns, Copyright: Sony/ATV Tree Publishing, Universal Music Publishing Mgb Ltd.,2003

LET IT GO!

Forgiveness

IT WAS THE SONG OF THE SUMMER. YOUTUBE WAS FLOODED WITH videos of people singing it: fathers and their daughters, a young girl with a church choir and even fathers riding together in a car. Much like "Butterfly Kisses" in the late 90s, "Let It Go" from the movie *Frozen* reached a point of saturation, where I personally thought *if I hear this song one more time* ... It did work as a good punchline for me at times, but even that wore off.

However, I could see Jesus singing the chorus. You know, where Elsa sings,

> Let it go, let it go
> Can't hold it back
> Let it go, let it go
> Turn away and slam the door[72]

That is a pretty good description for our next thread, which is *forgiveness.* I remember growing up with the phrase, "forgive and forget" as the standard definition of forgiveness. I struggled with the fact that even after forgiving someone, I *could* remember what they did. Let me give you a more biblical definition of forgiveness.

Forgiveness is *choosing to let go* of the emotions and attitudes we feel when someone has hurt us. Although there is a concept of forgiveness in some religions, John Stott reminds us, "No other system, ideology or religion proclaims a *free* forgiveness and a new life to those who have done nothing to deserve it but deserve judgment instead."[73]

The concept of forgiveness in other religions is at best of an *earned* forgiveness. One must *do* something to be forgiven.

---

72 Let It Go, words and music by Kristen Anderson-Lopez and Robert Lopez, published by Walt Disney Music Publishing Company

73 John Stott, Romans: God's Good News for the World, (InterVarsity Press, Downers Grove, IL; 1994). page 112

Even then, forgiveness was not guaranteed. In his book *Jesus and Muhammad*, Dr. Mark Gabriel[74] sums up the concept of forgiveness in Islamic teaching.

> In short, Allah alone decides whether a person is forgiven. If he commits a big sin, he is at Allah's mercy. If he commits a small sin, he can earn forgiveness through good works or going on hajj (pilgrimage to Mecca).[75]

Then, Dr. Gabriel defines Jesus' teaching on forgiveness. He writes,

> Jesus not only claimed to have the ability to forgive sins on behalf of God while he was on earth, he also claimed that his death would function as a substitute sacrifice, securing forgiveness for all humanity for all time.[76]

The message of Christ is that you can receive forgiveness freely through the Cross. Jesus has already paid the price for our release. Here is grace and mercy working in concert together. The Psalmist David understood the depth of forgiveness as he describes how God forgives our sins, "as far as the east is from the west, so far has he removed our transgressions from us"(Psalm 103:12). Let's look at some examples.

Let Me Go!

His life of deceit and manipulation was catching up with him. He had already been caught and confronted by his father-in-law, Laban, about secretly sneaking off with Jacob's family and flocks and heading back to Canaan. As his name would suggest, the "heel grasper" used his craftiness to wiggle out of the situation. In fact, at one point in the conversation, Jacob even makes it sound as if Laban himself caused the problem (Genesis 31:35-39).

Without apologizing for any of his actions, Jacob makes a covenant with Laban that would provide safety for his family and

---

74   Dr. Gabriel, once a devout Muslim, earned a doctorate in Islamic studies and taught at Al-Azhar University in Cairo before his conversion to Christianity.

75   Mark Gabriel, *Jesus and Muhammad*, (Charisma House: Lake Mary, Florida, 2004), page 87.

76   Ibid.

protection from harm without accountability. Laban may have left reluctantly, but at least he left. There was only one person Jacob now feared, his brother Esau. Tomorrow, Jacob was going to bring a face-to-face encounter with the one person whose life had been most effected by Jacob's unscrupulous trickery. Esau had sufficient reason for revenge.

Not once, but twice, Jacob had stolen the family birthright from Esau. Even though God had already promised Jacob that he would be the recipient of this family treasure, Jacob had taken advantage of his brother's hunger and their father's poor eyesight to take this gift from God by his own strength.

Jacob had reason to be terrified! Esau was joined by 400 men. Tomorrow was going to be a day of reckoning for Jacob. Stealing Esau's birthright twice was not something Jacob could deny or defend. He deserved Esau's entire wrath. There was no way home for Jacob without facing the consequences of his sin. The only hope that Jacob had was to wrestle away a blessing from God (Genesis 32: 22-32). Limping into battle, Jacob, the Heel-Grasper, becomes Israel, Triumphant with God.

Always a thinker, Jacob prepared an extravagant gift of animals to appease his brother. In the event that the gift didn't work, Jacob organized his family and flocks into two groups. The two handmaidens, Zilpah and Bilhah, were placed on the front line with their children. Next, the lesser-loved Leah and her family were placed third in line. Safely at the end of the line, Rachel and Joseph brought up the rear. If Esau attacked, at least Rachel and Joseph would be the last to go.

Much like the Prodigal Son, Jacob must have been practicing what he was going to say. Just like the Father running to the Prodigal Son, "Esau ran to meet Jacob and embraced him; he threw his arms around his neck and kissed him. And they wept" (Genesis 33:4). After all that Jacob had done to him, how could Esau not harbor bitterness and anger? Somehow, Esau had learned to let go of all the pain Jacob had caused. Esau was no longer a prisoner of an unforgiving spirit.

Letting Go Is Hard to Do

At 30 years of age, life could not have been better for him. He had everything a man could want: power, popularity, respect, a great job and a great family. When Joseph went out among the Egyptians, it was as if Pharaoh himself was there. In Genesis 41:41-57, it would seem that all the scars from Joseph's past had healed. The scars from thirteen years ago, when his brothers sold him into slavery, appear to have healed. Long forgotten is the accusation by Potiphar's wife or the imprisonment that followed, even the lapse of memory by the baker.

Then God brings Joseph's brothers back into his life (Genesis 42). Standing before him are the ten men who deliberately tried to destroy him. All the heartaches he has experienced during the last thirteen years resurface as if it were yesterday. There are hurts that can be forgiven quite easily. If you step on my foot and apologize, I can let that go. But there are also those experiences in our lives that hurt so deeply that forgiveness is not an automatic response. Why would God bring Joseph's brothers back into his life? Because Joseph needed to deal with the hurt his brothers had caused.

If you follow the word *wept* in Genesis chapters 42-46, there is an important lesson to learn about forgiveness. Forgiveness is often a process of letting go. Sometimes, it is more than a matter of someone apologizing and forgiving them. The work that God must do in our hearts probes deeper in order for us to let go. Let's look at the steps of forgiveness that Joseph experienced.

The first step is *re-opening the wound.*

Joseph has the advantage in the first meeting with his brothers, because Joseph recognized them; but they do not recognize him. What a great time to punish them for the hurt they have caused. Joseph accuses them of being spies and demands they bring Benjamin back in order to get food. The first time Joseph wept was in response to his brother's discussion of the events from thirteen years ago. As if it was yesterday, Joseph begins to feel those pangs of pain. Joseph is not ready to let his brothers see his tears.

He turned away from them and began to *weep*, but then turned back and spoke to them again. He had Simeon taken from them and bound before their eyes. Genesis 42:24

Joseph hides his tears, because he does not want to let his brothers know how deeply they had hurt him. He was ready to get revenge. The thought of forgiving his brothers without some sort of *paybacks* never crossed Joseph's mind. Joseph imprisons one brother and puts fear in the rest of his brothers by putting the silver they had paid for grain back in their bags. He also requests that the brothers bring his full-brother Benjamin back with them.

The second step of forgiveness is *releasing the emotions.*

The next time Joseph weeps is at the sight of his youngest brother. Although Benjamin was born before Joseph was sold into slavery, it had been thirteen years since he had seen his only full-brother. Joseph allows himself to feel things again. Even though the pain has gone to the very depth of his soul, Joseph feels joy, too. How much he must have wanted to throw his arms around his brother—but if the other brothers had not seen his tears of sorrow; they were not going to see his tears of joy. Instead,

> Deeply moved at the sight of his brother, Joseph hurried out and looked for a place to *weep*. He went into his private room and *wept* there. Genesis 43:30

The third step of forgiveness is *revealing himself.*

Joseph gave his brothers a hint about his identity when he throws a banquet for his eleven brothers and sits them in chronological order from oldest to youngest. After one last trick, Joseph can no longer keep his secret. He did not care who heard him cry as the last wall of unforgiveness falls. In Genesis 45:3, we read,

> And he wept so loudly that the Egyptians heard him, and Pharaoh's household heard about it. Joseph said to his brothers, "I am Joseph! Is my father still living?" But his brothers were not able to answer him, because they were terrified at his presence.

The final step of forgiveness is *releasing each brother individually.*

The last step may be the hardest. Joseph faces each of his brothers and forgives them. Benjamin was first. There was no need to forgive Benjamin. He had done nothing wrong. It might not have been too hard to hug Reuben. After all, Reuben had kept the brothers from killing Joseph. What about the brother who first thought of murdering Joseph? What about the brother who dipped Joseph's coat in goat's blood? Some of the brothers were more difficult to forgive than others, but

> Then he threw his arms around his brother Benjamin and wept, and Benjamin embraced him, weeping. And he kissed all his brothers and wept over them. Afterward his brothers talked with him. Genesis 45:14-15

Joseph's willingness to forgive opens up an opportunity for Pharaoh to bless Joseph and his family by giving them the choice land of Goshen. God will take Jacob's family from seventy people to the Promised Nation of Abraham. For the next four hundred years, the descendants of Israel will prosper and thrive.

Is there someone or something in your life that you struggle to forgive? Letting go can be hard, but with God's help, it is possible.

Letting Go of Limits

Jesus' teaching is filled with the call to forgiveness from God, of others and of ourselves. In the exemplary prayer we know as the Lord's Prayer, Jesus shares how forgiveness works in the Kingdom of God when He prays,

> *Forgive* us our debts, as we also have *forgiven* our debtors. And lead us not into temptation, but deliver us from the evil one. For if you *forgive* men when they sin against you, your heavenly Father will also *forgive* you. But if you do not *forgive* men their sins, your Father will not *forgive* your sins. Matthew 6:12-15

It is easy to grasp that our life in Christ will be marked by forgiveness of minor offenses. When someone apologizes for a little offense, it is not hard to let go. It was a conversation Jesus had with Peter that is a little bit more challenging. In the midst of Jesus' lesson on forgiveness, Peter asks an important question. What are the limits of forgiveness? How many times do I have to forgive someone? Peter actually doubles what the rabbis taught.

> Then Peter came to Jesus and asked, "Lord, how many times shall I forgive my brother when he sins against me? Up to seven times?" Jesus answered, "I tell you, not seven times, but seventy-seven times." Matthew 18:21-22

Seventy-seven times seems a little excessive, doesn't it? Jesus was not asking us to keep track of how many times we forgive someone. Jesus is taking the limits off! Life in Christ requires that by His power we are willing to live a lifestyle of letting go. There are no lines in the sand. In Christ, we give up our right to not forgive. That is a tough assignment! We can forgive most little issues and some bigger issues once, but Jesus is calling us to a lifestyle of forgiveness where not forgiving is not an option.

How can a person live that kind of life? We can't! Biblical forgiveness is not a human achievement, but a divine intervention. God does some of His best teaching in our lives when we are struggling with people and circumstances. It is in those times that God has our attention, because we know we cannot do it alone. "Bear with each other and *forgive* whatever grievances you may have against one another. *Forgive as the Lord forgave you*" (Colossians 3:13).

The last statement in that verse is not a call to discipline yourself to keep up with Jesus. It is describing how we forgive. It is only by His presence in our lives. Being a Christian is not an act of self-discipline. It is an act of surrender so that Christ can work through us.

Letting Go of Conditions

Throughout His ministry, Jesus forgave *when* someone asked for forgiveness, *before* someone asked for forgiveness and even if they *never* asked for forgiveness. When Jesus preached His final sermon from the Cross, His first words were, "Father, *forgive* them, for they do not know what they are doing" (Luke 23:34b). There were people in that crowd who mocked Him. There were disciples who cried for Jesus. There were Roman guards who were just doing their duty. Until the thief hanging beside Him asked to be remembered, there wasn't anyone who is crying out for forgiveness. However, Jesus forgave anyway.

Sometimes I can forgive people if they get some kind of punishment first. When my son Robb was about four, our family went to see my parents. At one point my mom had to verbally reprimand Robb about something. My son immediately fell to his knees and started praying. My first thought was, "What a sweet response!" That was until I knelt beside him and heard him whispering, "Get her God!" It's a human tendency to wish for the punishment of others. Only the presence of the Holy Spirit can enable us to let go of those people and things that have hurt us without any conditions.

If you look at the Seamless Robe that Jesus is wearing, you will see the phrase, "Let It Go!" Through Christ, we can. Remember, "If we confess our sins, he is faithful and just and will forgive us our sins and purify us from all unrighteousness" I John 1:9.

SHORT THREADS

WHAT ARE SHORT THREADS?

Do you know the difference between a plain golf shirt and the same exact shirt with a Nike check-mark logo sewn into it? About $20! That little bit of additional thread makes the shirt far more appealing to the consumer. It may not improve your score, but it sure makes people look at you differently when you triple bogey! That extra little thread makes all the difference in the world.

Along with the tightly-knit warp and woof pattern of the Bible, there are also short threads that make a passage of Scripture stand out more clearly. These threads may be contained in a single book of the Bible or may tie two or three books together. Short threads are threads that tie different chapters together. For instance, the phrase, "the just shall live by faith" ties Habakkuk 2:4 to Romans 1:17, Galatians 3:11 and Hebrews 10:38. The shortness of the use of these threads does not diminish their significance. Justification by faith was the main theme of the Protestant Reformation. Luther's discovery of this short thread revolutionized the Church!

Hopefully, these chapters will help you spot short threads throughout the Bible.

WHEN GOD'S HANDS WERE TIED

From the Cradle to the Cross

IT WAS AN UNUSUAL PLACE FOR THE SAVIOR OF THE WORLD TO make His entrance into time and space. One would think that this birth would take place in a kingly palace. However, the birth of Jesus in Bethlehem that first Christmas night took place in surroundings that were unfit for anyone, especially the King of Kings. Unlike the sterile hospital facilities we have today, this "delivery room" was filled with bacteria and germs. The smell in the air was a mixture of sweaty animals and their dung. There were no doctors or nurses to help this young couple in the delivery process. Rejected by the innkeepers in town, Mary and Joseph were thankful that they could find anywhere to be alone.

In the solitude of this stable, Mary and Joseph experienced the birth of God's child, Jesus. The angels had not sung to the shepherds yet. The wise men would not visit for a year or two. No one inside the city of Bethlehem knew that all of history had changed forever! The fulfillment of Isaiah's prophecy had come true when he wrote in Isaiah 9:6,

> For unto us a child is born, to us a son is given,
> And the government will be on his shoulders.
> And he will be called
> Wonderful Counselor, Mighty God,
> Everlasting Father, Prince of Peace

This night, the One that mankind had been searching for throughout the ages had arrived on Earth to set the captives free! The Word of God had become flesh and was dwelling among us! Later that night, the Good Shepherd would be greeted by a cluster of shepherds who had been working out on the hillsides of Bethlehem. It would be some time before the wise men brought appropriate gifts. Although the Old Testament Prophets had been predicting this event for hundreds of years, the birth went unnoticed by the throng that filled the streets of Bethlehem. They just wanted to pay their taxes and go home.

We tend to picture this night as silent and peaceful. We struggle with believing that baby Jesus would even cry. However, this was far from being a quiet or peaceful night! A war had now broken out. Satan certainly had taken notice of this event. Satan's greatest Enemy had now miraculously come to the Devil's turf: planet Earth. Strangely enough, Jesus had deliberately disarmed Himself of the heavenly arsenal He had at His beck and call. As Paul later wrote,

> Who (Jesus), being in very nature God, did not consider equality with God something to be used to his advantage; rather, He made himself nothing (emptied Himself) by taking the very nature of a servant, being made in human likeness. Philippians 2:6-7

The angels who had proclaimed Jesus' arrival had closed the portals of heaven, returning to their heavenly residence. God had never been more vulnerable. The only spiritual weapon Jesus had is *His love*! Jesus could not speak a word or move His arms and legs with any purpose. The only defense we have for our salvation is wrapped up in the hand of a little baby. What could He do? How could He save us?

As the battle lines are drawn, Jesus is completely outnumbered. On Satan's side were all the demons of Hell. His arsenal included sin, death and the grave. The Father of Lies must have thought that his moment of victory had come. On God's side, just the tiny hands and feet of a baby prepared to take on the enemy. Our confidence and hope is in the hands of Jesus.

One more step must be taken before the battle begins. Jesus' hands must be tied. As if it were not bad enough to have such a tiny Defense, God goes one step further. Luke records the next step when he writes, "And she gave birth to her firstborn, a son. She *wrapped him in cloths* and placed him in a manger, because there was no guest room available for them (Luke 2:7).

This detail is so important that the angels tell the Bethlehem shepherds that they are to look for "a baby wrapped in cloth." Although swaddling was a normal procedure when a baby was born, it has become even more popular with the young moms and dads of today. Of course, newborns are swaddled in the hospital nursery. There are even swaddling clothes that are specifically designed for this one purpose: to wrap the baby's hands and feet to their side and keep them feeling secure. Babies sleep better when they are swaddled. It is an important part of caring for a baby.

So why is the detail about the swaddling cloth so important? It is to remind us that even when God's hands are tied, Jesus has more than enough power to overcome the enemy. All that stood between all mankind and Satan's arsenal was a baby's hands. Even when Jesus could not walk or talk, even when his hands were tied, His hands were more than sufficient to hold Satan at bay.

As Satan lifted his sword in anticipation of the battle, the Prince of Peace slept. Even when Herod the Great tried to execute all the male children in Bethlehem, Jesus was kept safe by God forewarning Joseph to escape to Egypt. How frustrating it must have been for Satan to realize that our touchable God was untouchable to him.

After Mary and Joseph stayed in Bethlehem for an extended period of time, the wise men brought their costly gifts to give to this new King. Gold, frankincense and myrrh were laid at Jesus' feet. These gifts may well have provided resources for Joseph, Mary and Jesus to escape to Egypt.

Let us fast forward once again. We now stand by three Crosses outside the walls of Jerusalem. Two crowds have gathered to watch the crucifixion of the One on the middle Cross. There is a mob exhilarated by this horrendous act. There is a much smaller group standing by whose hearts are broken. Jesus has been tried by six different "juries" without being found guilty. Under the pressure of a riot, Pontius Pilate washes his hands of the dilemma and allows Jesus to be taken to the Cross.

When the four soldiers have walked Jesus down the Via Dolorosa, they complete the gruesome procedure of driving nails through Jesus' hands and feet, then lifting Him up on the Cross. Those same hands that were tied so close to Jesus' sides as a baby are now stretched out as far as are necessary to inflict the most pain possible. God has never been so vulnerable, even when Jesus was a baby, asleep in a manger.

For six long hours, Jesus preaches His final sermon[77] with what little strength He has. He requests forgiveness for those who never asked to be forgiven. Jesus makes arrangements for the care of Mary. He experiences separation from the Father that sin brings into our lives. Jesus' lips are moistened in preparation for a final victory cry, "It is finished" (John 19:30). At the very moment the priest blows the shofar sending the message it is time for the sacrifice to die, Jesus falls back into the Father's arms like a baby being held by his mother—and He dies.

`Because the time of Passover is quickly approaching, the bodies of the two criminals are taken down and removed. Joseph of Arimathea and Nicodemus ask permission to prepare Jesus' body for burial in Joseph's unused tomb. As they lay Jesus beside the Tomb, they begin a final swaddling process. Listen to John's account.

> Nicodemus [from John 3] brought a mixture of myrrh and aloes, about seventy pounds. Taking Jesus' body, the two of them *wrapped it*, with the spices, *in strips of linen*. This was in accordance with Jewish burial customs. John 19:39b-40

Using myrrh and other powerful spices, these two men wrapped the hands of Jesus by His side. Jesus' hands are no longer small and soft. Now they are marked by the scars inflicted by the nails used to Crucify Him. Instead of a manger, Jesus' body is placed in a tomb. He is unable to speak or move. The hands of God have once more been tied!

What a celebration must have taken place in Hell that night! Sin had no effect on Jesus, but Death and the Grave had double teamed Jesus to finally defeat Him. The hands of God seemed paralyzed to stop Satan's mission to "steal and kill and destroy" (John 10:10b). The plan of salvation appears to be stopped in its tracks.

The first and second day after the Crucifixion must have been filled with despair for every believer in Christ. But on the *third* day, the cloth that temporarily bound Jesus' body would lose its

---

77   What is known as the Last Seven Words of Christ are listed in the Appendix.

grip once and for all! God's Hands were no longer tied—nor will they be ever again. Satan had been defeated without God lifting a finger! Listen once again to John's account of this moment.

> Then Simon Peter came along behind him (the Apostle John) and went straight into the tomb. He saw the *strips of linen* lying there, as well as the *cloth* that had been wrapped around Jesus' head. The *cloth* was still lying in its place, separate from the *linen*. John 20:6-7

The funeral clothes could not restrain Jesus from His mission. The Tomb could not hold Jesus, because "the one who is in you is greater than the one who is in the world" (I John 4:4). The cloth around Jesus' head was lying in place as a sign that Jesus would be returning! There is no explanation for the Empty Tomb except that Jesus has been resurrected from the grave.

Ten of the disciples died for preaching that Jesus Christ was the Resurrected Christ. They did not have either the resources or the courage to overtake the Romans soldiers who were guarding the Tomb. If the Jewish leaders or Roman guards had stolen the body of Jesus, they would have produced Jesus' body at the first sign of trouble. The women who came to the Tomb would not have had enough weapons to overpower the guards or the strength to roll away the stone that sealed the Tomb shut. After all the persecution the Church has faced throughout two millennium, the Church still exists and will continue to exist until Jesus' return and into eternity.

In the book of Revelation, we see the hands of Jesus once again as the scroll of history is about to be revealed. Who would be worthy to break the seals and reveal how history would unfold? John records his vision by writing,

> But no one in heaven or on earth or under the earth could open the scroll or even look inside it. I wept and wept because no one was found who was *worthy* to open the scroll or look inside.

> Then one of the elders said to me, "Do not weep! See, the *Lion* of the tribe of Judah, the Root of David, has triumphed. He is *able to open the scroll and its seven seals.*" Then I saw a *Lamb*, looking as *if it had been slain*, standing in the center of the throne, encircled by the four living creatures and the elders.

He had seven horns and seven eyes, which are the seven spirits of God sent out into all the earth. He came and took the scroll from the *right hand* of him who sat on the throne. Revelation 5:3-7

If the hands of Jesus are strong and powerful enough to hold all of time and space, surely we can trust Him with what problems we are facing and even with our lives. There is no safer place for us to be than in the center of God's hands. One of my favorite verses is Psalm 49:16. It reads, "See, I have engraved you on the palms of my hands your walls are ever before me."

Is your life in His hands?

WHEN TWO WORLDS COLLIDE

The Shepherd-King

THEY CAME FROM TWO DIFFERENT WORLDS: SHEPHERDS AND Wise Men were at extreme opposites on the social scale. The shepherds were local boys who were waiting to grow up and get "real jobs." They would never have been on anyone's "A" list in Bethlehem. Although they were more acceptable than publicans and sinners, shepherds were not held in high regard. Spending your days working with sheep on the hillsides outside Bethlehem did not sharpen your social skills nor provide any money for gifts. Of all the people who had crowded into Bethlehem that night, these shepherds were the least likely to be chosen as eyewitnesses to this history-changing moment.

It could not be denied that God sent a special invitation for these shepherds to come to the manger. As the brilliant light of God's glory broke through the darkness of the night, the angel revealed, "I bring you good news of great joy that will be for all the people. Today in the town of David a Savior has been born to you; he is the Christ the Lord" (Luke 2:10-11). A heavenly host began to celebrate this glorious moment with praise. Forsaking their duties, these shepherds are not only the first visitors to see baby Jesus, but we find in Luke 2:16-17 that they become the first *evangelists* of this wonderful news.

On the other hand, the Wise Men seemed like the perfect choice. Not only were these men highly respected, but their search for knowledge placed them in a class of their own. They travelled from another culture far away, adding to the mystery of these Magi. They had position and wealth, but they were searching for something or Someone that could fill their hunger for truth. Little did they know they were following the star that would lead them into the presence of the Truth. They would stand in the presence of the One who placed the star in the sky.

The Magi also received a personal invitation from God to meet the Messiah. The Star that guided their travel would settle over the house in Bethlehem where Jesus, Mary and Joseph were staying. When they stopped in Jerusalem to seek help from Herod in finding this baby King, Herod gathered his chief priests and scribes. The writings of the prophet Micah held the answer when he wrote,

> But you, Bethlehem, in the land of Judah are by no means least among the rulers of Judah; for out of you will come a ruler who will be the shepherd of my people Israel. Micah 5:2

With the information they are given, the Wise Men travel the final five miles from Jerusalem to Bethlehem. In the hometown of King David, this new King would be found. Matthew records, "the star they had seen in the east went ahead of them until it stopped over the place where the child was. When they saw the star, they were overjoyed" (Matthew 2:9-10).

Unlike the shepherds, the Wise Men came prepared with gifts. Matthew reminds us, "Then they opened their treasure and presented him with gifts of gold and of incense and of myrrh" (Matthew 2:11b). These valuable gifts were fitting gifts to honor a king or deity in the ancient world: gold was the precious metal of kings, frankincense as perfume or incense, and myrrh as anointing oil. These gifts were certainly fitting to give to the new King of the Jews.

Spiritually, these three gifts had far deeper meaning. These three gifts tell the story of God's plan of salvation. It is doubtful that the Wise Men realized how perfect these gifts were to describe Jesus' ministry. One writer explains,

> In addition to the honor and status implied by the value of the gifts of the magi, scholars think that these three were chosen for their special spiritual symbolism about Jesus himself—gold representing his kingship, frankincense a symbol of his priestly role, and myrrh a prefiguring of his death and embalming.[78]

---

78   http://www.biblicalarchaeology.org/daily/people-cultures-in-the-bible/jesus-historical-j

Maybe the shepherds and Wise Men together are a perfect grouping to tell the story of Christ's birth! *Jesus is our Shepherd-King*. In fact, the history of Israel included some very important *Shepherd-Kings*. As discussed, Moses had once been a Prince of Egypt, but God called him to lead the Exodus when he was a shepherd. The prophet Amos had been called from his life as a shepherd at the pastures of Tekoa to become God's prophet. Most auspiciously, King David had his humble beginnings as a shepherd who God would anoint to become the greatest king Israel ever knew.

David would never forget his days sitting out on the same hillsides of Bethlehem where the shepherds heard the angelic announcement. The imagery of a shepherd was instilled within him. David saw God as the Great Shepherd. He writes,

> The Lord is my shepherd, I shall not be in want. He makes me lie down in green pastures, he leads me beside quiet waters, he restores my soul. He guides me in paths of righteousness for his name's sake. Psalm 23:1-3

Isaiah used shepherd imagery to draw a picture of how God cares for His people when he writes, "He [God] tends his flock like a shepherd: He gathers the lambs in his arms and carries them close to his heart; he gently leads those that have young" Isaiah 40:11.

The imagery of God as our Shepherd continues in the New Testament in Hebrews as we read, "May the God of peace, who through the blood of the eternal covenant brought back from the dead our Lord Jesus, that great Shepherd of the sheep" Hebrews 13:20.

Even John uses shepherd imagery to describe his vision of heaven. He writes,

> "For the Lamb at the center of the throne will be their shepherd; he will lead them to springs of living water. And God will wipe away every tear from their eyes" Revelation 7:17.

In John 10, Jesus Himself uses the Shepherd-King imagery as the Great I Am, adding that,

> I Am the good shepherd; I know my sheep and my sheep know me—just as the Father knows me and I know the Father—and I lay down my life for the sheep. John 10:14-15

Why would the King of Kings describe Himself in such lowly terms? What is it about the shepherd and his sheep that make the shepherds such perfect guests to attend the Nativity? The key can be found when we look at how shepherds relate to their sheep.

First, like a shepherd, *Jesus leads His flock, while they follow.* Unlike cattle, sheep are not driven from place to place. A shepherd does not get behind his sheep. Instead, he stays in front of them. The flock has to choose to follow the shepherd. Jesus always calls His disciples by saying, "Follow Me" (e.g., Matthew 4:19; Matthew 9:9; Mark 1:17; Luke 5:27; John 1:43). When Jesus describes the requirements to be His disciples, He says, "If anyone would come after me, he must deny himself and take up his cross daily and follow me" (Luke 9:23). Entrance into the Kingdom of God is not earned. It is accepted by choosing to follow Christ.

Secondly, like a shepherd, *Jesus knows His flock by name.* The Creator of the universe knows your name! You hold a special place in God's heart. In Christ, we are offered a personal, intimate relationship with God. We are called to follow our touchable God. Think of how many times in the Bible God calls someone by name. Abraham at Mount Moriah, Moses at the Burning Bush and the Apostle Paul on the Damascus Road are just three examples of God calling His followers by name. Jesus knows you and loves you anyway! The Great Shepherd knows where you are and what you are facing.

Thirdly, like a shepherd, *Jesus' voice is easily recognized.* At night, all of the flocks would be led into a common sheep pen for their protection. As a new day dawned, the shepherds would call out for their sheep. The flocks would follow the voice of their shepherd. Just as the Shepherd knew each sheep in his care, the sheep knew the voice of their shepherd.

I have often been asked how to tell the difference between God's voice and Satan's voice. There are some very definite ways to tell the difference. First, *God's voice will be clear not confusing.* When God speaks, He is definite and clear in what He tells us.

Satan specializes in confusion and doubt. Secondly, *God's voice will always be consistent with His Word.* God will never ask you to do something that is inconsistent with the Bible. Finally, *God's Voice will always be affirmed.* Paul reminds us,

> For you did not receive a spirit that makes you a slave again to fear, but you received the Spirit of sonship. And by him we cry, "Abba, Father." The Spirit himself testifies with our spirit that we are God's children. Now if we are children, then we are heirs— heirs of God and co-heirs with Christ, if indeed we share in his sufferings in order that we may also share in his glory. Romans 8:15-17

Finally, like a shepherd, *Jesus will seek out his flock.* The idea of a seeking God cannot be found anywhere else. In Bethlehem that night, the Shepherd-King came to us! Using the shepherd imagery again, Jesus tells the Parable of the Lost Sheep (Luke 15:3-7). Jesus describes His Shepherd's Heart when He says,

> Suppose one of you has a hundred sheep and loses one of them. Does he not leave the ninety-nine in the open country and go after the lost sheep until he finds it? And when he finds it, he joyfully puts it on his shoulders and goes home. Then he calls his friends and neighbors together and says, 'Rejoice with me; I have found my lost sheep.' I tell you that in the same way there will be more rejoicing in heaven over one sinner who repents than over ninety-nine righteous persons who do not need to repent. Luke 15:4-7

The word picture of the shepherd/king is essential in understanding the Kingdom of God. The Kingdom of God (God's rule in our life) will not be forced upon us. We must choose to accept Christ's offer to lead us in our life. Through the Holy Spirit, Christ offers us fellowship with Him, long before we accept Him. In what John Wesley called *prevenient grace* (grace that goes before), God brings people and circumstances into your life that make you aware of how much He loves you and how much you need Him in your life. Christ is working behind the scenes to bring us into fellowship and to keep us in fellowship with Him.

What a beautiful picture of how God longs to welcome us home. Right now, Christ is seeking you out. The shepherds and the Wise Men were the perfect guests to witness the Birth of Christ. Whether we are rich or poor, Jesus calls us into a life of fellowship with Him as we follow His lead.

If you look at Jesus in the Seamless Robe, you will notice that He holds a shepherd's staff in His hand and is wearing a crown. He will not force you into a relationship with Him, but He is working this very moment to invite you to walk with Him.

WHAT DID YOU SAY, JESUS?

John 2:4-5

MAKING SURE EVERYONE WAS HAPPY AT A JEWISH WEDDING reception was always nerve-wracking. The bride and groom were responsible to provide food and wine for their guests until the last guest went home. That could take a week or two! Running out of either food or wine was a social disgrace. It would be an embarrassment that the newlyweds would find hard to live down. Because the wedding was spontaneous,[79] the problem was calculating how much food and wine to purchase—what if Uncle Jedidiah never leaves?

In John's account of the Gospel, the changing of water into wine at this wedding would serve as the first *sign* that marked the beginning of Jesus' earthly ministry. It is not strange that this first sign took place on the *third day* (the day of deliverance) or that Jesus' first appearance is at a wedding (the celebration of a relationship). Even the secrecy of this miracle is not surprising. Jesus kept what is known as *the Messianic Secret* by often telling someone who had been healed, "Go and tell no one."

The focus of this miracle is Jesus, and rightfully so. In the changing of the water into wine, Jesus not only meets the immediate need, but visually teaches us that He has come to bring abundant joy. In John 13, Jesus will once again use water pots in the Upper Room to teach His final lesson on servanthood before He goes to the Cross.

It was a life-changing day for Mary as well. For thirty years, Mary had known Jesus as her obedient son. With the exception of staying behind in Jerusalem at twelve, Jesus had to be the perfect example of obedience. I am sure Jesus never looked at Mary and said, "Whatever!" There had never been any disrespectful words or

---

79   As we have discussed previously, the wedding started when the groom returned.

sassing. After the death of Joseph, Mary came to rely on her first-born Son on a daily basis. Mary had been comfortable knowing that whatever she asked of Jesus, He would do.

That is why I had trouble for years with Jesus' seemingly harsh response. It seemed like such a small request for Mary to come to Jesus when the couple runs out of wine. Mary just brought the need to Jesus like she had done hundreds of time before. My struggle is found in John 2:4, where we read, "*Dear woman*, why do you involve me?" Jesus replied. "My time has not yet come." What did you say, Jesus? Did you just call Mary, "dear woman?"

The only other time I heard the term "Woman" used in a similar context was by my friend Loreny. One day after school, I walked home with Loreny. When Loreny walked into his house, he yelled out to his mom, "Woman! Make me a sandwich!" I ran for cover! I did not want to be anywhere close to my friend when his mother choked him to death. Instead, she made him a sandwich. I only tried Loreny's approach once with my mom? It was not pretty! I never tried that again. How could Jesus speak to Mary so harshly?

I tried to fit Jesus into my theological "box" by trying to find an alternative meaning to the phrase, "Dear Woman." Surely, it was a term of affection spoken in love. I tried for years to find a way to make Jesus look good in this conversation. Finally, Jesus' words to Mary made sense! Mary was at the wedding as "Jesus' mother" (verse 1). When she brought the need to Jesus, she was "Jesus' mother" (verse 3). However, when Jesus responds to Mary's need, the one word Jesus uses transforms their relationship forever. By using the term "Woman," Jesus signals to Mary that His ministry has begun.

For thirty years, it was Mary speaking and Jesus doing what she asked. In one sentence, the relationship reverses. Mary transitions from being Jesus' mother to becoming a disciple. Jesus will step forward to lead and Mary will become His follower. Although I cannot prove it by the text, I see Mary taking a step back before she tells the servants "Do whatever he tells you" (John 2:5b). Mary steps out of the way and submits to Jesus' authority. Instead of trying to solve the problem herself, Mary puts her trust in Jesus.

What happened in Mary's life that day has to happen in each one of our lives. In our heads, we can accept that Jesus must be in charge of our lives. In our hearts, it is another matter. How often do we do all the talking when we pray? After we explain all of our petitions in detail, do we listen for His voice? Prayer is a two-way conversation. God will hear you, but He also wants to respond. Letting God lead is not a spiritual "Hail Mary!" when times get tough. It is the lifestyle that Christ made available to us on the Cross.

Too often, we live below the privileges God has given us through Christ. God never intended for us to tire ourselves by trying to find man-made solutions. On a daily basis, Jesus wants to reveal Himself to us. That requires us stepping out of the way. Mary's willingness to step back and let Jesus do whatever *He* wants is the call on every disciple's life.

Do you have problems right now? We all do. How are you handling them? I look back at over thirty years of being a pastor and realize that the times I remember most were not when I was working my own plan for bringing people to Christ. The best times were when I did not know what I was doing! What was happening could not be explained except that God was working. God is willing to work in your life, but you must be willing to step back and let Him be in charge.

Jesus calls Mary "Dear Woman" one more time. In one the most tender moments at the Calvary, Jesus speaks to Mary from the Cross. Listen to His words.

> When Jesus saw his mother there, and the disciple whom he loved standing nearby, he said to his mother, "Dear woman, here is your son," and to the disciple, "Here is your mother." From that time on, this disciple took her into his home. John 19:26-27

What began for Mary at Cana became a lifestyle for her, all the way to Calvary. Whatever you are facing today, could I give you some great advice? Step back and let God handle it! Always ask, "What did you say, Jesus?"

As Jesus stands before you in His Seamless Robe, He longs to hear you say, "Do whatever He says to do."

UPON THIS ROCK

IT IS THE MOST IMPORTANT ROCK ON EARTH. UNLIKE THE ROCK of Gibraltar, the significance of the Rock has nothing to do with its size or visibility. The building that houses the Rock is far better known than the Rock itself. When you look at Eastern Jerusalem from the Mount of Olives, the Dome of the Rock stands out as the most famous landmark in Jerusalem. You cannot miss spotting the gold-leaf painted roof or prominent location on the Temple Mount. However, the Rock is far more important than the building it's enclosed in.

The Hope Diamond has sold for millions of dollars, but this brown Rock is priceless! Although no amount of money could buy it, the authority over the Rock was given to a Muslim religious trust for free. When Israel took control over that part of Jerusalem after the Six-Day War in 1967, Israeli leaders (specifically Moshe Dayan) allowed an Islamic religious trust to have authority over the Temple Mount and the Dome of the Rock as a way of helping keep the peace. "Since that time non-Muslims have been allowed limited access to the area but are not permitted to pray on the Temple Mount.[80]" Jews are not allowed access at all.

The three major religions of the world meet at the Rock, each with their own significance. For Jews and Christians, this is Mount Moriah, where Abraham laid Isaac down to sacrifice him in Genesis 22. For Islam, this is the location where Mohammed's Night Journey ended as he rode a flying horse there in order to climb a golden ladder to heaven. The Rock and the ground around it has been the focus of wars throughout the ages.

The Temple Mount is the location where the Jewish Temple once stood. First by Solomon after David's death and then rebuilt by Zerubbabel after the Jews' return from Babylonian Captivity and finally by Herod the Great. Herod expanded the Temple

---

80   www.gotquestions.org/Dome-of-the-Rock.html#ixzz3I8kaRo47

Mount to make room for more people (and money) and walled it in. Herod's Temple was the Temple referred to in Jesus' ministry.

Because all three Temples stood on the exact same location, the Temple Mount is the holiest place in Judaism. Although the surface of the area is under Muslim control, archaeologists have dug underneath the surface and discovered Solomon's horse stables and other Jewish relics. Jews and Christians also believe this will be the site of the final Temple that is described in the book of Revelation.

Muslims view the Temple Mount as the third most sacred location in their religion (with Mecca being first). Muhammed's climb up a golden rope into the seventh heaven is viewed as taking place here. They view the area as the site of the Further Mosque mentioned in the Koran.

Because the location is central to the three major religions of the world, more battles have been fought over this location than anywhere else in the world. During the writing of this book, there were 15,000 Israeli soldiers surrounding the Temple Mount because of a large Islamic activity taking place outside the walls.

If this Rock could talk, it would tell us stories about some major events in both the Old and New Testament. In fact, this Rock is the setting for one of the strangest requests God has ever made. Remember, God's covenant with Abraham included three Promises: a Promised Son, a Promised Nation and a Promised Land. Of those three promises, Abraham will only see the Promised Son fulfilled in his lifetime. God's Covenant with Abraham hinges completely on Isaac. If Isaac dies, there will be no Promised Nation and no need for a Promised Land. Yet, in Genesis 22:2, we read,

> Then God said, "Take your son, your only son, Isaac, whom you love, and go to the region of Moriah. Sacrifice him there as a burnt offering on one of the mountains I will tell you about."
> Genesis 22:2

I have been guilty of reading Genesis 22 without understanding Abraham's emotions. I showed a video clip of the story of Abraham and Isaac on Mount Moriah to a Biblical Perspectives class. One of the students who had never read the Bible shouted out,

"Does his mother know they are doing this?" We know Abraham as a man of faith, but this was a heart-wrenching decision. How could God ask him to sacrifice his son? After waiting twenty-five years to see the first promise fulfilled, was that Promised Son to be taken away?

How could Abraham take his beloved son[81] and drive a knife through his heart? How could he set fire to the ultimate proof that God is faithful? Even though Abraham had six more sons after Isaac by his second wife, Keturah, Isaac was the Son of Promise. God's instructions did not make sense.

Nevertheless, the next morning, Abraham saddled up the donkeys and loaded them with the wood for the burnt offering, along with a sharp knife. I am sure his heart was filled with questions, but he chose to believe God was worthy of his trust. On the *third day* of their journey, Abraham sees Mount Moriah and realizes this is to be the place of sacrifice. Leaving the servants behind, Abraham places the wood on Isaac's shoulders. The knife that will be used to slay his son and the torch of fire that he will use to offer his son as a burnt offering, Abraham carries himself.

As Isaac evaluates the situation, he asks an obvious question, "The fire and wood are here," Isaac said, "but where is the lamb for the burnt offering?" (Genesis 22:7b). As Abraham prepares for the sacrifice of Isaac, I do not believe Abraham saw the ram in the thicket. He did not know how God was going to handle the situation. He simply knew that God was worthy of his trust. Yes, the Rock could tell the story of *God's faithfulness and Abraham's trust*.

I Run to the Rock

David remembered this same rock as a place of God's mercy. In II Samuel 24:1-17, we find David deciding to do a census of the number of fighting men in Israel. Other censuses are recorded in the Bible, but David's motive was problematic. In one of his final acts, David chose to trust more in the strength of men than the power of the Almighty.

---

81   Scholars estimate Isaac's age to be between 13 and 30, depending on interpretation of the Hebrew word for "son."

After the census, David knew what he did was a sin (II Samuel 24:10). God gives David three options for punishment. David can choose three years of famine, three months of fleeing from his enemies or three days of plague (II Samuel 24:13b). David chooses three days of plague. Over the next three days, seventy thousand people will die for David's disobedient act. It was near the rock that God commands the angel to stop the plague (II Samuel 24:16). Little did David know how important that location would become.

The Cornerstone of the Temple

Although David was not allowed to build the Temple, he was able to purchase the land where the Temple would be built. As we have seen, it is by the threshing floor of Araunah that the killing stops from the plague. As an act of repentance, David is told, "Go up and build an altar to the Lord on the threshing floor of Araunah the Jebusite" (II Samuel 24:18). David built an altar of sacrifice on the same Rock where Abraham had taken Isaac. God also sent fire on David's burnt offerings. The place of sacrifice for Abraham becomes a place of forgiveness and worship for David.

While David builds the altar, the owner of the threshing floor, Araunah the Jebusite[82] offers to give the land to David. David's answer is recorded in II Samuel 24:24 where we read,

> But the king replied to Araunah, "No, I insist on paying you for it. I will not sacrifice to the Lord my God burnt offerings that cost me anything." So David bought the threshing floor and the oxen and paid fifty shekels of silver for them. II Samuel 24:24

A few years later, King Solomon will build the Temple on this very spot. In fact, some have even suggested that the Rock was the place where the altar of the Temple was built. For certain, the Rock was a part of Solomon's Temple. Since the site of the Temple did not change, the Rock would also be a part of the rebuilt Temple under Zerubbabel and Herod the Great's expanded Temple and Temple Mount.

---

82   For the most part, Jebusites lived in and near Jerusalem.

Solomon's Temple is destroyed when Nebuchadnezzar and his Babylonian troops come to take captive the last group of exiles from Jerusalem. When the Israelites were allowed to return to Jerusalem and rebuild the Temple, Zerubbabel begins by building an altar of sacrifice on or near the Rock (Ezra 3:1-6). If the Rock could talk, it would describe the beauty of the gold-covered Temple. Maybe it would give a detailed description of the sights and smells of the Sacrificial System. I am sure part of the conversation would be about celebrating the yearly Day of Atonement and how God's Presence filled the Holy of Holies.

The Solid Rock

Above all the other events that took place at this location, the Rock would tell us about how Jesus walked on this sacred ground. Just a few hundred yards away, Jesus would be brought before Pilate by the Jewish religious leaders. Although not found guilty of any wrongdoing, God in human flesh would be flogged, mocked and sentenced to be crucified. The Son of God would become the final Sacrificial Lamb. The crowd shouting for Jesus to be crucified would still echo from the Rock. Some have even suggested that this place is where Jesus' body was prepared for the Tomb.

What was an altar of obedience for Abraham and an altar of forgiveness for David would become the altar of salvation for us all, through Christ. God's plan from Creation to the present can be traced back to this spot. The covenants of God, both Old and New, are threaded through this holy place. The Rock of Ages chose this place to exhibit His love for us. It was a love that took Him to the Cross to be sacrificed for our sins.

You may never get to see the Dome of the Rock or the Rock itself, but they are not the focus of the Bible anyway. When we see pictures of the Temple Mount, we are called to focus on the Cross. When Jesus laid His life down for us on the Cross, it changed all of history. Nothing can compare to the fulfillment of God's Divine Plan of Salvation. It is not Abraham or David or the Temple that makes this place sacred. It is the Death and Resurrection of Christ that can change our lives!

And the story is not over! It is on the Temple Mount that the Third Temple will be built someday. Events described in the book of Revelation will be fulfilled on this very spot. There is a present-day Sanhedrin in place. There are websites today that provide live 24/7 camera coverage of the Temple Mount. It is upon this rock that God will do His very best work!

The thread of Jesus' Seamless Robe is certainly woven into this Rock as a foundational place where history returns time and time again.

THE TOWEL AND THE BASIN

The Call to Servanthood

IT HAD TO BE A VERY AWKWARD MOMENT! WITHIN HOURS OF the whirlwind that would take Jesus from the Garden of Gethsemane to the Cross, the disciples were fighting over who was the greatest among them. The verbal competition showed clearly that the disciples did not hear a word of Jesus' teaching. You know that Peter's voice could be heard above all the others. In a moment that was meant to be an intimate time with His disciples, Jesus watched the Twelve as they tried to push and shove their way to the top.

Jesus did not say a word, but what He did brought an embarrassing silence to the room. He simply moved to the water pot that was sitting by the door of the Upper Room. John tells us what happened next,

> So he [Jesus] got up from the meal, took off his outer clothing, and wrapped a towel around his waist. After that, he poured water into a basin and began to wash his disciples' feet, drying them with the towel that was wrapped around him. John 13:4-5

What would be so awkward about Jesus washing the Disciple's feet? Why did the argument stop so quickly as a holy hush fell over the room? What Jesus was doing was a lowly act typically left to servants. When someone came into a Jewish home, there were three acts of greeting each visitor would expect as a part of the welcome. First, the host would greet each person with a kiss on each cheek. Second, the host would anoint the visitor's head with oil. The oil would not only refresh the guest, but the smell of the oil would cover-up the personal's body odor. Most hosts would have had no problem with kissing and anointing the guests.

It was the third act of greeting that was left for the servant to carry out. The water pot sitting beside the door was there so the servant could draw water from it, kneel down to unfasten the guest's sandals and wash their feet. How disgusting! How humbling an act was that? Because most people walked from place to place, their feet were dirty and smelly. Washing someone's feet was never pleasant.

Jesus was fulfilling the role of a servant. Instead of arguing about who was most important to Jesus, the disciples should have taken over this responsibility. As the disciples hung their heads, Jesus began dipping the towel into the basin of water and washing the feet of each disciple. The Disciples silently watched their Master without saying a word. Peter breaks the silence! Thinking he understands Jesus' message, Peter refuses the foot washing.

> "No," said Peter, "you shall never wash my feet." Jesus answered, "Unless I wash you, you have no part with me." "Then, Lord," Simon Peter replied, "not just my feet but my hands and my head as well!" Jesus answered, "A person who has had a bath needs only to wash his feet; his whole body is clean. And you are clean, though not every one of you." John 13:8-10

Peter reverses his position from total refusal to extreme acceptance. Peter asked for a bath! He missed Jesus' lesson both times. Jesus was summarizing His ministry through a living illustration. The lesson was about intentional *servanthood*, not spontaneous reactions. When the foot washing is finished, Jesus explains His actions, "I tell you the truth, no servant is greater than his master, nor is a messenger greater than the one who sent him" (John 13:16).

The lesson on servanthood Jesus taught in the Upper Room was certainly not the first lesson on that topic. Jesus had been teaching servanthood throughout His ministry. Before Jesus sent His disciples out for the first time, He shared key Kingdom Principles when He told them,

> "A student is not above his teacher, nor a servant above his master. It is enough for the student to be like his teacher, and the servant like his master" (Matthew 10:24-25).

When Jesus described the Kingdom of God, He always turned the world's system upside down. God's Kingdom is not about being first, but being last. Following Christ means I choose to be His servant. Instead of trying to be noticed, a disciple of Christ must constantly remember, "For you died, and your life is now hidden with Christ in God" (Colossians 3:3). The definition of "success" for disciples of Christ is the opposite of the world's definition. Listen,

> Jesus called them together and said, "You know that the rulers of the Gentiles lord it over them, and their high officials exercise authority over them. Not so with you. Instead, whoever wants to become great among you must be your servant, and whoever wants to be first must be your slave—just as the Son of Man did not come to be served, but to serve, and to give his life as a ransom for many." Matthew 20:25-28

The thread of servanthood is found in the Old Testament as well. When the prophet Isaiah describes the coming Messiah, he describes him as a Suffering Servant. "See, my servant will act wisely; he will be raised and lifted up and highly exalted" (Isaiah 53:13). We live in a culture that moves upward towards success. The Kingdom of God is based on working our way downward as we are willing to do whatever Jesus asks of us.

Jesus called us to be *losers*. We are called to lose ourselves in Christ. Jesus stated it best when He said, "Whoever finds his life will lose it, and whoever loses his life for my sake will find it" (Matthew 10:39). The call to being a servant for Christ is hard in a culture that is "climbing the ladder" or "at the top of their game."

During the late 19th century, an American preacher named Samuel Logan Brengle traveled to London to join forces with General William Booth, founder of the Salvation Army. Because of his excellent preaching and teaching skills, Brengle had been offered some of the largest Methodist Churches in America. Instead, he chose to join the Salvation Army in England. Booth was skeptical of Brengle's willingness to come under authority.

Booth's first assignment was to teach Bengle that his role with the Salvation Army would require he learn to be a servant for Christ. We read, "There one of his first duties was to blacken and shine the boots of his fellow cadets, a job that was considered menial."[83] Brengle carried out his assignment without complaint. Can you imagine the thoughts that could have crossed Brengle's mind? "I am one of the best preachers in the world and you want

---

83   en.wikipedia.org/wiki/Samuel_Logan_Brengle

me to polish and shine muddy boots? Never!" Instead, Brengle did as he was asked. Brengle humbled himself to be a useable instrument in God's Hands. He is not remembered for his preaching as much as he is for his life of service to those in need.

The biggest struggle the disciples had in following Christ was competing for the "Most Important Disciple" award. James and John asked for the left and right side of the Throne (Mark 10:35-37).[84] When the other disciples found out about the request, they got angry because they were vying for those positions! This competitive spirit would be divisive all the way to the Cross.

If you look at Jesus' Seamless Robe, you will notice there is dirt on the sleeves. The Kingdom of God means we will have to "roll up our sleeves" and empty ourselves of *self* in order to be useable. As Paul reminds us, "For you know the grace of our Lord Jesus Christ, that though he was rich, yet for your sakes he became poor, so that you through his poverty might become rich" (II Corinthians 8:9).

Are you a servant of Christ? There are ladders to climb even in the church. Too often, we focus more on where we are going rather than where God is leading us. Being a Servant of Christ may not bring us fame, but humbling ourselves enables God to use us to touch lives for eternity.

---

84   In Matthew's account of the event (Matthew 20:20-21), it is James and John's mother that make the request.

CALVARY STILL STANDS

The Crucifixion

IT WAS A BEAUTIFUL TREE! LOCATING IN THE MIDDLE OF THE Garden of Eden, it is one of the two trees that are mentioned by name in the Bible. Eve was correct when she "saw that the fruit of the tree was good for food and pleasing to the eye, and also desirable for gaining wisdom" (Genesis 3:6b). The problem was not with the tree. The tree of the knowledge of good and evil was forbidden because it was reserved for God alone. Only God can define what is good and evil.

As Genesis 3 shows, the ability to define right and wrong is a deadly weapon in man's hands. When man is in charge, there will always be an attempt to make "good" conform to our lifestyle, and apply the word "evil" to what others do and think. Thus, morality becomes determined by majority vote. The end result is consistently an "anything goes" mentality. As James Garlow notes, "The individual's attempt to eat from the tree indicates a desire to preempt God and to determine what is good and what is evil."[85]

The only condition of God's Covenant with Adam and Eve was that they could not eat the fruit from this one tree. The condition for the relationship was very clear. Adam and Eve could not claim ignorance. God had created Adam and Eve with a spirit. Why did God give Adam and Eve a choice? It was because God started at the greatest point of trust. All that held the relationship together was love. There had to be a *choice* made to love God back.

Trees are another thread that can be traced throughout the Bible. If you follow this thread, it will take you through the Bible from the Garden of Eden to Mount Moriah to the Cross—and you will end up in Heaven. As one writer reminds us, "A tree was involved in the entry of sin into humanity (through the tree in the

---

85   James Garlow, The Covenant: A Study of God's Extraordinary Love for You, (Beacon Hill Press: Kansas City, Missouri, 2007), page 72.

Garden), the answer to sin for humanity (through the cross), and the ultimate removal of sin in eternity (through the tree of life)."[86] Let's examine four trees that changed history.

The Curse (Genesis 2-3)

The Tree of the Knowledge of Good and Evil is first mentioned in Genesis 2:17 and we have studied it already. By partaking of the forbidden fruit, Adam and Eve not only brought a curse on themselves, but caused the tree to be cursed as well. Although the Tree of the Knowledge of Good and Evil is not mentioned after Genesis 3, this tree will serve as a symbol of the curse God placed on all mankind. The curse of Adam will play a role throughout the rest of the Bible.

For instance, as Moses gives final instructions to the Israelites, he reminds them, "If a man guilty of a capital offense is put to death and his body is hung on a tree, you must not leave his body on the tree overnight. Be sure to bury him that same day" (Deuteronomy 21:22-23a). Why would these instructions be so important? Moses explains, "because anyone who is hung on a tree is under God's curse" (Genesis 21:23b). The Tree of the Knowledge of Good and Evil serves as a symbol that we are born under the Curse of a broken relationship with Christ.

The author Rico Ho points out that "in the Old Testament laws, when a man is hung on a tree, it represents a special mark of the curse of God, or what the Apostle Paul in Galatians puts it as, the 'curse of the law.'"[87] Hanging on a tree was the ultimate humiliation. Being displayed in such a despicable manner was the main reason Saul fell on his sword (I Samuel 31:4). Having your decapitated body on display was what every king feared the most.

The Covenant (Genesis 22)

The second tree is less obvious than the first. Isaac carries this tree on his shoulders as he accompanies Abraham to the top of Mount

---

86   www.gotquestions.org/curse-hanging-tree
87   Rico Ho, http://bit.ly/1Bh9o62

Moriah[88]. God has asked Abraham to sacrifice his son Isaac as a burnt offering to God. The *tree* represented the sacrifice that must be made for our salvation. The scene on Mount Moriah serves as a foreshadowing of the Cross. On Mount Moriah, we get a glimpse of the hope to come as God provides a ram to die in Isaac's place. Can you imagine the joy in Abraham's heart as he is given back his son?

Within a stone's throw of Calvary, we see Jesus' Crucifixion acted out. What was asked of Abraham was to be *willing* to sacrifice his son. In Christ, the Father would willingly sacrifice His Son. To some degree, Abraham understood the emotions of the Cross. Is the story of the Cross so familiar to us that we no longer feel the story?

A few years ago, I attended a Christmas pageant. Having grown up in the church, I had seen lots of pageants. That night, the story came alive to me. I felt the presentation in my heart. As if it was the first time I had heard about Jesus, I found myself moved to tears. May we never become so familiar with the Story that we lose our passion for what Christ has done!

Long before the Cross, Abraham knew that God was worthy of his trust. He staked his present and future on God's faithfulness. Abraham was not disappointed. As James Garlow states, "When the Abrahamic covenant was sealed and confirmed that day, God was essentially saying to Abraham, 'Since you have honored this covenant by giving your only son, I can honor this covenant by giving my only Son.'"[89]

The Cross (Matthew 27:33-44)[90]

How do you break the Curse on mankind? God takes the weapons of the enemy and uses them against him.[91] (This principle is also

---

88   James Garlow shares that the Hebrew word for "wood" and "tree" are the same.

89   Garlow, page 74.

90   Also Mark 15:22-32; Luke 23:33-43 and John 19:17-24

91   In comparison, being crucified was the Roman's vilest punishment and being "hung on a tree" was the Jewish equivalent.

a thread throughout the Bible: David fought many of his battles with the sword of Goliath Isaiah 21:9]; when God punishes the Israelites by sending venomous snakes among them [Number 21:6-9], God's antidote is to "make a snake and put it up on a pole; anyone who is bitten can look at it and live" [Numbers 21:8].)

We all know John 3:16, but in the two verses before that wonderful proclamation, Jesus draws us back to the *snake story*. As He explains the born-again life, Jesus tells Nicodemus, "Just as Moses lifted up the *snake* in the desert, so the Son of Man must be lifted up, that everyone who believes in him may have eternal life" (John 3:14-15). No matter what Satan uses against us (even snakes), God turns the powerful weapon of the Enemy to bring victory.

Jesus defeats Death by dying! Jesus confronts Satan's ultimate weapon face-to-face. Jesus experiences death in its fullest form. The death of Christ is an intentional attack of love. Jesus explains, "Greater love has no one than this, that he lay down his life for his friends" (John 15:13). It was not because of our worthiness. In Romans 5, Paul reminds that Christ died for us when we were *powerless* (verse 6), *sinners* (verse 8) even *enemies of God* (verse 10).

The Resurrection of Christ is the antidote for the grave. Easter is a celebration of the fact that the Tomb is empty! Jesus faced the grave and won the victory once and for all! Satan has been disarmed. We have the calm assurance that there is life beyond the grave. Paul writes, "If we have been united with him like this in his death, we will certainly also be united with him in his resurrection" (Romans 6:5).

But how do you break the Curse of the Forbidden Tree? Jesus faces the ultimate Cursed Tree of all time, the Cross. Crucifixion can be traced back to the Persian Empire. The Greeks borrowed it from the Persians. When the Romans borrowed crucifixion from the Greeks, they perfected it to an art form. Roman soldiers prided themselves in being able to inflict the maximum pain over the longest period of time. Crucifixion was such a terrible way to die that Roman citizens were exempted from being executed in such a manner, no matter what crime they might commit.

Unlike most forms of execution, crucifixion was not meant to kill the person immediately. Crucifixion was not designed to make the person bleed to death. Success was measured by *how much* pain was inflicted and *how long* it took for the person to die. As the condemned hung in public display, they would experience the effects of dehydration and collapsing lungs. The agonizing process could take days. The horrifying cries of the condemned served as a warning to others about disobeying Caesar. The crosses were placed outside the entrance gates so that all could see and hear.

Why is this the perfect way for Jesus to die? *Spiritually*, Jesus uses Satan's most vile weapon as the means of our redemption. Jesus breaks the Curse of the Forbidden Tree by defeating Death on the Cross. The ugly symbol of sin becomes the beautiful symbol of life. As Paul writes, "Christ redeemed us from the curse of the law by becoming a curse for us, for it is written: "Cursed is everyone who is hung on a tree" (Galatians 3:13). Rico Ho summarizes,

> We are all cursed in our sins and the just punishment is death and to be hung on a tree. But Jesus came to redeem us from the curse of the law by becoming a curse for us, and in that sense to be hung on the cross, or tree, on our behalf. He took our sins on His body, and hence the curse, literally implicating Himself with Deuteronomy 21:22-23.[92]

Physically, Jesus died on His own terms. The Roman soldiers did not *take* Jesus's life from Him. He *gave* His life for us. In order to quicken the process of death before Passover began, the Roman soldiers broke the legs of the two criminals at 3 p.m. These men would no longer be able to gasp for air by using their legs to push up. By their cruelty, the soldiers caused the criminals to die.

However, when they approached Jesus to break His legs, they realized Jesus had already died. Jesus has already called out with a loud voice, "Father, into your hands I commit my spirit" (Luke 23:46). With the words of Psalm 31:5 on His lips, Jesus breathed His last. The sword thrust into Jesus' side only verified that He was already dead. The Cross was an intentional act of God.

Symbolically, the Cross was the perfect way for Christ to die, because it *suspended Him between Heaven and Earth*. For us, Jesus is the only One worthy of building the bridge back between God

---

92   Rico Ho, http://hungryforgodsword.blogspot.com/2009/05/jesus-hung-on-tree-or-cross.html

and man. With His Death and Resurrection, Jesus pays the price for us to return to God.

The Celebration

The final Tree is found in both Genesis and Revelation. The Tree of Life found in the Garden of Eden reappears in John's vision of Heaven. "He who has an ear, let him hear what the Spirit says to the churches. To him who overcomes, I will give the right to eat from the tree of life, which is in the paradise of God" (Revelation 2:7).

There is a major difference in God's reaction to the Tree of Life in Genesis 3 as compared to His response in Revelation 22. Instead of being driven away from the Tree of Life after the Fall, those who have put their trust in Christ are welcomed to come to the Tree of Life. Jesus says, "Blessed are those who wash their robes, that they may have the right to the tree of life and may go through the gates into the city" (Revelation 22:14).

James Garlow asks a key question when he asks, "What's the difference? What happened between the first few pages of Genesis and the final few pages of Revelation?"[93] The answer is that Jesus, "having canceled the written code, with its regulations, that was against us and that stood opposed to us; he took it away, nailing it to the cross" (Colossians 2:14).

Through Jesus' victory on the Cross, all those who have been cleansed by the Blood of Christ can partake of the fruit of the Tree of Life. The reason for our celebration is explained further in the next verse when Paul writes, "And having disarmed the powers and authorities, he made a public spectacle of them, triumphing over them by the cross" (Colossian 2:15).

Peter concludes, "He himself bore our sins in his body on the tree, so that we might die to sins and live for righteousness; by his wounds you have been healed" (I Peter2:24). The Blood of Jesus shed on the Cross becomes a cleansing agent of our sins. Listen to the words of rejoicing over the One Who defeated sin, death and the grave!

---

93   Garlow, page 74.

Then the angel showed me the river of the water of life, as clear as crystal, flowing from the throne of God and of the Lamb down the middle of the great street of the city. On each side of the river stood the *tree of life*, bearing twelve crops of fruit, yielding its fruit every month. And the leaves of the *tree* are for the healing of the nations. No longer will there be any curse.

The throne of God and of the Lamb will be in the city, and his servants will serve him. They will see his face, and his name will be on their foreheads. There will be no more night. They will not need the light of a lamp or the light of the sun, for the Lord God will give them light.

And they will reign for ever and ever. The angel said to me, "These words are trustworthy and true. The Lord, the God of the spirits of the prophets, sent his angel to show his servants the things that must soon take place. Amen!" Revelation 22:1-6

Jesus' Seamless Robe has splinters in it, because Jesus hung on the Tree (the Cross) to break the curse of sin. The Cross is an offensive symbol to those who are enemies of Chrsit. Many have sacrificed their life, because they were "people of the Cross." Calvary still stands!

A SOLDIER'S STORY

dedicated to Wanda Carr

Can you imagine what it must have been like for the soldiers who crucified Jesus? "A Soldier's Story" is about viewing the Crucifixion of Jesus through the eyes of the Centurion who oversaw the four men who led Jesus to the Cross. This story is not in the Bible, but does use several of the threads included in the Gospel accounts.

I HAD NOT SLEPT WELL THE NIGHT BEFORE. I NEVER LIKED COMing to Jerusalem for Passover. It was always packed with people who hated Roman soldiers. The days were long and tense. The atmosphere could change from celebration to violence in just seconds. It did not help that Pontius Pilate had massacred 19 Jews near Jerusalem not long ago. Pontius Pilate's abuse of the Jewish people not only caused him to be hated by the Jews, but he was also in trouble with Rome! Caesar had warned him that if one more thing happened, Pilate would pay a price.

To make matters worse, all of us—Pontius Pilate, we Roman soldiers and even the criminals who faced execution—were housed in Antonio's Fortress. Some called it the Praetorium. Whatever name you chose, it could not change one fact—it was too small. We were sleeping within a stone's throw of the men we were going to execute in a matter of days.

The building was built by Herod the Great so he could spy on activity inside the Temple walls. Herod intentionally built the walls higher than the Temple walls for that very reason. The four towers gave us an excellent vantage point to watch activity inside the Temple walls. For just Herod, it would have been more than adequate space. However, when you try to crowd hundreds of Roman soldiers into the same area, we not only had to worry about the actions of the Jews; but the reactions of our fellow soldiers. More than one life had been lost from the infighting within this building.

But my restlessness was not caused by my fellow soldiers. I had already fallen asleep when I was awakened at midnight by the sound of Jewish men singing. I did not understand their words, but I could hear them clearly as they walked out the main gate of the city directly below my quarters. It was unusual for people to be out this late, but it was the joy in their singing that haunted me. It made it difficult to close my eyes. What did they have to be joyful about? As their voices faded, I tried to get some much needed rest. Of all nights, I needed my sleep that night! Tomorrow was the beginning of Passover. The emotions of the Jews would reach the boiling point.

Shortly before 1 a.m., I heard loud noises as my room lit up like daylight! I ran to the window to see hundreds of soldiers accompanying the High Priest and some of his cohorts out the same gate the Jewish men used earlier. They were carrying torches and swords as they headed east out of the City. Where were they going so late at night? What was so important that required so many soldiers? All that mattered to me was that I had not been called to be involved. I returned to my bed.

Within the hour, the mob was back! When I looked down at the gate, I only saw one man being brought in. He'd been beaten, but did not put up any resistance to the abuse. As the light of one of the torches illumined his face, I recognized it as the one they called Jesus. This Jewish teacher had been a problem for the Jewish religious leaders throughout the week, but he had caused us little problem. He had turned over some tables and chased out the Jewish moneychangers on the Temple grounds, but thankfully the people were angry at Jesus, not us.

It was the middle of the night, but the voices soon faded as the mob moved to the south and west. Whatever happened to Jesus did not involve me, so I finally fell sound asleep. I knew nothing of the injustices carried out by the Jewish religious leaders against Jesus. All of their so-called *trials* were held on the opposite side of town. Most of them took place inside homes or some other buildings.

Shortly before sunrise, I heard the sound of an angry mob as they approached Antonio's Fortress. Whatever was happening, I could no longer ignore it. This was a blood-thirsty crowd. I could barely distinguish Pontius Pilate's voice as he tried to appease the crowd. There was no question about what the mob wanted. They wanted someone to be crucified! I made sure I had my sword as I got dressed to go outside.

What has a person done that would cause this crowd's response? Surely, I was about to see a murderer or a thief. Instead, there stood Jesus. Calling for him to be crucified seemed excessive for turning over some tables. Jesus had not broken our law and had even healed some people throughout the week. What charge could be brought that would make Jesus worthy of death? *Blasphemy* was the charge brought to Pontius Pilate. This was a Jewish religious offense. The Roman Empire was home to a panorama of gods. We never crucified for religious practices. You could worship whatever god you want.

In a very smart political move, Pontius Pilate sent Jesus to the west side of town to the Palace of Herod Antipas. Let Herod the Great's son deal with this religious issue! Since Jesus was a Jew being charged by the Jewish religious leaders, why not send him to the present King of the Jews? Unfortunately, Herod Antipas had no power to crucify. Only the Roman government had authority to carry out a crucifixion.

In order to force Pontius Pilate to act, the religious leaders came back with a new charge, *Treason*! Threats against Rome were charges worthy of crucifixion. I could see beads of sweat beginning to form on Pilate's brow. If this crowd riots, Pilate will be removed from power at best or even worse, executed by Rome. However, he had to take the charge of treason seriously. How could he both satisfy the crowd and keep this mob in line.

In one final attempt to appease the crowd, Pilate remembered that Jewish custom allowed a prisoner to be set free during Passover. Wisely, Pilate offered Barabbas as an alternative choice for the crowd. We had tried for years to catch this low-life. Barabbas did not have a conscience. He had murdered numerous of his enemies, including both Romans and Jews. I had even looked forward to watching Barabbas die the slow, painful death we would inflict on him. Jesus or Barabbas? The choice seemed so obvious.

But the crowd shocked all of us when they cried for the freedom of "Barabbas! Barabbas!"

I was going to enjoy leading my squadron of four to the scourging for Barabbas! I longed to see the crowd take their opportunity to beat him and curse him. I wanted to drive the nails into his hands myself. Then I heard the order, "Julius, go release Barabbas and set him free!" You should have seen the look on Barabbas' face when I stood at his prison cell with my keys. There was terror in his eyes. If anyone was worthy of being crucified, it was Barabbas. Now the serial murderer cowered in the corner of his cell.

I nearly choked on my words when I told Barabbas, "I have come to set you free. One named Jesus is going to die in your place. You are free to go." It took a moment for the words to sink into his head. Cautiously, he got up and walked out into a freedom he did not deserve. He looked over his shoulder the whole way out of the building. No one would understand the salvation that Jesus would bring on the cross more than Barabbas. The middle cross had been intended to be his place of death.

When I returned to my station near the mob, I heard Pontius Pilate ask, "What shall I do with the King of the Jews?" The crowd answered, "Crucify him! Crucify him!"[94] Pilate was physically shaken, because he could not find Jesus guilty of any wrongdoing, Pilate washed his hands in front of the crowd trying to relieve himself of any responsibility for what was about to happen.

Although he knew it broke Roman law, Pilate announced that Jesus would be crucified. "Julius, take four of your men and escort the prisoner to his flogging." Me? All of my anger had been spent on Barabbas. I had no desire to see this Jesus crucified! Doing my duty had never been so hard. I watched four of my best men surround Jesus as they walked him to the place of flogging.

My men were good at their job! They knew how to strike a criminal just hard enough to inflict the greatest pain and yet not kill him. It was a fine line between near death and death, but we were experts at going just far enough.

Jesus's back was stripped of any clothing. The soldiers picked up their whips and waited for my count. Each time I counted,

94   Matthew 15:12-13

the soldiers would hit Jesus with the sharp metal at the end of their whips. I began the count, "1, 2, 3, 4 …" Each time the end of the whip would rip flesh from Jesus' back. The cries of pain usually made me hungry for more. Today, I cringed inside. I was so relieved when I called out, "39!"[95] Blood trickled down Jesus's back as we dressed him and prepared him for the next step.

Although Jesus was staggering from the agony of the flogging, I ordered my men to place the crossbeam on Jesus' shoulders. The crossbeam was heavy to carry in normal circumstances, but after being beaten nearly to death, the pressure was unbearable. For the first time, I felt sadness for a prisoner as I watched Jesus stumble, trying to take each step. I eventually ordered a man out of the crowd to help him bear the crossbeam.

We never took a prisoner directly to the site of the crucifixion. That would be too easy. With the crossbeam on his shoulder, the prisoner would begin the walk down the Via Dolorosa. The path was configured so that it would provide the longest route to the crucifixion site.

Also known as the Way of Sorrow, the narrow path wound around the streets of Jerusalem. This gave the people of the city opportunity to abuse the prisoner personally. I have never seen someone treated with greater contempt than Jesus.

When we finally arrived at the crucifixion site at Golgotha, I ordered my men to begin the crucifixion process. They laid Jesus on his back across the vertical bar of the cross and joined the horizontal piece to it. Having borrowed this method of execution from the Greeks, we perfected the crucifixion process that had originated with the Persians. We were experts in how to make sure the arms were stretched out to the point of inflicting the greatest pain and limiting the movement of the arm. My men knew exactly how to find the opening in the wrist bone where a nail could be driven without causing much blood loss or without breaking a bone.

---

95   Forty minus one was found to be the breaking point between extreme suffering and death. Whipping someone 40 times could end in death. The purpose behind crucifixion was to make the pain last as long and as intensively as possible without causing death.

The feet of Jesus were next. The correct positioning of the legs was vital. The last thing we wanted was to allow the prisoner to push up with his legs and catch a short breath of relief. The fear of not being able to breathe was much more terrifying. Once again, my men placed Jesus' legs in the most uncomfortable position possible and found the hole in the anklebone that allowed a nail to be driven through the ankle without blood loss or breaking bones. Each hammer blow made me feel nauseas! I found myself unable to look at Jesus while he was being crucified.

Using a rope system, my men lifted Jesus' cross into place. There is a moment in the lifting process where temporary paralysis sets in. The splinters of the wood digs into the raw back at the same time the body goes numb. The panic of not being able to breathe sets in. Why was I trembling? I had seen this pain inflicted hundreds of times before. Why was I shaking as I watched Jesus being lifted up?

It was nine o'clock in the morning when the crucifixion of Jesus began. Two other prisons were suspended in air on either side of Jesus. Even the doomed prisoners began mocking Jesus. The religious leaders stood at the foot of the Cross and challenged Jesus to call angels to take him down. I had never seen such hatred expressed for a prisoner under my care.

In the midst of all the chaos, Jesus began to speak. His words were soft, but clear. I heard him say, "Father, forgive them, for they do not know what they are doing."[96] How could this man who had been treated so unjustly pray for forgiveness for those who unashamedly hurled insults at him? No one was even *asking* for forgiveness! From that moment forward, it was if I became deaf. I could see Jesus talking to one of the criminals and to his family, but it was as if I was having a dream. In that surreal setting, Jesus' words of forgiveness kept ringing in my ears.

When Jesus died, it was like a child falling asleep in his father's arms. Such peace! Such purpose! Jesus was unlike anyone who I had ever known. A sense of love and acceptance fell over me. I began to weep unashamedly. Then the sky became dark and an

---

96   Luke 23:34

earthquake shook the ground around me. Terrified, I knelt and exclaimed, "*Surely he was the Son of God!*[97]

As I knelt at the foot of the Cross, I felt drops of the blood of Jesus fall on me. For the first time in my life, I felt free!

---

97   Matthew 27:54

APPENDIX

THE BREATH OF GOD

By Gabriela Rodriguez

THE MORNING OF MAY 20TH 2013, STARTED OFF IN A WONDERFUL way. It was my birthday week and I always look forward to my birthday. It was a gloomy Monday morning, but even that couldn't erase the anticipation I felt for the week ahead. By mid-morning the weather had cleared up and it was sunny and humid. I went to lunch with my husband. Shortly after returning back to the office after lunch it started raining pretty hard.

My husband called me and told me that it was hailing outside really bad where he was at and that he had heard that there was a tornado heading to Norman/Moore. He suggested I leave the office and head to the kid's school to check them out. I struggled with the decision, because I felt that perhaps they were safer in the school building. I kept thinking, "they are safe in that building." Regardless, I closed down the office quickly and headed south to check out my kids. My husband was on the north side of town and we agreed to meet and "ride out" the bad weather at home.

By the time I left the parking lot of the church where I am employed, the weather had taken a turn for the worse. Hail was threatening to break the windshield of my new Honda Civic that we had recently purchased. I felt nervous and frazzled, because I could hardly see anything in front of me. Fortunately, the streets were empty. I kept flipping through stations trying to hear the weather but couldn't find anything. The rain and hail were deafening and blinding by this point.

Three different times I tried to stop and take cover, first under the portico of a church, but someone beat me to it just as I was pulling in. Then I tried to take shelter at two different gas stations, but just as I was pulling in someone would take the only open spot, so I just kept driving. I had lost all communication with my husband by that point and I was just concentrated on getting to my children's school, Briarwood Elementary.

When I finally arrived at their school about 20 minutes after leaving my job, I looked as if their school had been deserted. It felt like the scene of a *Left Behind* movie. Cars were randomly parked everywhere in the parking lot. Some cars were running and doors were open on others. I couldn't find a parking spot so I followed the flow and left my car and ran the rest of the way to the front office. To my dismay, no one was there. It was pitch black and it seemed everyone was already taking cover.

I ran to my daughter's class first and knocked on the door. I told the teacher that I was there to check out Abby. The teacher quickly gave Abby to me. We then rushed to find my son Estaban who was in the kindergartener's classroom. They were taking cover in a dark hallway and so I basically was shouting his name in the dark trying to find him. When I got to him I was still fully expecting to get in my car and take my kids home. At that exact moment I got a text from my dad that said "please tell me you are in a shelter somewhere, because a tornado is coming your way right now." His text convinced me to take shelter with my kids at the school rather than to leave. Almost immediately, I started to hear louder sounds outside and quickly had the kids assume tornado position in the hallway.

I heard a teacher or principal with a walkie talkie in hand say, "it just hit Stone Meadows" which is the edition where we live and was very close to the school. I immediately threw myself on top of my kids and just kept saying "Oh God, please protect us and everyone here." It then felt and sounded like a runaway train was headed our way. The speed of the wind picked up more and more. Then I felt as if a train hit us from every direction, ran over us and left us trapped among rubble and debris. All the while I could hear myself comforting my children. "It's okay, my loves, God is with us. We are going to be okay…God is with us….we are going to be okay…God is with us."

After the tornado passed, we were trapped under rubble and debris for what seemed like hours, but indeed it was not that long at all. A nice older gentleman removed rubble from on top of us and created a small passage for us to get out from under the mess we found ourselves in. We immediately found ourselves outside and unprotected from the elements. All I could hear all around were the shouts and terrifying screams of young children. I just embraced my own terrified children and tried to comfort some of their classmates whose parents were not there.

My heart was racing with so much adrenaline. My mind was racing with so many questions. So many questions. Did my husband make it home in time to get out of the tornado? Was he caught in the storm while driving? Should I go home or stay at the school? Do we even have a house to go to? What can we do to help others?

Everything outside was a clean sweep. The parking lot that had been full of cars 15 minutes beforehand was completely clean. No traces of cars remained on it. We couldn't find our vehicle. I started to walk home with my kids. With what seemed like a war scene all around us, we saw my husband running towards us. We embraced as a family as we were finally reunited.

We prayed thanking God for his protection over us and prayed for everyone else around us and those even more affected by the storm. We found our house still standing, heavily damaged but standing. All our cars totaled, our community forever changed.

A few days later, we processed the tornado experience with our children. I asked my daughter if she felt any debris hit her at all? Neither she or my son had even a little scratch on them. She said, "no I didn't feel any pain at all. All I could *feel was your breath on top of me* and that *made me feel safe.*"

I immediately thought about that short text that came from my earthly father shortly before the tornado hit. The text had convinced me to stay at the school and take cover there rather than try to rush home in the mess. Had that text not come when it did, I would probably not be alive to write this at this time. My kids and I would have been caught in that storm outside, unprotected and in a car that was totally deformed in the storm.

I thanked God for not just my earthly fathers' very opportune text, but for His perfectly-timed guidance, direction and wisdom every step of my journey through life. At just the right time, He whispers to me if I just simply take the time to stop in the midst of the craziness and business of life and simply listen to His voice and take the time to read His text to me.

My daughter's comment about feeling safe because my breath was upon her also made me think of God's breath on me. As I lay there, on top of my children trying to protect them from the F-5 tornado tearing through our house, school, and community, God's very present breath was upon me. I've since thought of so many moments when God's breath was visibly upon me. Of times when in the *overwhelming-ness* of life, His peace surrounds me. When in times of despair, His love sustains me. When in times of loneliness, His presence is near. His breath was and indeed has been upon me; calming me and making me feel safe in His embrace.

His breath marks the difference in my life. His breath helps me to breathe when the demands of the world around me threaten to suffocate and overwhelm my soul. His breath of peace, love, serenity and grace surround me and allow me to breathe and therefore live life and live it to the full. Thank God for that sweet breath from heaven here on earth!

THE STEPS OF MAKING A BLOOD COVENANT[98]

A series of events are set into motion when two people decide they want to "cut the covenant." It is referred to as the blood covenant ceremony and is considered a most serious and solemn event.

1. *An animal is sacrificed*: Usually a bull, a goat, or a lamb is killed and cut in half down the center. The two halves are separated with a pool of blood between them.

2. *The exchange of coats*: Each participant removes his coat, a sign of the tribe's identity and authority, and gives it to the other participant. By doing so, each is saying, "Everything I am, everything I represent now belongs to you."

3. *The exchange of weapon belts*: Each participant removes his weapon belt, which included his sword and bow. They would exchange these belts and, by so doing, declare to each other, "All my strength now belongs to you. My enemies are now your enemies." It was saying that when an enemy attacked then my blood covenant brother had a responsibility to defend me the same as he would himself.

4. *The exchange of names*: Each participant takes the other's name on himself. A person's name represents his individuality. This exchange of names demonstrated a death to being an "individual." Remember that covenant is the union of two people. In covenant you are no longer concerned only with yourself. Your concern now includes your blood covenant brother. You care for your blood brother the same as you care for yourself because the two of you are now one.

5. *The walk of blood*: Each participant walks a path in the shape of a figure "8" between the halves of the slain

---

98 www.rockofoffence.com/myst4.html

animal, then stops in the middle in the midst of the pool of blood to pronounce the blessings and the curses of the covenant. The curses would be brought to bear upon the one who broke the blood covenant. It basically said, "the one who breaks this covenant will die just like this animal has died." A pledge was also made that said, "Just as this animal gave its life so I will give my life for you if necessary."

6. *The cut of the covenant*: A knife is used to make an incision in either the palms or the wrists of each participant. This was to allow blood to freely flow. The Bible teaches that life is in the blood. The two participants then engage in a handshake allowing the free flowing blood to intermingle. This symbolized the two bloods, the two lives, being joined into one blood and one life. In some cultures, the blood from each participant is mixed into a cup of wine. Each would drink from the cup demonstrating their union. The actual practice of "cutting the covenant" varies in its methods depending on the culture. When this event was finished, a substance would be rubbed into the wounds so they would never heal cleanly. This was done so that a permanent "mark" would be left. Wherever these men would go, they would be identified as a "covenant man" by the visible mark on their bodies.

7. *The covenant meal*: This is usually a meal of bread and wine. Each fed the other signifying that "all that I am is coming into you." The covenant meal usually ended the blood covenant ceremony. At this point a new relationship is born. It is a love relationship. This kind of love is called "Hesed" in Hebrew and "Agape'" in the Greek. It is a love that says, "I will never leave you or forsake you."

THE SEVEN LAST WORDS OF CHRIST

JESUS' CRUCIFIXION BEGAN AT 9 A.M. ON FRIDAY MORNING OF Passover week and ended at 3p.m. that same Friday with Jesus' last breath. During the six hours of hanging on the Cross, Jesus spoke seven sentences that are known as *The Seven Last Words of Christ*. They are the seven statements that are recorded in the gospel accounts of Christ's death. In the midst of the hostile crowd and the agony of being crucified, Jesus carries on a private conversation with the Father.

In his powerful sermon *Were You There?* Dr. Peter Marshall, former chaplain of the Senate, describes Jesus being lifted up on the Cross as Jesus "mounting His final pulpit."[99]

Jesus' final sermon may not have been as long as the Sermon on the Mount, but it was just as powerful. Here are the Seven Last Words of Christ in chronological order and with some footnotes to explain the timing and significance of each word.

1. "Father, forgive them, for they do not know what they are doing." Luke 23:34

This word was spoken shortly after Jesus was lifted up on the Cross. There are two crowds at the Cross: an angry mob that is mocking Jesus and a small group of disciples who are crying. No one was asking to be forgiven. Jesus forgave *before* He was asked to forgive, *when* He was asked to forgive and even if He *never was asked to forgive.*

This word was spoken at 9 a.m. which is the first time of prayer for the Jews and the time when the Temple gates were opened. Jesus probably prayed this prayer several times throughout His crucifixion. The sky becomes dark at this moment. *See Stephen's parallel prayer in Acts 7:60.

---

99 To hear the whole sermon, go to www.sermonaudio.com/sermoninfo. asp?SID=924082030352

2. "I tell you the truth, today you will be with me in paradise." Luke 23:43

When the Cross of Jesus is first lifted into standing position, Matthew tells us that the two criminals being crucified on either side of Jesus both join in the crowd's mocking of Jesus (Matthew 27:44). Remember that only the worst of criminals were crucified. It is ironic that they would find fault with Jesus.

At one point, one of the criminals has a change of heart. Luke's account records that moment when Luke writes,

> One of the criminals who hung there hurdled insults at him: Aren't you the Christ? Save yourself and us!" "But the other criminal rebuked him (the other criminal). 'Don't you fear God,' he said, 'since you are under the same sentence? We are punished justly, for we are getting what our deeds deserve. But this man has done nothing wrong. Luke 23:39-41

John records the conversation between Jesus and the seeking criminal. The criminal makes a special request of Jesus when he states, "Jesus, remember me when you come into your kingdom" (Luke 23:42). Jesus' words apply Jesus' willingness to forgive. Jesus answers, "I tell you the truth, today you will be with me in paradise" (Luke 23:43).

3. "Dear woman, here is your son," and to the disciple, "Here is your mother." John 19:26-27

This third word is spoken as the soldiers are divvying up Jesus' clothing. There were four soldiers who guarded a prisoner and actually crucified a person. One of the rewards for their participation in this gruesome process was taking the clothing of the person being crucified. There were four soldiers and five pieces of clothing. The seamless robe of Jesus was the remaining article of clothing. This robe was usually made by a man's mother when the man left home.

The robe represented a special bond between Mary and Jesus. While the soldiers are casting lots for the special robe, Jesus makes sure that Mary is taken care of. Jesus hands the care over to the "disciple whom Jesus loved." Throughout John's Gospel account, this phrase is what the Apostle John uses to refer to himself. The same phrase is used in the recording of Jesus' conversation with Peter about forgiveness for his denial of knowing Jesus during Jesus' trial. At the end of Jesus' conversation with Peter, we read, "

> Peter turned and saw that the disciple whom Jesus loved was following them. (This was the one who had leaned back against Jesus at the supper and had said, "Lord, who is going to betray you?") John 21:20

4. "*Eloi, Eloi, lama sabachthani?*"—which means, "My God, my God, why have you forsaken me?" Mark 15:34

This word of Jesus is the most difficult to understand. To hear these words spoken by the One who knew no sin is heart-wrenching. We are reminded of the burden that Jesus was carrying at this moment when the Apostle Paul wrote, "God made him who had no sin to be sin for us, so that in him we might become the righteousness of God" (II Corinthians 5:21).

It helps to realize that Jesus is quoting the first line of Psalm 22. Since there were no chapter or verse markings in Jesus' day, the Rabbis would teach their students by using the first line of a particular Psalm. Psalm 22 describes many of the events of Jesus' death but ends with a message of hope. This word was spoken at noon.

5. "I am thirsty." John 19:28

Here is proof of Jesus' humanity. Like all mankind, Jesus experiences thirst. Having refused a medicated drink at a prior time in the crucifixion (Mark 15:23), Jesus now requests this water on a hyssop branch in order to wet his lips in preparation of His next shout of victory.

A bunch from the hyssop bush was used by the Israelites (Exodus 12:22) to place the blood of the Passover lamb on the doorposts before the tenth plague that came on Pharaoh and the Egyptians. This was the death of the first-born of every person and all animals if blood was spread on the doorpost. The pattern of marking the doorpost was in the shape of a Cross.

6. "It is finished." John 19:30

Jesus' mission to pay the price for our salvation is finished. Noticed, that he shouts this word. Jesus's lips have been parched by the Crucifixion and the hot sun. Wetting his lips with the water from the hyssop enables Jesus to lift His voice in this shout of triumph.

7. "Father, into your hands I commit my spirit." Luke 23:46

Jesus is quoting Psalm 31:5. It is 3 p.m. on Friday when Jesus breathes His last breath. This is the exact time when the shofar (animal's horn) is blown to announce that it is time for each family's Passover lamb to be slain. Jesus becomes our last Passover Lamb.

HOW TO FIND THREADS

LET'S TAKE THE MIRACLE OF THE WATER CHANGED INTO WINE in John 2:1-11 to show part of the process of finding threads in a passage. Here are some of the questions that should be asked as we examine a Scripture passage along with answers for this miracle. First, let's look at the passage.

> On the third day a wedding took place at Cana in Galilee. Jesus' mother was there, and Jesus and his disciples had also been invited to the wedding. When the wine was gone, Jesus' mother said to him, "They have no more wine."
>
> "Dear woman, why do you involve me?" Jesus replied. "My time has not yet come."
>
> His mother said to the servants, "Do whatever he tells you."
>
> Nearby stood six stone water jars, the kind used by the Jews for ceremonial washing, each holding from twenty to thirty gallons.
>
> Jesus said to the servants, "Fill the jars with water"; so they filled them to the brim. Then he told them, "Now draw some out and take it to the master of the banquet." They did so, and the master of the banquet tasted the water that had been turned into wine. He did not realize where it had come from, though the servants who had drawn the water knew. Then he called the bridegroom aside and said, "Everyone brings out the choice wine first and then the cheaper wine after the guests have had too much to drink; but you have saved the best till now."
>
> This, the first of his miraculous signs, Jesus performed at Cana in Galilee. He thus revealed his glory, and his disciples put their faith in him. John 21:1-11

1. Read the passage *three* times, *twice* silently and *once* out loud. Speaking the words out loud helps to truly hear the passage.

2. What is the main focus of the passage? The miracle of Jesus changing the water into wine.

3. What are details that would not have to be mentioned to convey the main focus?

- On the third day (the day of Jesus' Resurrection).

- At a wedding (the word picture of unity and celebration).

- Cana (Nathaniel's home town, the name means "place of reeds" plus reed is mentioned in one of Isaiah's Messianic passages in Isaiah 42:3).

- Water Pots (used for foot washing; a servant's role; one was used by Jesus in John 13 for the washing of the disciples' feet; six water pots would suggest that it was a large wedding).

- Mary referred to as Jesus' mother in verse 1 and 3, but addressed by Jesus as "Dear Woman" (Transition for Mary from her role as Jesus' mother to stepping back to become a follower of Jesus)

- Water and wine (water represented cleansing and wine represented joy).

- The quality of the wine is noticeably better (there is greater joy in living for Christ; abundant life in John 10:10b).

- The use of the word *sign* (used throughout John to describe the miracles of Jesus that are recorded; each miracle is pointing to who Jesus is).

- Revealed His glory (in John 1:14, John declares we will see God's glory in Jesus' life).

4. Where are we? Cana (Nathaniel's hometown, the name means "place of reeds" which is the word picture used in Isaiah 42:3 to describe the work of the Messiah).

5. Are there any numbers in the passage? Yes, three or third (a divine number and the number of life and resurrection).

6. Are there any colors in the passage? No

7. How would you summarize the conclusions that can be drawn from this passage?

- Jesus wants to cleanse our life (water) and bring us joy (wine).

- Jesus wants to bring us abundant life (120 to 180 gallons available).

- We can bring our needs to Jesus, but we must be willing to let Jesus lead (Mary in verses 4-5).

- Jesus is our Resurrected Lord (On the third day).

- We can celebrate our life in Christ (a wedding).

What do you see? Every passage has threads in it. Pray that the Lord will help you see the threads that make the passage come alive.

WHAT DID I FORGET?

AFTER EVERY SERMON I PREACHED AT MY LAST PASTORATE, MY friend Terry would shake my hand and then ask, "Do you know what you forgot?" He would go on to share some other insight that he had seen in my sermon text. It took a little adjusting for me, but I came to appreciate Terry's question. Within every passage of Scripture, there is so much Truth that 30 minutes (or less) cannot contain it all.

I am grateful for all the people God has used to awaken me to the depth and richness of His Word. After 36 years of preaching, it becomes tempting for me to think I knew the Bible inside and out. Worse yet, I found myself just reading the Bible for sermon preparation. I read more out of duty than delight. I have to be careful now that I don't share too much information that people get that "deer in the headlight" look in their eyes.

The hardest thing in writing this book has been trying to "contain" the lessons that God is teaching me about His Word. Please know that this book is not *exhaustive* in any way. We have just scratched the surface of the thousands of threads interwoven into the Bible. My goal has been to begin the journey with you. Learning about God and His Word is a never-ending process.

Let me be honest, I "forgot" thousands and thousands of threads. As examples, I did not deal with the Sabbath day principle, the 10 steps of making a covenant, the importance of water and mountains or God as Creator versus Darwinian evolution (even though I read Darwin's *Origin of the Species* all the way through). I wanted this book to be concise, easy-to-read and affordable.

My prayer is that God can use something I have shared to help you have a renewed desire to know God's Word. The Bible was sewn together by God for you! Open the letter! You will be surprised at what God is waiting to teach you!

ACKNOWLEDGEMENTS

OVER FIFTEEN YEARS, GOD HAS USED A NUMBER OF PEOPLE TO teach me about the seamlessness of Scripture. I am grateful for patient friends who waited while I tried to put into words what God was showing me. Thank you for listening when you were receiving a longer explanation than you expected.

Although they may not have always understood my enthusiasm when God "turned on the lights" during class, I want to thank every student who sat through my Biblical Perspectives classes at Spring Arbor University, Southern Nazarene University and Oklahoma Wesleyan University. It was energizing to see the Bible through the eyes of veteran Bible students as well as students who were picking up a Bible for the first time.

I want to thank the congregation at Oklahoma City Trinity Church of the Nazarene. The four months I spent with you were both healing and affirming for me. What fun it was to preach without having to attend a single Board Meeting! Thanks also for the recent feedback you gave. You will never know what an encouragement it is to have sermons "stick."

I want to thank two Sunday School classes at Edmond First Church of the Nazarene. In spite of my inability to draw and poor handwriting, you let me communicate my heart. You stayed with me when I was in "rapid fire" mode.

I want to thank Gabby Rodriguez, Executive Pastor at Trinity for the Bible studies we had during my four-month interim. Not only were you such a quick learner, but you showed me how the seamless concept works in English and Spanish!

I also want to thank my editor and friend Adam Robinson. Although we have never met face-to-face, Adam has proven that he is a Publishing Genius! He has patiently worked with me through two books now. Thank you Adam for lovingly remind me that I was trying too hard to write this book by myself. It was so much easier when I let God lead. I am so glad Robb convinced me that you should be my first choice.

When I first started writing this book, I asked several friends to give me feedback concerning the early chapters. I want to thank Pastor Joe Shreffler for his great insights. They were both fair and kind. When I was thinking of giving up, the excitement that my dear friend Lela Patton expressed encouraged me to press on.

I want to thank Dr. Leonard Sweet for his encouragement to write this book. Although we have had limited time face-to-face, his emails of guidance and encouragement helped me to have the confidence to write. Thanks for teaching me about narraphors and being my Lead Pneumanaut!

I want to say a special thanks to my wife Bonnie for allowing me to spend so much time in my Man Cave writing. Thanks for believing in me and being such a great cheerleader! You are the best!

ABOUT THE AUTHOR

Dr. Randy Schuneman spent 33 years in ministry as a pastor in Kansas, Michigan and Oklahoma. He has also served as an Adjunct Professor at Spring Arbor University, Southern Nazarene University and Oklahoma Wesleyan University. He is presently serving as a Hospice Chaplain in Mercy Hospice in Oklahoma City, Oklahoma.

Randy is the author of the book *Conversations with an Angel* which recounts the story of the life of his late daughter Jennifer. It reveals the lessons about life, love and loss that Jennie taught her Dad through her life as a childhood cancer survivor, a pediatric oncology nurse and a terminal cancer patient.

Randy is a life-long New York Yankees and Green Bay Packers fan. He is also an avid fan of the Oklahoma City Thunder.

Randy lives with his wife Bonnie in Edmond, Oklahoma. Their son Robb also lives in Edmond.

Made in the USA
Charleston, SC
13 July 2015